As If!

THE ORAL HISTORY OF

CLUELESS™

AS TOLD BY AMY HECKERLING, THE CAST, AND THE CREW

JEN CHANEY

TOUCHSTONE

NEW YORK LONDON TORONTO SYDNEY NEW DELHI

To my best friends from Tilden Intermediate School and Walter Johnson High School, who remain my dearest friends today. And to every preteen or teen who ever watched *Clueless* and wondered whether the Chers, Dionnes, Tais, Murrays, Travises, and Joshes in their lives will still matter to them twenty or thirty years later. I can assure you, from experience: they will.

Touchstone
An Imprint of Simon & Schuster, Inc.
1230 Avenue of the Americas
New York, NY 10020

First Touchstone trade paperback edition July 2015

Interior design by Jill Putorti

Manufactured in the United States of America

10 9 8 7 6 5 4 3 2 1

Library of Congress Cataloging-in-Publication Data has been applied for.

ISBN 978-1-4767-9908-7
ISBN 978-1-4767-9909-4 (ebook)

Contents

• • •

Introduction

• • •

In mid-July of 1995—when American culture was fixated on such matters as O. J. Simpson's ill-fitting glove, TLC's insistence on not chasing waterfalls, and the box office domination of *Batman Forever*, *Pocahontas*, and *Apollo 13*—the fact that a modestly budgeted teen movie called *Clueless* was about to arrive in theaters, become a major hit for Paramount Pictures, catapult the careers of its stars, influence fashion for two decades, and become a permanent cultural touchstone for multiple generations . . . well, let's just say it was something most people couldn't predict at the time. (You can't blame them, really. They were very busy focusing on the rivers and the lakes they were used to.)

Executives at Paramount Pictures—the studio that took on the film after others, regretfully, it would turn out, passed on the project—had great confidence in writer-director Amy Heckerling's shiny, girly comedy about a shopaholic Beverly Hills teenager with a few Jane Austen DNA molecules in her genetic code. Sherry Lansing, then the head of the studio, liked it so much that after screening it, she didn't have a single story note. "She said, 'This is fantastic. I don't have anything I think you should change,'" remembers Adam Schroeder, one of the film's producers.

It's not like *Clueless* was flying entirely below the public's radar. The comedy benefited from some serious promotional juice courtesy of MTV, which, like Paramount, was part of the Viacom family, and pitched the film heavily to its *Real World*–

addicted Gen X and Y audience. Media buzz about the breakout potential of Alicia Silverstone—then best known for her appearances in a trio of Aerosmith videos and the thriller *The Crush*, in which she stalked a post–*Princess Bride*, pre-*Saw* Cary Elwes—also started to build well before the film's release. *Entertainment Weekly* splashed an image of Silverstone in a shimmery baby-doll dress on its cover in March of '95, headlining it with the supremely confident statement "A Star Is Made." "If all goes as planned, the coming months will witness Silverstone's transformation from gym-locker pinup to household name," the story read. "En route to theaters are Silverstone's *True Crime*, a thriller in which a Catholic schoolgirl turns gumshoe; *Le Nouveau Monde*, a Gallic coming-of-age story directed by Alain Corneau; and, most notably, *Clueless*, a teen comedy due this July that's described by its creators as a Rodeo Drive version of Jane Austen's *Emma*." "Most notably" was, it turned out, an understatement.

But in Hollywood, even a gorgeous, on-the-rise young starlet and a director with a track record for making profitable hits (see Heckerling's *Fast Times at Ridgemont High*, *European Vacation*, and the *Look Who's Talking* pics) do not guarantee success. Given the landscape for teen movies at the time, it's understandable that industry insiders and observers weren't necessarily sure that *Clueless* would click with ticket buyers. While TV shows and movies about adolescents and young adults had not disappeared entirely from the landscape, the high school movie as a bankable genre had more or less petered out by 1995.

Then *Clueless* made its debut on July 19, 1995 (a Wednesday), and became the number one movie in the country that day. The weekend of July 21–23, it generated $10.6 million—it was the number two movie in America for that three-day period, right behind *Apollo 13*—and immediately was branded as one of the summer's most unexpected triumphs. "In the midst of a summer of mostly desultory films, along came 'Clueless,'" said a *New York Times* piece that ran the Monday after that strong debut, confirming in print that it had emerged as "a sleeper hit of the summer."

The movie went on to earn $56.6 million in the US and Canada, a figure that Hollywood data-tracking site Box Office Mojo equates to $105.7 million in contemporary inflated dollars. That's a nice return for a film whose production budget landed in the $13 million range. Reviews were positive as well. "Heckerling walks a fine line between satire and put-on, but she finds it, and her dialogue could be anthologized," wrote Roger Ebert. *New York* magazine critic David Denby proclaimed it a "comedy of goodness" that made "the nastiness of a 'smart' teen movie like *Heathers*" seem "like a failure of imagination." In the *New York Times*, Janet Maslin called the movie "as eye-catching and cheery as its star."

More importantly, *Clueless* touched a chord in the culture that was clearly primed and ready to be struck. Preteen and teen girls—some of whom would eventually grow up to share their *Clueless* love with their own daughters—raced to malls in search of plaid skirts and knee-high socks, surprising higher-ups at major department stores who had not anticipated the hordes of wannabe-Cher shoppers. Almost immediately, Paramount began working with Heckerling to develop a TV show adaptation. Within a year, the movie's soundtrack would sell enough copies to be certified gold; it would eventually reach platinum status. The success of *Clueless* also would defibrillate the barely breathing high school movie genre, resulting in a flood of teen movies in the late '90s and early '00s, many of which featured Cher-esque female protagonists and blatantly targeted the young-and-XX-chromosomed demographic that had made *Clueless* such a smash.

Career doors began to open wider for almost everyone involved after the movie came out, most notably Silverstone. At the age of eighteen and mere weeks after *Clueless* sent her industry stock into the stratosphere, she inked a reported $10 million deal with Columbia Pictures that made headlines in the trades and elsewhere. Suddenly, it felt like the whole world was making a cameo at the Val party.

Coverage of Silverstone went from excessive to inescapable, with stories and photos of her everywhere: in *Vanity Fair*, *Time*, and *New York* magazine, and on the cover of *Rolling Stone*, where she dressed in all pink and parked her frilly-bikini'd bottom next to the headline "Ballad of a Teen Queen." *Entertainment Weekly* name-checked both Austen, whose *Emma* inspired the *Clueless* narrative, and Silverstone in its year-end list of the most significant entertainers of 1995, while *Vanity Fair*'s 1996 Hollywood issue featured Heckerling in an Annie Leibovitz photo spread focused on the industry's most influential female filmmakers. Heckerling also won an award for best screenplay from the National Society of Film Critics and was nominated for best original screenplay by the Writers Guild of America. The media credited *Clueless* for, as *New York Times* columnist Peggy Orenstein put it, proving there's a market for movies "in which girls are in charge of their own fates, active rather than reactive."

What's even more remarkable is that twenty years later, *Clueless* is still as omnipresent in American culture as it was back then. Thanks to its presence on cable, DVD, and streaming services like Netflix and Amazon Instant Video, *Clueless* is still watched on a regular basis by longtime fans as well as young people discovering the magic of Murray's freshly shaved head for the first time. Tributes to the movie—in the form of Twitter accounts, Buzzfeed listicles, and start-up tech companies that encourage users to dress their bodies just like Cher does in *Clueless*—are ubiquitous in the digital sphere. Fashion designers and labels continue to riff on the costumes created for the film by Mona May. (Are you in a Macy's, H&M, or Urban Outfitters, like, right now? Stop. Look around. There's probably a sheer shirt, a pleated miniskirt, or some knee-highs in your field of vision that, thanks to the circle-of-life nature of fashion trends, easily could have been yanked out of Cher Horowitz's ridiculously substantial closet.)

The idea of molding Jane Austen's narrative structures and themes into something more modern? That has been *everywhere* post-*Clueless*, from *Austenland* to Web series like *The Lizzie Bennet Diaries* and *Emma Approved.* The influence of the film can be seen in the pop cultural creations of some high-profile influencers of today's girls and young women, including Katy Perry, Lena Dunham, Tavi Gevinson, Mindy Kaling, and Iggy Azalea, just for starters. I mean, when Azalea, the Aussie rapper, decided to make a music video for "Fancy," otherwise known as the most inescapable song on planet Earth during the year 2014, to what 1995 film did she opt to pay homage? Hint: it wasn't *Waterworld*, y'all.

Clueless, then, isn't merely a touchstone for the nineties generation. It's a teen movie that continues to be passed from one generation to the next and is just timeless enough for every generation to think it's speaking directly to them.

So how did it all happen? How did Amy Heckerling come up with the idea to bend and twist nineteenth-century England into an exaggerated, luminescent version of Beverly Hills circa the mid-1990s? How did Silverstone, Paul Rudd, and others get cast in this movie and who else was considered for their roles? What was the vibe in the classroom during the filming of the debate scene that taught us all how to mispronounce the word *Haitians*, or during the robbery scene that taught us all what an Alaïa was? Why does this movie still resonate so much, with so many people, two decades later?

Those are all questions that this book will answer, along

with some incredibly nitpicky ones that only serious fans would be inclined to ask. Questions like: Who painted that picture of Cher's mother that hangs in the foyer of the Horowitz household? What's the deal with the hair clip that Cher wears on her date with Christian, and in what way is it connected to Amanda Bynes? (Swear to God: there really is a connection.) What happened to all of Cher's costumes after production wrapped? Who described his experience at the premiere of *Clueless*—held on Malibu's Zuma Beach and broadcast on MTV—by noting that he got "white-boy wasted"? (Forget it, I'll just tell you the answer to that: Coolio. It was Coolio.)

But this complete history of *Clueless* is about more than just fun pieces of trivia. Using material gathered from more than eighty interviews with people who worked on the film, as well as professors, fashion experts, industry insiders, cultural critics, and fans of the movie, this book will tell the story of how hard it was—and often still is—for a female filmmaker with a point of view to get a movie green-lighted in Hollywood. It will explain why so many Jane Austen scholars consider *Clueless*, a film some initially and wrongly dismissed as nothing more than a fun romp about a ditz with a credit card, the best Jane Austen adaptation ever made. It will shed light on the amount of work, creativity, and craft that went into making *Clueless* look so effortlessly bright and glossy. It will delve more deeply into how *Clueless* used fantasy to create a world that, in a way, achieves a social ideal that reality can't quite match: a place where a gay kid is accepted among his peers, where young girls are empowered to be their confident selves, and where the best friendship between a white girl and a black girl is so natural that no one bothers to bat a heavily mascaraed eyelash in its direction. This book will do a lot of other things, too, as you'll see when you start turning these pages.

As If! couldn't explore any of those subjects without the

generosity of the many, many people who spoke with me as part of this project. Please peruse the long list of *Clueless* oral history sources, which acknowledges their contributions and also tells you more about the impressive things many of them have accomplished since graduating from Bronson Alcott High School. (I'll thank a few particular individuals even more effusively in the acknowledgments.)

This book is written primarily in an oral history format. The material in that oral history was gathered from interviews conducted while I was working on a 2013 Vulture piece about the Val party scene (the director's-cut version of that piece is in part 2) and during extensive interviews conducted specifically for the book.

Memories of things that happened twenty years ago can sometimes get a little fuzzy. When cast or crew members occasionally recollected the same event a little differently, I have presented both sides of the story. I also relied heavily on the movie's 144-page production report to verify information, particularly regarding exactly when and where certain scenes were shot.

When writing a book like this, it's inevitable that some key people—including cast members and musical artists who contributed to the soundtrack—will either not wish to participate or won't be available to do so to the extent that I hoped. For that reason, I occasionally use quotes from interviews published or broadcast by other media outlets. Those have been appropriately footnoted and sourced within the text. Some quotes, from both my interviews and elsewhere, have been condensed in order to allow the narrative to flow more seamlessly. This has always been done in a way that keeps the meaning of the source's words intact.

One final thought (for now) on what makes *Clueless* so special: as I spoke to various people about the film and rewatched it—both in pieces and in its entirety, repeatedly—while working on this book, I was struck by how much it exists within the context of its era as well as outside of it. As many Tumblrs, tweets, and online comments can attest, *Clueless* is one of those movies that really gets nineties nostalgia motors revving. Which makes total sense. But, at the risk of sounding, like, *way* philosophical, one of the more remarkable things about *Clueless* is that it seems to exist almost across time.

This is a movie that uses a story first published in 1815 as its narrative blueprint. Yet it's also a movie that's steeped in the music and pop culture references of the 1990s, the time of Marky Mark pants-dropping and catchy Mentos ads. And somehow, it's *also* a movie that, through a combination of Heckerling genius and glorious accident, managed to predict how we live now. In 1995, the idea that two friends would stand right beside each other while talking on their cell phones was a hilarious joke. Now it's a snapshot of our daily existence, although now we speak less and text more. When Amy Heckerling decided that Cher should activate a snazzy computer program that allows her to dress herself like a virtual paper doll, do you know what Amy Heckerling did? She invented the freakin' fashion app.

Young women certainly asserted their opinions with Cher's brash confidence before *Clueless*, and, culturally speaking, were doing so pretty actively around the time the movie was released. But on the Internet, an even broader swath of female voices can be heard, in outlets like Jezebel, the Hairpin, *Rookie* magazine, and Slate, as well as on various social media platforms. Often, the women sharing the most compelling and well-reasoned points are women who grew up on *Clueless*, which suggests that even if Cher doesn't know how to say *Spartacus*, she may have, in some small way, shown young ladies how to stand up and speak for themselves.

Clueless, then, is something that's simultaneously past and present and future. Watching it may sometimes make us ache for a "back then," when we had just graduated from college, or were in high school, or watched it during our first middle school sleepover. But the reason it's so good, as good as only a handful of teen movies can legitimately claim to be, is because every time you turn it on, it also feels very right now.

Part One

BEFORE *CLUELESS*

From Yes to No to Yes Again: How *Clueless* Got off the Ground

Amy Heckerling kicked off her career as a Hollywood director with a movie that became a perennially quotable teen classic: 1982's *Fast Times at Ridgemont High.* Though its sensibility was different from that of *Clueless*—*Fast Times* was steeped in much more reality than Cher's fluffy, feathery fantasy land—the movie became culturally significant for many of the same reasons *Clueless* later would, too.

Like *Clueless*, *Fast Times* launched the then-still-early careers of several impeccably cast, promising young actors, including Sean Penn, Jennifer Jason Leigh, Phoebe Cates, and Forest Whitaker; it featured dialogue, as scripted by Cameron Crowe, that seemed to enter the lexicon the second it emanated from cineplex speakers; and it forever embedded several iconic movie moments—most notably, Phoebe Cates's slo-mo removal of that red bikini top—into the collective memory of a generation. *Fast Times* became a touchstone movie for teens of the 1980s, the same way that *Clueless* would for teens in the decade that followed.

Though Heckerling would spend the rest of the 1980s exploring other cinematic worlds—including ones involving gangsters (*Johnny Dangerously*), Griswolds (*European Vacation*), and babies that sound like Bruce Willis (*Look Who's Talking*)—it wasn't surprising that in the early 1990s, she would again feel compelled to revisit high school hallways. Initially, that was something that 20th Century Fox actively encouraged her to do.

In 1993, Heckerling began developing a TV show for Fox that focused on the popular kids at a California high school, including a central female character fueled by relentless reserves of optimism. At that point, the project was called *No Worries*, one of several names used (*I Was a Teenage Teenager* was another) before *Clueless* earned its official title status. Given Heckerling's established skill and success with coming-of-age comedy, it seems like *No Worries* should have come together with . . . well, no worries, or at least very few. But that wasn't the case.

In its formative stages, the project eventually known as *Clueless* went from potential Fox TV show to potential Fox feature film, and then—for a short but frustrating period before landing at Paramount—almost didn't happen at all. Its path to the big screen is a tale about a filmmaker inventing a very positive character, then dealing with frustration, Hollywood sexism, and rejection, but ultimately finding the support to make her movie by staying true to her vision. It's also a tale in which Heckerling explains the connection between her own family and the ex-stepsibling romance between Josh and Cher.

Amy Heckerling, writer-director: I remember reading *Emma*. I remember reading *Gentlemen Prefer Blondes*. Those characters: what I gravitated to was how positive they could be. There's a word that's thrown around a lot now—*entitled*—which is a way older people can look at young people in a kind of negative way. But I always feel like people that have that optimism and feel like they can do things, there's something so endearing and charming about that, because you know life will beat everybody down eventually. Maybe not everybody, but many people. There's something very life-affirming to see that quality in people. So I liked those characters.

One of, obviously, my favorite characters in *Fast Times* is Spicoli because it doesn't occur to him that, oh, the teacher will think badly of him for coming in late, wanting to surf, any of that. He doesn't mean anything negative about anybody else, and it wouldn't occur to him that they're thinking that about him.

There was an episode of *Gidget* that I saw, obviously, when I was a little kid. A friend of Gidget's father's had a student from Sweden or something come to stay with them. She was a big nerd and completely didn't know how to dress or act with boys or anything. Gidget took it upon herself to make her over.

When Gidget made this girl over, the girl became very popular and actually started to go after Gidget's boyfriend. So I recall when I was first reading *Emma*, that I was thinking, *This is like that episode of* Gidget. *[Laughs]* There are a lot of things in *Gidget* and *Dobie Gillis* and *The Patty Duke Show*, where the teachers are referencing great literature and then the characters go off and have their own take on it.

Twink Caplan, associate producer of *Clueless* and Miss Geist: We started working together way back when she was doing *European Vacation* . . . we were best friends, Amy and I. She directed me when I acted and then we became producing partners and they were just wonderful, wonderful years.

After *Look Who's Talking*, *Look Who's Talking, Too*, and a couple TV shows that we tried to do, Amy came up with this idea of *Clueless*, that was a takeoff on *Emma*. It was so exciting. I was the sounding board . . . it was all Amy—her brain. I just loved her brain.

Amy Heckerling: Sometimes you're working on things and you think, "Oh, I have to write this" or "I'd better look at my notes." And other times you just want to. That was how I felt writing Cher. I just wanted to be in that world, and in her mind-set.

All of [the *Clueless* characters] were in [the original TV pilot]. Well, not all the guys. But Cher and Dionne, and her father, and the teacher, Mr. Hall. [In the pilot] she was a rich girl that wanted a high-fashion grunge outfit so that a boy would think that she was smart. Because that was what she thought smart people wore.

Eventually the TV people put it in turnaround and I was very frustrated. I had moved to a new agency then. That's when Ken Stovitz became my agent and I showed him that pilot, and he said, "This is a movie."

Ken Stovitz, Amy Heckerling's agent: You know, when you get into business with someone, you find out what really is the home run, dream come true. And early on, she told me about this project. So I said, all right, if I can do *anything* for her, I'm going to do what I can to get this made.

Amy Heckerling: Then Fox movies bought it from Fox TV.

Ken Stovitz: I think it was under [Fox film executive] Elizabeth Gabler's [purview]—and she was nothing but totally supportive and everything. But eventually she couldn't get it made there.[1]

Amy Heckerling: She was a real champion of the project: a smart woman, familiar with Jane Austen, and somebody you could talk to about characters and structure, and really loved it. She was a pleasure to work with. She was so passionate that when her bosses put it in turnaround, she was so upset, like in tears. So I love her.

Twink Caplan: I remember one of [the Fox executives] thought it would be better if the boys were more prominent. It wasn't about that. It was about these girls.

---

1 Elizabeth Gabler was an executive vice president at Fox during the 1990s. She is currently the president of Fox 2000, a division of 20th Century Fox responsible for bringing *Life of Pi* and *The Fault in Our Stars*, among others, to the screen.

Amy Heckerling: During the development there was a concern that it was too much about one female, and that I should make Josh a bigger part, and he should be living next door, and his mother [should be] in love with her father, they weren't ex-stepbrother and ex-stepsister. They thought that was incestuous. Like: "What if the Brady Bunch got involved with each other?" I didn't watch *The Brady Bunch*, so I couldn't really argue.

The thing is, my grandparents were stepbrother and stepsister. In the Jewish ghetto in the Pale of Settlement in Europe, it was pretty verboten to have a female that was [perceived as] loose. My great-grandmother was a widow with children. For a female to be alone with children, there weren't opportunities. In this small little world, a woman that was not in a marriage was going to become destitute and there'd be children [involved]. I mean, I'm not Isaac Singer so I can't tell you exactly how life went there. But if there was a free-floating female—if your brother died and he had a wife and children, you would marry the woman and take care of the kids. Everybody took care of things rather than looked for the big love experience.

My grandmother's father was a widower, and my grandfather's mother was a widow. [My great-grandparents] both had children, and so they got married; they all had grown children. Then my grandmother was a teenager, and she had an older stepbrother. Totally not blood-related. When I was a kid all she did was complain about her stepmother to me, her evil stepmother and how mean she was to her and would hide her in the closet when the social worker came so she wasn't sent to school and she could be kept at home to do the cleaning. But her stepbrother, whom she later married, was always a protector. They were married. They knew each other from the time they were teenagers. He was almost one hundred when he died; she was in her late eighties. So they were fighting for, like, eighty years. I mean, *fighting*. But when one got sick, they were completely lost. They were so dependent on each other and so angry all the time with each other. Anyhow, they cracked me up. So it did not seem like a crazy thing to me [for Josh and Cher to be together].

When the studio tells you, ooh, this is incestuous and you're going: this is my grandparents. I mean, it's the Jewish ghetto. You don't leave a woman out on the street, because she has no money and how will she feed the kids? Widowers marry widows and that's how it is, and [their respective children] are not related.

Twink Caplan: So we went into turnaround. And I guess we started working out of Amy's house, actually. Which wasn't a bad thing because I got a dog, Leon, a Maltese, and he played with Sir Mix-A-Lot, her Maltese. . . . We were very depressed, though.

Ken Stovitz: We had set it up at Fox. We couldn't get it going. I took it out once, twice, maybe three times to the rest of the community. And only the last time did we attach Alicia Silverstone based on the music video.

What we submitted was the screenplay and the music video. I told everyone it was a $13 million movie. I gave them the budget, I gave them Amy's track record, which was—I mean, if you look at her ratio of cost to success, I think *Look Who's Talking* was done for $6.5 million and I think it did $285 million.[2]

In those days, $13 million for a really polished movie—that

2 Actually, *Look Who's Talking* did even more than that: it made $296.9 million worldwide, on a budget that the *New York Times* reported was closer to $8 million. Still: pretty great cost-to-success ratio.

movie today would cost, I'll take a guess and say, $35 million. Because everyone actually got paid. It wasn't like doing a movie where everyone worked for no money.

We got rejected so many times it was a joke.

Amy Heckerling: [Ken] just refused to let it die. I mean, he was a bulldog in pursuing it and pushing and not making me feel like it wasn't good or I should be thinking of other things. He really was a champion.

Ken Stovitz: Everyone in Hollywood wants to do what is in vogue at that time, and an unheard-of teenage-girl movie that looks at the lunacy of how we live our lives, and what importance we place on things, and her crazy friends—I don't think they thought that people cared about it that much. Whatever was happening at that time wasn't that.

Amy Heckerling: Well, there was a moment in time where a number of movies seemed to be about, for lack of a better word, stupid young people. There was a movie called *PCU*. Actually, I thought it was a very smart movie, commenting on the political correctness craze. David Spade and Jeremy Piven—I thought they were wonderful. But I guess it didn't perform the way they wanted. There was another movie, *Airheads*, which was about a rock band that wasn't doing well, [with] Adam Sandler and Steve Buscemi and I think Brendan Fraser. Which was a really funny script and a funny movie, but the fact that it's called *Airheads* and here's another thing called *Clueless* . . . [*Airheads*] didn't do well, so by association, we're not making another one that sounds like that. They didn't get the irony. You could say *Beavis and Butt-Head* is not about smart people, but it's a very smart cartoon.

Adam Schroeder, *Clueless* coproducer and then president of Scott Rudin Productions: Teen movies were just not happening. It was almost like a relic of the John Hughes movies in the eighties.

Amy Heckerling: Everybody passed on it. Then Scott Rudin liked the script. Then there was a bidding war for it, without anything being different.[3]

Ken Stovitz: When you're an agent, that's what you do. As soon as you get interest, you let everyone else know. "Hey, man, I've got a thing going on over here. I'm going to be dating this girl. If you want to come out with me, you gotta . . ."

Amy Heckerling: There were two different people who showed it to [Rudin]. One was my ex-boyfriend from film school who was working as, I think, an assistant cameraman on a movie Scott was doing. And one was a music supervisor who had gotten ahold of it, who was a friend of Scott's. So separately, those two people showed it to him and he responded. That stamp of approval was enough for the town.

Ken Stovitz: I gave [the script] to Scott. And by the way, they may have also. But I know I gave it to him.

Adam Schroeder: Fox was not going to do it and they gave them, let's say, a limited turnaround. That's where we were able to kind of get into it. We were at Paramount at the time. Again, it wasn't one of those safe bets either. But Scott was so prolific in terms of the movies that he was doing—really big

3 Scott Rudin is one of the most prolific and successful Hollywood producers of the past two decades; his credits include *The Truman Show*, *The Hours*, *No Country for Old Men*, and *The Social Network*.

studio movies, and they would be kind enough to let him do smaller movies, usually more artsy-fartsy movies. But this was something really special and different.

Barry Berg, coproducer and unit production manager: Just having [Scott's] name on the film meant so much to so many. It became an important film the moment he signed on to produce it.

Adam Schroeder: I had read it when it was [called] *I Was a Teenage Teenager*, and we were quoting passages from it all the time, the assistants [in Rudin's office] and the junior executives. We were big fans of *Fast Times*. That was such a benchmark movie for me and for my youth.

The fact that Amy had mined this kind of territory before in such a seminal way with *Fast Times*, and here she was doing it again but on such a sophisticated level—and not sophisticated in a way that was going to alienate teenagers, but potentially embrace adults in a nostalgic way. It was based on *Emma*. It was more than just a teen comedy and set pieces and sex and all. It had real, deep characters and other layers.

Amy Heckerling: When Scott read [the script], his notes were pretty much what brought it back to the way it was [originally].

Ken Stovitz: I didn't just sell the script, we got a production commitment. These days they have to have a green-light committee. Everyone in the world votes on it: the head of marketing and distribution, head of international. It just doesn't happen like this anymore, unfortunately.

Twink Caplan: Maybe I shouldn't even add this, but it is part of the history for me personally that I was a producer with Amy at 20th Century Fox. But by the time it went to Paramount, Scott had hired—he gave a producer credit to Adam, who worked with him, and to line producer Barry [Berg], who, I guess, got a producing credit. And they didn't have enough producer [credits] to give me one, who was with Amy the whole time. So they gave me [the title] associate producer even though, you know, whatever.

Ultimately, I think I set a precedent for being associate producer and being on the one-sheet at Paramount, because I had parity with the other men and that was the deal that I struck: at least give me parity.

The upside of that was I've never worked with so many incredible people in my life.

Ken Stovitz: Rejection can either be the thing that kills you or the thing that inspires you to just say, "I'm not going to take no for an answer." We chose to do the latter. We chose to say, "We know we've got something good here. We're not going to take no."

Five Key Pre-*Clueless* Teen Movies

In order to understand how the cinematic stage got set for Cher's big-screen debut, check out these five significant teen movies released during the decade that invented the modern teen movie genre: the 1980s. These are not the only important or good teen films that came out during that period. But they're the ones that seem most *Clueless*-relevant and, therefore, beg to be watched (or rewatched) by all Cher Horowitzian scholars.

Fast Times at Ridgemont High (1982)

Arriving just a few months after *Porky's*, Amy Heckerling's portrait of California high schoolers was initially dismissed by some as just another teen sex comedy. But *Fast Times* actually dared to do something that few movies at the time attempted: it treated its female characters (and their sexuality) with a sensitivity and frankness that valued their experiences as much as the experiences of the boys.

Valley Girl **(1983)**

Another female filmmaker, Martha Coolidge, is responsible for taking this indie about seemingly dim California ditzes with credit cards (sound familiar?) and turning it into a sweet, *Romeo and Juliet*–inspired story about young love and LA culture clashes. In Deborah Foreman and Nicolas Cage—who had just gotten his career started the year before with a small role in *Fast Times*—Coolidge found a pair of star-crossed romantic leads who generated a palpable, zingy chemistry.

The Breakfast Club **(1985)**

In *The Breakfast Club*—the most important teen film released during this decade—John Hughes and Molly Ringwald gave us Claire Standish, the stereotypically rich, snobby, entitled girl who turns out to be as complicated and confused as her less wealthy and popular peers. *Clueless* would later flip the script on the "rich kids are our enemies" theme, one that was very prevalent in eighties movies. *The Breakfast Club*—and, a short time later, *Ferris Bueller's Day Off*—allowed us to imagine how such a flip might be possible.

Pretty in Pink **(1986)**

Written by Hughes and directed by Howard Deutch, this is an obvious exception to the previous assertion that John Hughes never depicted the popular crowd as a pack of flagrant douchebags. Actually, *Pretty in Pink*'s Steff might be the most deliciously contemptible rich douchebag in all of cinema history. What makes *Pretty in Pink* *Clueless*-relevant is the way it celebrates Andie (Ringwald again, God bless her) and her sense of bold, thoroughly vintage style. Before *Clueless* put fashion at the absolute forefront in a high school movie, Ringwald was paving the way by stoking young girls' appetites for thrift-store chic.

Heathers (1988)

Like *Clueless*, *Heathers* is a satire that pokes fun at the spoiled and privileged. But while *Clueless*'s wry commentary is illuminated by happy beams of optimistic sunshine, *Heathers* marinates in a cesspool of dark cynicism. With this film about a sadistic Christian Slater (referenced in *Clueless*!) and a reluctant Winona Ryder bumping off their ultra-snotty, lunkheaded classmates, the high school genre's aforementioned sticking-it-to-the-rich-kids trend got pushed about as far as it could go. Which meant that in the not-too-distant future, things had to go in another direction.

When Emma Met Cher: *Clueless* and the Spirit of Jane Austen

Jane Austen's *Emma* was first published in 1815, long before complaint rock, *Ren and Stimpy*, and Alaïa dresses were invented. But in *Clueless*, Amy Heckerling found a way to bridge the gap between Austen's story about a privileged, provincial, nineteenth-century English woman matchmaking and meddling in the lives of others, and the story she was telling, about a privileged, often oblivious late-twentieth-century Beverly Hills fifteen-year-old eager to make over anyone who enters her orbit.

Clueless was by no means the first attempt to adapt *Emma*. The comedy of manners became a BBC TV movie for the first time back in 1948; various films and miniseries based on it and other Austen works have trickled out every decade since.

But during the mid-1990s, there was a sudden onset of Austen mania, both in film and on television. In addition to *Clueless*, the year 1995 alone delivered numerous more traditional Austen adaptations: *Persuasion*; Ang Lee's *Sense and Sensibility*, starring Emma Thompson, Hugh Grant, and a pre-*Titanic* Kate

Winslet; and, in the UK, the BBC's much revered take on *Pride and Prejudice*, which cast Colin Firth in the role of the wet-shirt-wearing Mr. Darcy, a part he would (kinda sorta) reprise in the film version of *Bridget Jones's Diary*. Two more takes on *Emma* would follow in 1996: one starring Kate Beckinsale that aired on Britain's ITV and a motion picture in which Gwyneth Paltrow's Emma Woodhouse attempts the early-nineteenth-century version of a makeover on Toni Collette's Harriet Smith.

In a *New York* magazine interview in July of 1996, when Paltrow was promoting her *Emma*, she spoke dismissively of the awareness *Clueless* had already raised about Austen's novel: "'I think it's sad,' she says, lighting up her first Camel, 'that America's first cultural reference to this movie will be *Clueless*. I mean, *honestly*.'"

But here's the truth, *honestly*: *Clueless*, then Hollywood's sole attempt to thoroughly modernize the author's work, is now, in retrospect, a pioneer. Over the next two decades, a seemingly never-ending parade of contemporary, sometimes cheeky, occasionally zombified Austen updates has wound its way through the worlds of literature, film, TV, and the Internet. But even with so many adaptations, both classic and unconventional, to choose from, many Austen scholars—including four represented here—continue to embrace *Clueless* as not only a very imaginative spin on *Emma*, but one of the more thematically on-point Jane Austen updates ever.

Amy Heckerling, writer-director: Obviously one thing about seeing a [character] who's so sure of themselves [is] they're going to run into something eventually that's going to make them doubt themselves. That is what the arc [of *Clueless*] kind of wanted to be. That made me remember *Emma*. So I reread it, and it was just like: *Oh my God, this is so good. This is so perfect. How lucky am I?*

Dr. Inger S. B. Brodey, professor of comparative literature at University of North Carolina–Chapel Hill and co-organizer of UNC's annual Jane Austen Summer Program: Oh, I loved [*Clueless*]. I thought it was very clever, and I still think it's one of the best, if not the best, adaptations of her novels.

Dr. Devoney Looser, professor of English at Arizona State University and former member of the Jane Austen Society of North America (JASNA) board of directors: It gets tone right and it gets the satirical elements right. I think it makes Emma a more genial, lovable character, perhaps because she's more accessible as a type. It's easier to love her, so I think part of why I enjoy the adaptation has to do with my own sense of young women and what I find amusing, infuriating, and entertaining about them.

I think it spoke to me as an adaptation that was, in some ways, more true than the ones trying to be historically true.

Dr. Juliette Wells, associate professor of English at Maryland's Goucher College and current member of the JASNA board of directors: The little fishpond of self-regarding Beverly Hills rich people turns out to have a whole lot in common with the self-regarding rich people of Austen's time and place. So yeah, it's an amazing hook: *Emma*—in Beverly Hills! Which is kind of like: *Pride and Prejudice*—and zombies!

Amy Heckerling: I mean, it's not a real adaptation. It's not: "And then [Cher] meets a guy and he's engaged and she doesn't know it and there's a farmer." I was going for equivalence that made sense to me to tell the underlying story, in a way that made sense for what we're living through now, or [were] in the nineties. So I wasn't trying to say, "Here's *Emma*." I was trying to say that *Emma* makes perfect sense now. There's so much that hasn't changed—[Austen] was so brilliant, it's timeless.

Juliette Wells: I think you appreciate the film more if you know *Emma*, for sure. I've definitely had students, not my finest students, but students who come and say, "I'm taking this course because of *Clueless* and my goal for this course is to appreciate *Clueless* more." And I say, "You will meet that goal." If nothing else, the transformation of Frank Churchill into Christian is the most inspired stroke of adaptation in the entire history of adapting Jane Austen.

Amy Heckerling: Well, I knew Cher had to believe that she was going to have a relationship with somebody that everybody else would know she wasn't going to have one with. So naturally I figured: gay. I liked the idea of one of the people in her world also being a gay friend. It seemed like the perfect reason, so she's not jealous or mad at some other girl or something. It was: *Oh my God, I didn't even notice this*. Because I don't think [Emma] was ever really mad at Jane Fairfax.[4] She just didn't get it. And in a way, if she was honest with herself, she didn't really love [Frank] anyway. She just loved making up stories and living out drama.

I liked the idea that Emma is so into her own stories and machinations that she doesn't see the obvious, which is that these two people are engaged. She can, from the slightest hint, decide that somebody is madly in love with her. And it's not that crazy, because it was a world where there were not a lot of hints. People weren't sexting each other, you know? You had to build something out of, like, a touch without a glove.

Dr. Joan Klingel Ray, former English professor at the University of Colorado–Colorado Springs and former president of the Jane Austen Society of North America: [Josh] is like the college-guy version of Mr. Knightley. He's wonderful and

4 Jane Fairfax is a character who is secretly engaged to Frank Churchill in *Emma*, making him unattainable to Emma.

he sees the flaws in Cher the same way Mr. Knightley sees the flaws in Emma. But like Emma, who denies his pointing out her flaws, Cher, too, thinks that he doesn't really understand her. She doesn't understand her own attraction to this character any more than Emma understands her attraction to Mr. Knightley.

Inger S. B. Brodey: [Austen] has this three-step process with Emma, where Emma first observes something very correctly, and then she says, for example, "Mr. Elton is not upset that Harriet isn't coming to dinner." So she notes it carefully enough and well enough that we readers can share that same observation. Then she remarks how strange that is: "Isn't that strange?" And "Could it be that he doesn't love her? No." And she immediately rejects that idea because men—there's no accounting for men and their stomachs, I can't remember exactly what her rationalization is. But I feel like "as if" does something similar to that. [Cher]'s usually acknowledging something that's actually true and then says, "As if," to distance herself from it or reject it. There's lots of things like that, that are really clever adaptations of how the narrative [in *Emma*] itself functions.

Amy Heckerling: The "How are we going to get home?" [question] was a big part of what the [Val] party needed to accomplish for me, story-wise, and that is strictly from Jane Austen. When Emma goes to a party, there's [the question of] who will go home with whom in which carriage, and which neighborhood it's in. Which is exactly the situation that worked for the cars and the freeway and who lives where and how you were going to get there. Whenever I sort of bumped into something like that where I thought, *That's exactly what still happens*, I really loved it.

The burning of [Tai's Elton] souvenirs is exactly a scene

with Harriet [in *Emma*]. I think she had some plaster [from Mr. Elton]. I guess, when they didn't have bandages [back then], it was plaster and material that they used to clean up blood. You start to learn about day-to-day life, and you imagine: *Somebody had that and they saved it?* It's like saving somebody's Breathe Rights or bandages. It's like: bleh. It would be good DNA evidence, but, you know: ick. But that's precious to [Harriet]. And you think: *Well, what else would be precious to [Tai]?* That [Elton] put the ice in a towel, and the song that they listened to.

Joan Klingel Ray: I love the line in *Clueless* where Josh says to Cher, "You're playing with her like she's a Barbie doll" . . . The way I always taught *Emma* well before seeing *Clueless* was that she is playing with Harriet Smith as if she's a doll. And if you look at Jane Austen's description of Harriet Smith, she has golden hair and a lovely round face. When I push my students and say, "What does Harriet Smith's description remind you of?" suddenly even the young men in the class go, "She looks like a doll."

Juliette Wells: Both of these, the film and the novel, are working within the ancient conventions of classical comedy. Comedy is the one that ends with marriage. So in *Clueless*, the grown-up characters are the ones getting married in the end, whereas Austen's *Emma* begins with the marriage of those characters. Austen's *Emma* ends by marrying off all the remaining characters of marriageable age, including Harriet Smith and Robert Martin. So Amy Heckerling's film gestures toward the happy-ending conclusion that we all know marriage to be.

Inger S. B. Brodey: It leads the audience to think it's going to be Cher's wedding and [Heckerling] punctures it neatly with the narrative voice. That's fun, and that's very Austen-ish.

Juliette Wells: I think *Clueless*, more than any other adaptation that I'm aware of, is really an independent work of art. It is also an adaptation, but it didn't need to sell itself as an adaptation.

Now, my students are born in 1995, some of them, so if they know *Clueless* it's because an older sister introduced them to it or somebody hooked them on it. But they respond to it as if it had been made yesterday, and that's not true of the other 1990s Austen adaptations, which the students treat as historical artifacts. I'm serious. We watch *Pride and Prejudice* with Colin Firth, and my students who were born in 1995 say, "Is that supposed to be sexy?" I say, "At the time, it was considered very sexy." And they say: "Oh." But they still laugh at *Clueless*, and they still get what a clever take on Austen it is.

Joan Klingel Ray: It shows that people are always the same. You look at 1815, you look at 1995, it's: people behave the same.

From Beverly Hills to Bronson Alcott High: The Real Teens Behind *Clueless*

Like any thorough writer, Heckerling did her research, spending time in actual California classrooms so she could get a feel for the way real teens spoke, thought, and behaved. She spent the most time at Beverly Hills High, thanks, in part, to a teacher there who took particular interest in her project: Herb Hall. Hall primarily taught theater but also served as the coach of the speech team and taught classes in speech and debate.

If that name and job description sound familiar, they should. Mr. Hall, the speech and debate teacher played in *Clueless* by Wallace Shawn, was named after Hall, who retired from Beverly Hills High in 2014 after twenty-eight years on staff there. Hall also acted outside of school hours. So that guy who plays the principal of Bronson Alcott High in *Clueless* and introduces new student Tai Fraser during gym class? Yes, that's him.

As both he—the real Mr. Hall—and Heckerling explain, the students at an actual Beverly Hills high school definitely added more color to the fanciful Beverly Hills high school Heckerling invented in her screenplay.

Amy Heckerling, writer-director: I sat in on classes, mostly at Beverly Hills, but I also went to different schools, too, just to get a sense.

There was one school in the Valley where the kids were very, very motivated. But I think they had just really edited what they were showing me. They showed me their honors class and it was a class of the people, out of the whole school, that were getting all of the benefits. It was their way of showing me their best.

Herb Hall, the "real" Mr. Hall and the *Clueless* principal: I was actually at lunch in the faculty lounge one day and our principal, Ben Bushman, came through. He was giving a tour to a young lady. Ben wasn't one of those real glad-handy, hand-shaky type of people. So he wasn't crazy about doing those types of things. He walked through, and he saw me, and he just went: "Here. Go with Herb." It was the end of lunch and he didn't introduce us, so I had no idea who she was, and then he ran out the door. So I said, "Okay, what are you doing?"

[Amy]'s very, very shy and very quiet. So she said, "Well, I'm doing a film and I want to do some research because it takes place in this school environment." My first reaction in my head was *Oh, we get this all the time*. You know, I get e-mails and calls from people asking me if I can make them famous, if I will introduce them to movie stars, they want to come and make movies—all kinds of strange things. So I thought she was, maybe, a USC film student, because she was very young, very youthful looking. So I said, "Okay. Have you done anything? Is this your first film?" She goes, "Oh no. I've done some work before." It was clear she didn't want to say anything. So I said, "Well, like what?" And she said, "Oh, I did a movie called *Fast Times at Ridgemont High.*" And I just went, "*What?* You're Amy Heckerling!"

After lunch I had a public speaking class, and the irony was that about three-fourths of the kids in that class were theater students. She said she just wanted to sit in the back. She didn't want anybody to know who she was. . . . So I said, I won't teach, I'll just get them started on something and we'll see what happens.

We went in and I had no idea what I was going to do. I just started a conversation with a couple of them and it evolved from there, and they were just being themselves. We just pretty much BS-ed the majority of the class.

Shortly before the bell rang, one of the kids went, "Who's that lady in the back?" And I just said, "Well, I don't know. Why don't you ask her?" And he goes: "Who are you?" These are really outgoing theater kids. She said, "My name's Amy Heckerling and I'm just doing some research for a movie."

One of the kids said, "Is it about Beverly?" She goes, "Yeah." [The kid] goes, "You'd better not be doing *90210*." Because that had just come out and the school community was incensed and insulted by the way it was portrayed. So [the students] said, "Okay, we'll talk to you, but you have to promise us that you will do this movie right. And you won't just do the stupid stereotypes, you'll actually make the movie look the way the school does." So she said okay. She had told me she wanted to come for that class period, which was fifty minutes. That first day, she stayed an hour and a half.

Amy Heckerling: One of the girls told me a story about some friends of hers who were always fighting. They were a couple, but they were always fighting. But their fights seemed to be sort of for show. They had a dramatic edge to them. She told me about how at one prom . . . the girl and the guy had a fight and she locked herself in the bathroom and that was how the prom went for her. But it's something that people remember because it was the big fight at the prom. I liked that aspect of a couple, that their identity that they've picked out and they keep reenacting is they're the dramatic, *Who's Afraid of Virginia Woolf?* couple. [For the Val party scene] I thought, *Well this would be a good place—[Dionne and Murray have] got a captive audience for them to have a big fight.*

Herb Hall: There's a scene in the movie where a kid gets his report card—I think it was his report card—and Mr. Hall is telling him something about how he's one of the worst students he's ever had or something, and the kid starts cussing in Farsi. That's something that actually happened in my class.

I had given out grades or whatever it was. And I said, this is the lowest grade point average in the history of education. The kid looked at his paper and started cussing me out in Farsi. The whole class just fell apart. It was hysterical. So she used that. That's where that scene came from.

Amy Heckerling: There was a girl [in class] who was doing a debate on whether or not animals should be used in scientific experiments. She was standing in front of the class, and one arm would make a circular motion and then the other arm would make a circular motion. She really wasn't saying anything. It was: "We shouldn't use animals because we can do other things. Like, we can use computers." That was all she had and she just milked it for all it was worth. And I thought: *What? How can you be so damn lazy? How can you show up with an assignment and have nothing and with total confidence just get up in front of the* *class?* There was just such a nonchalance about her. They were in school but it wasn't like there was any quest for knowledge or ambition to go to a college . . . it felt like they were just schlepping around and putting on makeup.

The way I went to school [at a high school for art and design] was quite different and it wasn't typical, either. So maybe I just expected too much.

Herb Hall: Beverly High has this enormous front lawn. It looks like a college campus. And the kids do really spread out based on what groups they hang out with. At the time, there was this gigantic tree, which has since fallen down, that was called the Persian Tree. There are a lot of kids at that school that are of Persian descent. That was one of the things [the students] said to her: you have to put this in the movie because everybody thinks everybody at Beverly is this white, Anglo-Saxon-looking kid, like they are in *90210*. And they said, "That's not true. Make it look real."

I didn't [know there was a character named Mr. Hall] at all until I saw the script. And then I went, *Oh, this is interesting*. Then I went: *Oh, he's a speech teacher*. Now a whole bunch of stuff makes sense. She never told me. She didn't say anything.

Amy Heckerling: The name was just sort of an honor to him.

Herb Hall: The irony is that most of the kids she talked to in my class graduated. So I didn't see them [after the movie came out], but the kids who were there overwhelmingly thought it was really funny. You would always get the ones who didn't get the point. Who would go, "That's not what it's really like."

But the kids who got it overwhelmingly said yes, she got it right. The kids at Beverly liked the fact that there were little in-jokes that they knew nobody else was going to get except them.

Even now, it's a big deal . . . Once a month, the principal

would have tours of Beverly where prospective parents would come to the school. He would take them around the school to show them different parts of school programs and stuff. And when he would come to the theater department, he would let me walk them around the two theaters and tell them about how our program works. He would always insist that I tell them about *Clueless*. We would mention that in our particular department, all of us worked professionally outside of education. The music teachers did professional work and so forth, and then I would tell them about *Clueless*. And invariably they would go, "Oh, I've got to go run home and watch that again because I love that movie. We have eighteen copies of it." I would always tell them, "That's good, because you're paying my residuals. So go watch it on Netflix a few more times. That's good for me."

The Language of *Clueless*

Amy Heckerling's *Clueless* screenplay pulls off the neat, rhetorical magic trick of seeming both familiar and wholly new. Simultaneously, Heckerling managed to capture the way 1990s kids talked while also telling them how they were going to sound before they even knew it yet. "Some of the strange language that the girls use was put in because it's funny," says Wallace Shawn, the actor who played Mr. Hall, and also happens to be a noted playwright, screenwriter, and close friend of Heckerling's. "The next thing you knew it became part of the language Americans use in speaking to each other."

From an early age, Heckerling says she was fascinated by language, studying and collecting words and phrases from a variety of sources. That well-honed ear for slang and incessant curiosity about conversational idiosyncrasies informed the words she put in the mouths of her *Clueless* characters. Their unique dialect was inspired by all kinds of things, including the slang dictionary published by the linguistics department at the University of California–Los Angeles, classic movies, rap songs, Shawn's manner of speaking, and Heckerling's own creative mind.

Amy Heckerling, writer-director: Since I was a kid, any time I would see any article on slang and lists of words, I saved it. I have a folder with rusted paper clips and things from *Time* magazine from when I was a little kid.

My mother would take me to the movies when I was little. So in *West Side Story*: "He's a real down guy." "Down": that means good. So when [Christian] goes, "You're a down girl," that's from *West Side Story*. I've been compiling this shit my whole life.

Every way that you say something positive says something about who you are, how old you are, where you live, how much money you have—which is sometimes why I can't even talk, because everything's too revealing.

I made [a slang dictionary] for *Clueless* when I was writing it. So I have that one for that moment in time. Also, [I had] to have a separate category for Christian-speak because that was Rat Pack language. Rat Packian, 1940s to '60s, film noir, Dashiell Hammett, Frank Sinatra.

I had a jive-talk dictionary that I found in the library and xeroxed, from, I guess, the seventies. But it was words from the army and prison and musicians. I compile things from a lot of places. Also, a lot of songs. Obviously rap music, but even going back to Cab Calloway.

I wanted to make the kids smart and expressive and stylized. So . . . there's a black couple that sound like an old Jewish couple, and there's skaters, and then there's a girl whose father is a prominent attorney and has an intelligent teacher. She's steeped in their vernacular and also, separately, [in] teen-speak.

"Brutally rebuffed" was not something that teenagers were

saying. That's how Wally [Shawn] speaks. Wally's a smart guy. A lot of the way he speaks is in Cher's vernacular. When she says, "I tried to show the teacher my scholastic abilities and I was brutally rebuffed"—that's the way Wally talks. I just think his language is so beautiful and funny.

Wallace Shawn, Mr. Hall: I didn't know that. I don't know how I talk. So anybody is welcome to steal it!

Plenty of people use words that came to them from *Clueless* and they don't even know that they do. They haven't the faintest idea.

A Glossary of Selected *Clueless* Terms

AS IF

Amy Heckerling: "I had done a pilot with my friend Meredith Scott Lynn. She was in New York when I was writing [*Clueless*] and we'd hang out and do stuff [with her gay best friend, Andrew]. I think a lot of [sayings] come from the gay community and then get spread to kids and then to the general public. 'As if' and 'whatever' came from that gang of people."
Definition: The definition is pretty self-explanatory; it's the Cher Horowitz way of saying "no way!" or "not even."
Use it in a *Clueless* sentence: Cher, pushing away an amorous high school boy that she would never date: "Ew, get off of me! Ugh—as *if*!"

AUDI

Amy Heckerling: "Audi . . . where did I hear that? . . . That must have been from [students at] school."
Definition: The phrase also appears in *UCLA Slang 2*, the 1993 edition of the university's sporadically (sporadically—Tai shout-out!) updated slang dictionary. There, it is defined under "be Audi/

be Audi 5000/be 5000: v. to be leaving immediately. *I'm Audi.*" The reference, obviously, is to the car, which sounds like "outie."
Use it in a *Clueless* sentence: Both Cher and Tai exit scenes by announcing, "I'm Audi."

BALDWIN

Amy Heckerling: "I don't know if that was in the UCLA slang [dictionary] or if that was just from Baldwin brothers. I mean, it's obviously from Baldwin brothers, but I don't remember if I brought it up or if I read it."
Definition: It's not in the UCLA slang dictionary, so let's go ahead and give Heckerling credit for this one. Obviously it means a cute guy, as in the Paul Rudd kind.
Use it in a *Clueless* sentence: Cher, referring to Josh: "Okay, okay, so he's *kind of* a Baldwin."

BARNEY

Definition: Heckerling confirmed that this was taken from the UCLA slang dictionary, which defines it in multiple ways. The *Clueless* definition is the second one listed: "n. stupid or inadequate male: (male) loser. *That guy is a real barney*." *UCLA Slang 2* also points out that *barney* comes from the *Flintstones* character named Barney.
Use it in a *Clueless* sentence: Cher, referring to the douchebag guys Tai befriends at the mall: "I don't know where she meets these barneys."

BETTY

Definition: Heckerling confirmed that this also was taken from UCLA's *Slang 2*. The definition reads, in part: "n. very physically attractive female. *You should have seen this girl—we're talking major betty. The Flintstones.*" This, too, comes from *The Flintstones*; sadly, Betty married a Barney.
Use it in a *Clueless* sentence: Cher, referring to the portrait of her mother: "Wasn't my mom a betty?"

<u>BUGGIN', AS IN "TOTALLY BUGGIN'"</u>

Amy Heckerling: "*Buggin'* was around. *Totally* has been since the eighties."

Definition: It's just another way of saying "freaking out."

Use it in a *Clueless* sentence: Cher, describing her father's fiftieth-birthday party and making a pro-immigration argument: "People came that, like, did not RSVP. So I was, like, totally buggin'."

<u>HYMENALLY CHALLENGED</u>

Amy Heckerling: "That I made up, because a lot of the handicapped things were turning into challenges."

Definition: Totally virginized. (Related term: *ensembly challenged.*)

Use it in a *Clueless* sentence: Dionne: "Besides, the PC term is *hymenally challenged.*"

<u>IN ON THE HEAVY CLAMBAKES</u>

Amy Heckerling: "'Clambakes,' where did I get that from? I think from my jive-talk dictionary."

Definition: Essentially, it means being up on the social scene.

Use it in a *Clueless* sentence: Christian, to Cher: "I'm new, but I thought maybe you had an in on the heavy clambakes?"

<u>JEEPIN'</u>

Amy Heckerling: "That must have come from rap songs."

Definition: As the movie makes clear, this is a synonym for doing it in a car.

Use it in a *Clueless* sentence: Murray, to Dionne: "What's up? You jeepin' behind my back?" Dionne: "Jeepin'? No. But speaking of vehicular sex . . ."

<u>KEEPING IT REAL</u>

Amy Heckerling: "It's hard to remember: I think 'I'm keeping it real' was in the script. And 'It's the bomb.'"

Donald Faison: "She said that was in the script? No, that's not true. It was not in the script. I put that in the script. She didn't write *I'm keeping it real*. I heard that from my neighbor. Some kid in my neighborhood said, 'Just keep it real. Just make sure you keep it real.' And I was like, *Oh. That's what the kids are saying now*. And so I put that in there myself: 'I'm keepin' it real. Because I'm keepin' it real.' [She] didn't write that—damn it, Heckerling! Come on, old buddy!"

Amy Heckerling: "It might have been [Donald]. It could easily have been."

Donald Faison: "I said it because he was trying to be, like, a hoodlum. And when you keep it real in the hood, you keep it as gangster as possible. So when [Dionne] asks him, 'Why would you shave your head?' his response is, 'I'm keeping it real,' because he's gotten all gangster."

Use it in a *Clueless* sentence: Murray himself just did. Because he *still* keeps it real.

MONET

Amy Heckerling: "That one is from UCLA."

Definition: From *Slang 2*: "n. person who seems desirable from a distance, but isn't up close . . . [from Claude Monet]."

Use it in a *Clueless* sentence: Cher, referring to Amber: "She's a full-on Monet. It's like a painting, see? From far away, it's okay, but up close, it's a big ol' mess."

RATIONED

Amy Heckerling: "That's from World War II movies. Because rationing was a big thing."

Definition: It's another way of saying that one is socially unavailable or that one's time is limited.

Use it in a *Clueless* sentence: Christian, asking Cher if she's free this weekend: "Hey, Duchess, you rationed this weekend?"

SURFING THE CRIMSON WAVE

Heckerling couldn't recall whether she cribbed this term from a random slang dictionary, heard someone else say it, or made it up herself.

Amy Heckerling: "If you look through any slang dictionaries, there are tons of terms for sex, for being drunk, and for having your period. People are very expressive about that. In fact, I was going through some slang sites recently for a thing I'm writing now, and for getting your period, the new one that I loved is *Shark Week*. There's always something, you know: from *visit from Aunt Flo* to *Shark Week* to *surfing the crimson wave* to *riding the*, whatever, *the red corvette*—I just made that up."

Definition: It's surfer code for menstruating.

Use it in a *Clueless* sentence: Cher, explaining at least one of her tardies: "Mr. Hall, I was surfing the crimson wave. I had to haul ass to the ladies'."

TOE-UP

Amy Heckerling: "I'm not sure where it came from. I don't think it came from a song. I don't think it came from the UCLA slang study; it might have come from there. Maybe it did come from a rap song. *Toe-up* is like saying somebody's ugly."

Use it in a *Clueless* sentence: Dionne, objecting to Cher's suggestion that they adopt Tai: "Cher, she is toe-up. Our stock would plummet."

WAY HARSH

Amy Heckerling: "Using *way* as a qualifier—like *very*. That's the other one you have to have a lot of in your back pocket. That will change the feel of any word, by how you say it's 'very.' *Harsh* was just *harsh*. That wasn't like a new word."

Definition: Pretty self-explanatory, but: it's another way of saying extremely hurtful.

Use it in a *Clueless* sentence: Cher, after Tai calls her a virgin who can't drive: "That was way harsh, Tai."

WHATEVER, PREFERABLY WITH W HAND GESTURE

As Heckerling previously explained, that came from her friend actress Meredith Scott Lynn and her group of friends.

Amy Heckerling: "I remember that there was a lot of this. [*Heckerling makes the traditional* W *sign*.] This was like, early nineties. Then sometimes we'd both hold our hands up like this—[*Heckerling makes a bigger* W *sign with all fingers outstretched*]—because we'd make a big *whatever*."

Definition: You think this requires an explanation? *What-ever*.

Use it in a *Clueless* sentence: Amber to Cher, after Cher makes a flimsy debate point about the Haitians: "What-ever."

YOU GOT MY MARKER

Heckerling: "Oh, *marker*: That's, you know, *Guys and Dolls. Little Miss Marker.*"

Definition: *Marker* is another word for IOU. Which means this is Christian Stovitz–speak for "I owe you one."

Use it in a *Clueless* sentence: Christian, to Josh after he says he'll drive Cher home from the Bosstones party: "Thanks, man. You got my marker."

Casting *Clueless*: A Tale of Two Studios and Many Actors

Imagine Reese Witherspoon as Cher Horowitz, announcing that she "totally paused" at a stop sign. Imagine Cher arguing over the remote control with Josh, but with a Josh played by Ben Affleck. Picture the moment when Murray gets his head shaved at the Val party and his braces-a-sparklin' smile fills the entire frame. Now picture that face and that smile belonging to . . . Dave Chappelle.

Technically, the actors mentioned in this Bizarro World version of *Clueless* did not all audition for the real *Clueless*. Affleck did, reportedly reading for Josh when the project was still at Fox, while Witherspoon and Chappelle merely met casually with Amy Heckerling during the casting process. But the fact that they and others were either considered or mentioned, at least in passing, as possible fits for the roles now forever associated with Alicia Silverstone, Paul Rudd, and Donald Faison is a reminder of how widely the net gets thrown when the actors in a Hollywood movie are being chosen. Because everyone turned out to be so natural and right for their parts, it's easy to forget that there was a time when the canvas of *Clueless* was still blank, waiting to be colored in by faces plucked from head shots, TV pilots, casting tapes, auditions, and, of course, Aerosmith music videos.

This is the long, name-droppy story of how that canvas got its color via a casting process that began when the film was being developed at Fox, then continued after the project parked itself at Paramount Pictures. The people involved in that process included: two casting directors, writer-director Amy Heckerling, several producers, studio executives, and a flotilla of bright young actors who landed on the radar of all those key *Clueless* decision-makers. Obviously, only a handful of those actors would actually wind up in the movie. But even some of the ones who either dropped out or didn't make the cut would later become some pretty high-wattage people in the entertainment industry—the kind who would star in major summer blockbusters, appear in popular films and/or TV shows about vampires, and become Academy Award winners.

The Fox Sessions

Once Fox decided that the project eventually known as Clueless *should be a theatrical feature rather than a TV show, casting got under way. Carrie Frazier, a longtime friend of Heckerling's who got her start by acting as the director's assistant on* Fast Times at Ridgemont High, *was then working as a casting director who had staffed up the ensembles in films like* River's Edge *and 1994's* Little Women. *During the two months Frazier worked with Heckerling on* Clueless, *they, along with producer Twink Caplan, would audition several actors who would eventually get cast after the project moved to Paramount, Brittany Murphy, Donald Faison, and Jeremy Sisto among them. But there was one actress that Frazier and Heckerling insisted on locking down immediately: Alicia Silverstone, who both women agreed was the perfect Cher, full stop.*

Carrie Frazier, *Clueless* casting director at Fox: I brought in Alicia Silverstone. I sent Amy, I guess it was a videotape at that time, of a young actress that I felt was really terrific. Which was Alicia.

Amy Heckerling, writer-director: I was watching an Aerosmith video of "Cryin'." That was the first video she was in. And I just fell in love with her. Then my friend Carrie Frazier, who's a casting director [and] who was [casting it] when we were doing it at Fox, said, "You have to see this girl in *The Crush*." And I was like, "No, I want the Aerosmith girl." Well, it was the same girl.

Carrie Frazier: That is exactly what happened—totally. Totally!

Amy Heckerling: Carrie always says, "Why do you always tell people that you were on the treadmill watching her? I was the casting director and I told you to see her." That's true. My casting director Carrie told me to see that girl, who I also saw while I was exercising on the treadmill to an Aerosmith video. Then people would say, "[Alicia] was discovered while Heckerling was exercising to Aerosmith," which sounds more fun than saying, "A casting director told you to see her." But that's the same girl and that's who I loved.

Carrie Frazier: It's so funny about the whole Alicia thing because I keep telling Amy, "I'm the one who sent you the videotape, who told you to watch her," you know, and she goes, "No, no, I knew about her before," and I'm going, "Right." You know, that sort of stuff. [*Laughing*] But she's my dearest friend and it's like, you know, it's always that kind of stuff [between friends].

Amy Heckerling: When I finished the script, they were up to the "Crazy" video. So I videotaped it when it came on, and I gave [the producers] the script and the videotape. And they said: "Oh, the dark-haired one?" Which was Liv Tyler. I said: "No, no, no. *This* one."

[Alicia] came in with her manager at the time. She was, like, seventeen, and she was just so adorable and sweet and really innocent. Not a person that has been making movies for a long time, but like a real kid, although she had been making movies for a while. In fact, I think my ex-husband might have worked with her before when she was a little kid on *The Wonder Years*, as a girl that Fred Savage was in love with.[5]

Twink Caplan, associate producer and Miss Geist: Alicia was at lunch with [Amy] and she was drinking out of a straw. But you know when you're older, how you bring the glass to you, and when you're younger you bend down to where the straw and the glass are? That was like this little moment where Amy thought, *Oh my God, is this kid the part?* Alicia just, she really did have a—she still does—she's got this purity of spirit, you know?

Alicia Silverstone, Cher: [Amy] seemed so cool and laid-back—dressed in all black with her strong New York accent. As a California girl with English parents, [that accent] was really unique to me. She was warm and easy to talk to.

Carrie Frazier: It was a situation where she was going to have to do this big screen test. But I knew she was really young at the time. She had just come back into town and I secretly went over to her house and ran lines with her because I knew she

5 Heckerling's ex-husband, Neal Israel, did direct a couple episodes of *The Wonder Years*, but not the one that featured Silverstone. That 1992, season-five episode—in which Silverstone played a Kevin Arnold–attracting hottie named Jessica—was directed by Thomas Schlamme, who would go on to executive-produce and direct many episodes of *The West Wing*, among other TV shows.

needed someone to run lines [with]. It's like having someone do homework with you.

I didn't give her any real direction other than just making sure she, kind of, was a little up to speed. She had found this dog that she was adopting—she was a kid! She was just lovely. So we ran lines a bunch and sat and talked for a little while and then I said, "Okay, I'll see you tomorrow, you know, on the screen-test set." And we went down and she tested. I was reading with her in the screen test. I was just dreadful, but she was wonderful.

Alicia Silverstone: I remember when I read the script the first time, thinking, *Oh, she's so materialistic*. That I was, like, judging [Cher] instead of being delighted by her. I remember thinking, *This is so funny and I'm not funny*. That's what I thought at the time. But once I was playing her, no, I fully—I just had so much fun being her.

I loved how seriously she took everything. That's essentially how I played it. The woman that I worked with at the time said to me, when I said I'm not funny, she said, "Oh my God, you're the funniest person I know." And I said, "Why?" She said, "Because you take everything so seriously." And I really went with that. I felt like that was what Cher was. She was so sincere and so serious. And that's what I think makes her so ridiculous and lovely all the time, you know?

Carrie Frazier: After Alicia did [the] screen test, as I remember—and I might get some of this wrong—it went to Fox and they were kind of like, "Oh, she's okay." You know, it wasn't like, "Oh my God, this girl's fabulous." It was like, "Oh, she's okay," and, "Who else is there?" and—you know, the project was still kind of in flux and we weren't screen-testing anybody else. So that was the girl as far as I was concerned. I was like,

"This is the girl! If you don't grab her, you're nuts." This is the perfect casting and perfect time in an actor's life where you go, she's just the right everything for this role.

Amy Heckerling: I had my heart set on Alicia. When Fox was thinking of doing it, they wanted me to explore all the options—you could say, "Here's who I want and here's the script," and they go, "Yeah, fine. Now start casting." And they'll consider that person [you want], but they want you to see who's out there.

Carrie Frazier: I had just finished [casting] *Little Women* for MGM. I was really up on the young-girl scene, so I knew all the girls that I thought were really special. And you want to make sure you explore all of them. So that's what was happening.

Amy Heckerling: I saw Alicia Witt, the redheaded one. And who else? Tiffani Thiessen. The one that—she was in that show at NYU and she cut her hair and everybody was mad? Keri Russell, yes. Then they go, "You've got to see the girl in [*Flesh and Bone*]." I never got to see her, I guess she was off on other things. That turned out to be Gwyneth Paltrow.

Carrie Frazier: It was the first time I'd seen Angelina Jolie . . . and it was like, oh my gosh. But she was too knowing for what was needed for *Clueless*. I needed someone who was completely unknowing and Angelina was so knowing. It was an interesting moment. Angelina never came in [to audition] for the project. I was just looking at her tape, her videotape of music videos she'd been doing, [and saying], wow, that girl's really interesting! I remember an agent pitching her and I'm going, "No, no, no, this is exactly the opposite of what I need for this."

Later on, when I started heading up the casting department

for HBO and I got the script for *Gia*, I said, "I've got the girl." That was Angelina. And it was like, they didn't know who she was, they had someone else in mind for the role, they had already supposedly given the role away, and I just beat them senseless until they said, "Oh, I see what you mean. This is the right girl." It happens.

Amy Heckerling: I met with Reese [Witherspoon] because everyone said, "This girl's amazing. She's going to be huge." I went, "Okay." But [I was told,] "She's not going to read. You can meet with her."

Carrie Frazier: I had her meet Reese over at the Four Seasons hotel in Los Angeles, on Doheny, in the bar. I'm a huge Reese Witherspoon fan. I just thought she was terrific.

Amy Heckerling: I saw some movie where she had a Southern accent. Maybe it was on TV, a movie of the week, I don't know. But I did see some scenes of hers and went: *Wow. She's amazing.* But Alicia is Cher.

Carrie Frazier: So much of casting is about catching the actor or actress at the right time in their life. And even though you end up going, "So-and-so can do the role," there was something about Alicia that was a little bit younger and a little bit more naive in a way that we felt was really the right girl.

I brought in Brittany Murphy. She was just so similar, again, to the character. She was really sweet, really had that slightly didn't-have-a-lot-of-confidence kind of quality, trying to do the right thing. She just was wonderful.

She got halfway through her reading, and I said, "You can stop." And usually when someone says that, a casting director, they're like, "Nah, you're not right, get out of here." Or "Let's do something else," or something. She looked at me with those big eyes like, *Ohhh no, I didn't make the cut*. I said, "You can stop because you're coming back for the director." She goes, "*Really?*" She's like, all smiles. And I go, "Absolutely. You thought I was going to stop you because I didn't like what you were doing." She goes: "Yeah!" I go, "No, no no. You're coming back. I don't want to touch what you're doing, I just want Amy to see it." So then she came back and it was just lovely.

Oh gosh, who else did I bring in that ended up in the movie? Is it Jeremy Sisto? Yeah, Jeremy Sisto. I feel like—oh, the maid, the woman who played the maid, do you remember? Aida Linares. Yeah, I brought her in. [Donald Faison]—he's so nice. Yeah, I cast him in it, too.

Donald Faison, Murray: I remember auditioning for it twice, or three times, and nothing coming out of it. Then them coming back maybe a few months later and being like, hey, so it's the same movie but we're with a different studio now. So I auditioned again.

Amy Heckerling: Ben Affleck told me [later that] he read. But I don't remember that. I don't remember him reading for me. He might have read for a casting director.

Carrie Frazier: I brought in Ben Affleck, for the role of Josh. I thought he would be fabulous for it. I was really trying to get Ben Affleck the part.

I was so upset [when the project went into turnaround] and so kind of like, *Oh no!* Again, because I thought, *Oh, I've got the perfect girl for the role*, you know. A lot of it's just the luck of who is right there. And she was right there.

I just was kind of, like, confounded. But nothing surprised me making movies.

Alicia Silverstone: I do remember after being cast, getting a fax—this was pre-e-mail—from Amy, while I was shooting in Paris with James Gandolfini, saying something to the effect of, "The studio has decided they don't want to make it, but we're not going to give up!"

Carrie Frazier: Then, when I got the call that it was going over to Paramount, they wanted to have me work on it for no money. They said, "Oh, we paid you for two months already at the other studio, so we're not going to pay you over here." And I was like, "That's awful." I'm a real proponent of casting directors and I feel that they've been taken advantage of over the years, incredibly, and have been paid badly.

I said, "I'm not doing that. I'm just not doing that." It's like, "This is a really good movie. I've worked my butt off and now you want me to work a whole bunch more but not pay me? What are you thinking? You wouldn't do that to any other person in any other department." And I said I wouldn't do that, they'd have to pay me, and they said, "Oh, well, we really can't do that." So I went off and did *Leaving Las Vegas*. I figured if I'm going to do something for no money, I'm going to do it for some place that really doesn't have any money.

I was really heartbroken about that on every level. Every level.

On to Paramount

When Clueless *eventually landed in the hands of producer Scott Rudin and Paramount Pictures, Frazier was off the project, and Marcia Ross—a casting veteran who had worked in both television and film, and most recently had been the head of casting for the TV division at Warner Bros.—was brought on as the new casting director. Ross says she had left the Warner Bros. job to go back to casting independently, but had been paid out of the last year of her Warner Bros. contract. That payout put her in a situation where she didn't need to worry about the fact that, by Hollywood standards, she would not be paid much for her work.*

With Ross, a new set of producers—including Rudin, Adam Schroeder, Robert Lawrence, and Barry Berg—and Heckerling, Caplan, and Paramount executives all now at the decision-making table, the second attempt to cast Clueless *began as the fall of 1994 got under way. Thankfully, Ross never threw away her notes from that time period. In the account that follows, she reads from selected portions of them and confirms the identities of some of the actors under* Clueless *consideration. It's important to remember, again, that some of the actors mentioned below actually auditioned and some of them did not. But the mere fact that all of their names ended up in the* Clueless *casting director's notes speaks to the level of talent eager to be part of Heckerling's second high school classic.*

Marcia Ross, *Clueless* casting director at Paramount Pictures: I got a call one day just out of the blue saying, "Would you be interested in this movie? It's at Paramount. Scott Rudin is producing." Scott Rudin: he already was a huge producer. I knew Scott Rudin when he was a nineteen-year-old casting director. He's younger than me . . . When I was working at a small talent agency, he was casting.

And Amy Heckerling—well, I loved *Fast Times at Ridgemont High*. But the thing is, they have no money. They have $10,000 for a casting director. To me, I was like, *You know what? That's fine. I just got paid off for a year at Warner Bros., and I want to get back into the movies and I want to do a studio feature*. I would have done it for free, you know what I'm saying?

Carrie Frazier: Marcia was very generous about [the transition] with me personally and I still, to this day, appreciate it. Marcia's fabulous.

I don't begrudge her anything, I just think that casting directors should be paid. But I think it's getting better. I hope it's getting better.

Marcia Ross: When the movie left Fox and went to Paramount, with now Scott as producer, the budget was quite reduced. I never knew why Carrie did not continue as the casting director. We went back and reread and then tested some of Amy's candidates from the Fox readings. They were in the mix with everyone else that I was bringing in.

Adam Schroeder, coproducer: The casting was going to be so important. When you think about the benchmark of the cast of *Fast Times*, not to talk about *Fast Times* so much, but man: look at the careers that those guys ended up having, and it was the first movie for most of them.

Marcia Ross: [*Flipping through her notes*] It's so funny to go back and see some of these people you read.

There were a number of people, like Freddy Rodriguez, Norman Reedus, Mekhi Phifer, Jeremy Renner . . . where [it] was the very early days of their careers.

My first preread session was Monday, September twelfth, 1994. The very first person it looks like I read the very first day was Freddy Rodriguez. He was reading for Travis. He was nineteen at the time. He looks very young but adorable.

On October sixth, I put together a demo for [Amy] and on this demo was Eric Close, for I don't know what part; Breckin Meyer from something called *The Jackie Thomas Show*; Chris Demetral; Johnny Whitworth from *Party of Five*; Paul Rudd from *Sisters*; Jeremy Renner, reading the role of Travis; and Michael Cade.

While Ross, Heckerling, and others searched widely and thought carefully about all the roles, they agree that deciding who should play Josh was the toughest decision they had to make.

Amy Heckerling: [Casting Josh] was the hardest. I had a vision in my head and it wasn't gelling with people out there. When I'm writing, I usually have little pictures of what I imagine the guy looking like. And I had the Beastie Boy: Adam Horovitz.

There was something smart and funny about him. The way he looked and the songs: that was in my brain.

Marcia Ross: Because I was always reading actors, I knew a lot of people and I knew a lot of young actors and I was able to come up with a bunch of thoughts for parts and sort of come in with ideas and show her these ideas. Paul Rudd was one of those people.

Paul Rudd, Josh: When I auditioned for it, I had also asked to read for other parts, [including Christian and Murray].

I thought Murray was kind of a white guy wanting to be black. I didn't realize he was actually black. Also I thought: *I haven't seen that character before, the white guy who's trying to co-opt black culture*. But, well: *That character is actually going to be African-American*. Oh, okay.

I think I read for Elton as well. But Amy said, "What do you think of Josh? Do you want to read for that?" So I did.

Amy Heckerling: I remember I saw Paul, and I really liked him. There were still more people to be seen. Sometimes you see somebody, you love them but there's five others or ten others on the list that you're still going to be seeing.

Adam Schroeder: He needed to be older and [Alicia] was young, but we didn't ever want it to feel not natural when they ended up together. There was the whole stepbrother thing, even though they weren't related at all, so we really wanted to be careful and cast that perfect person. We read a lot of actors.

Twink Caplan: Amy and I loved [Paul] right off. We did. We *loved* him. He hadn't done that much, but he was cute and he was sweet. He reminded me of George Peppard. Not in his acting, but, like, the nose. You know, his nose and stuff. But he was the sweetest guy, very engaging. That giggly-eye smile, his eyes would just, you know . . . he was wonderful, really wonderful.

Adam Schroeder: He'd done mostly television but Scott and I had seen a TV pilot, a busted TV pilot that didn't go, called *Wild Oats*. We would always watch the pilots that didn't go just to see what new actors and writers [were out there]. It's almost more interesting to see what didn't go and why. You can really discover things that way. And he really was just a standout from this pilot, half-hour sitcom, for Fox. He came in and was so interesting. We tested him and we knew he was very, very top of the list.

Paul Rudd: I knew that they must have been kind of interested, because they had me back a few times. Honestly, what I remember when I was auditioning and meeting Amy for the first time is making some joke about Shakespeare preparing something from a monologue. I'm sure it was not a very good joke or anything. But I remember she really laughed at it. Almost more than anything else, I remember, in talking with Amy in the auditions, I was like: *Oh, she's cool*. And feeling like: *Oh, I click with her*.

Marcia Ross: We had him on hold—we had him on hold for a long time, but they weren't really ready to decide. Then . . . finally, they decided—they cut him loose, actually. And it was hard. They really liked him but they just couldn't commit to it and he was offered another movie. Finally, we couldn't hold him anymore. He took this *Halloween* movie [or] something. I remember he cut his hair for that and the whole thing.[6]

Paul Rudd: I had done that *Halloween* movie before *Clueless*. That *Halloween* movie was my first movie, which I wasn't so sure I wanted to do. I had a manager at the time, who was like, "You should do this." And then I remember I got *Clueless*, and he's like, "You shouldn't do this." That's how good that manager was. But anyway, I cut my hair for the sake of cutting my hair.

I remember really vividly where I was, just kind of walking down the street, and I was like, "Man. I don't know. Why don't I just cut off all my hair?" And I just walked into a barber shop and they just buzzed my head. Then I want to say, a week later or something, I was in a restaurant and Amy Heckerling was there.

6 Rudd starred in the sixth *Halloween* movie, *Halloween: The Curse of Michael Myers*. He played Tommy Doyle, the grown-up version of the boy Jamie Lee Curtis babysits in the original *Halloween*.The movie opened two months after *Clueless*, on September 29, 1995. Even when figures are adjusted for inflation, it remains one of the lowest-grossing films in the *Halloween* franchise.

Amy Heckerling: I ran into him in a restaurant and he had cut his hair really short. I went, "What the fuck did you do?" He said, "I didn't think I had the part." I said, "Oh my God, hardly any time went by, I didn't finish seeing everybody. Yeah, I want you. You cut your hair?" I knew I wanted him and we hadn't finished seeing the people we were going to be seeing. And in that time, he assumed that it was over.

Paul Rudd: I was very, like, weirdly cavalier about it. I just go: "Oh, I didn't know." In a way, it wasn't really on my radar. And I remember I said, "Well, you know: if it's supposed to work out, it'll work out." Saying that to Amy—you kind of want to say, "No, that's not the way it works!" *[Laughs]* Because she had said, "If you hadn't cut your hair, you might have gotten this part." And I was like, "Oh. Oh, okay." It was weird, I wasn't—yeah, I think I might have just been a little too casual about the whole thing. Which, in retrospect, is probably a good approach for most things.

Marcia Ross: We still kept seeing more people. We kept seeing more people and [were] not sure we had it, and seeing more people and [were] not sure we had it, and seeing more people.

Michelle Manning, executive vice president of production at Paramount Pictures: Maybe [casting] it was hard, [and] I just didn't realize they were going through so many people.

They would just bring me who they wanted [and] we said yes.

Marcia Ross: I'm fairly sure Zach Braff read for Josh. I had hired a casting director in Chicago to put people on tape for the role while I was still searching for an actor to play the role. He was going to [Northwestern] at the time. My note was that he was good.

Look at this here: [*Reading from notes*] "To all concerned"—this is from me—"Amy and Twink have plans to be in New York City on Tuesday, October eleventh. I would like to set up an audition taping session of the following actors starting at ten a.m. that day. Please advise about arrangements: Lauryn Hill; Donald Faison . . . Billy Crudup—reread script, didn't think it was right [for him]; Rafael Petlock; Sarah Gellar; Michael Imperioli; Peter Facinelli; Adrien Brody; Steve Zahn; Damon Wayans; Diego Serrano; Sam Trammell; Donovan Leitch; Justin Theroux; Gabe Olds; Holter Graham; Danny Morgenstern . . ."

I'm not saying all these people came in, but that's the memo I sent out about auditions.

Amy Heckerling: There's so much [that goes into casting]. Sometimes you feel like [the actor is] too similar to somebody else that really is going to play one of the other roles, and you need more of a contrast. Sometimes you just—your heart goes out to a person and you go, *Oh my gosh, I just really love that person. I want to watch them.*

Marcia Ross: [*Reading from notes*] "Larenz Tate. Margaret Cho—meeting only." It's so funny to go back and see all this.

Amy Heckerling: Other times, God knows there's a sexual element to it. You just think, *Oh my God, they're so hot.* Which I would have for guys and I know most guys have for the girls that they cast. You could see being in love with them. That doesn't mean you are in love with them, but that part of your brain works to see how that's possible. I feel like in a way, I could see being in love with all those people that are in [*Clueless*].

Marcia Ross: [*Continuing to read from notes*] "The following is a list of actors that are scheduled [to read in New York]." [*Stops* *reading*] Again, I can't say they all auditioned. [*Resumes reading*] "Anthony Rapp; Steve Zahn; Peter Facinelli; Justin Walker; Lauryn Hill; Donald Faison; Justin Theroux; Gabe Olds; Holter Graham; Josh Hamilton; Matt McGrath; Michael Imperioli; Adrien Brody."

A lot of these guys read for Josh.

[*Again, reading from her notes*] "Dear Adam: As per Scott's request, I spoke with Carolyn Kessler at Premier Artists about the possibility of Alicia coming in for a casting session on Monday, October seventeenth, to read with Josh Charles. . . ."

Adam Schroeder: Josh Charles was talked about. Did anybody mention him? I'm trying to think. He was a friend at the time. I don't know if he came in, because he was kind of making movies.

Donald Faison: I went on the audition in New York and I ran into people I went to high school with, like Josh Charles, who, I think we were in Spanish together. He was auditioning for Josh.

Marcia Ross: [*Reading from another section of her notes*] "If [Alicia]'s available, it might be a good idea to have her also read with the following actors: Eric Close, Henry Thomas . . ."

Adam Schroeder: I think [Henry Thomas] came in for Josh, yeah. He just didn't seem right for it. He was the right age. He wasn't young enough, I think, to play any of the other kids. I don't know, Josh had to have that kind of, cool, but not.

Marcia Ross: [*Still reading from her notes*] "Jason London, David Lascher, Dalton James, Paul Rudd, Johnny Whitworth . . . For Christian: Chris Demetral . . . Jamie Walters, Justin Walker. For Heather: Natasha Wagner. For Tai: Alanna Ubach, Brittany Murphy. Stephen Baldwin for Christian. Stacey Dash. Call somebody about Donald Faison. Bring out to read. Bring out Justin Walker. Bring back Justin Whalin."

Well, there you go . . . It was a callback session.

We screen-tested at the end, and that's really how it ended up with Paul. We screen-tested several guys with [Alicia] on film, and she and Paul—he really was good with her. He was great with her.

Adam Schroeder: [It came down to] Stephen Mailer, who is Norman Mailer's [son]. He was an actor. I'd seen him in a production of *Sophistry*, a Jonathan Marc Sherman play here in LA, and he'd done a couple of movies. He was a really, really good actor. I don't know what he's gone on to since. This is kind of funny: Richard Grieco's brother [David] . . . who was a really good-looking, charismatic kid who hadn't acted before.

He was actually an artist and I don't know how he came to us. Marcia must have found him. He came the very last time we were doing these tests with Paul and Stephen Mailer and then another guy named David Kriegel—I think his name was David Kriegel, who I think had been in *Speed* . . . Those are the guys it came down to.

Marcia Ross: From the minute he came in to the minute he got the part—and it was such a long journey, really, that one in particular—there was always this sort of harking back to: remember Paul? I can't explain it to you. He never went out of consciousness.

Paul Rudd: I don't remember the actual call saying I got the part. I do remember shooting *Halloween* 6 and having a conversation with my manager at the time and talking about it, and how they wanted me to do it. And he wasn't sure. It was my first movie. No one was getting paid anything, and it wasn't a big budget or anything. They made the offer, and he asked for less than they made the offer for in exchange for second billing. It was just all up in the air. *[Laughing]* He had a funny, unorthodox approach.

With *Halloween*, which I treasure. I really do. I think it's hilarious. That was one, I wasn't sure about that. But *Clueless:* no, I wanted to do that one. And that was the one that they were like, "I don't know."

Donald Faison: I met Paul then [during auditions]. I met Breckin Meyer; I'd seen him in *A Nightmare on Elm Street 4* or 5 or some shit like that. I thought that was really freakin' cool. I was like, *Holy cow, that's the dude from* Nightmare on Elm Street*!*

There are conflicting recollections about exactly who, aside from Breckin Meyer, was an "official" finalist for the role of Travis Birkenstock. It is clear, however, that several actors were strongly considered for the part, including one who is now an Avenger, another who is currently starring in The Big Bang Theory, *and a third who happens to be Meyer's best friend.*

Adam Schroeder: You know, it was also funny when Breckin Meyer came in and Seth Green came in and it was down to the two of them for Travis. And it turned out they were best friends.

Marcia Ross: I know that Seth and Breckin are great friends and I have spoken to both of them about auditioning for the same role.

Adam Schroeder: It was really sweet. Breckin and Seth were best friends and really supportive of each other. But I'm sure each wanted the part. Then one of the top contenders for Tai was an actress named Alanna Ubach. Alanna was Seth Green's girlfriend [at the time]. So there was a version of Seth Green and his girlfriend playing Tai and Travis, at one point. But obviously they cast Breckin and Brittany and we were so happy.

Marcia Ross: Jeremy Renner was the other choice for Breckin's part.

[*Later, as she's scanning her casting notes*] Ooh, Johnny Galecki! Johnny Galecki—he came down to the final two on that part. He was the other one.

Adam Schroeder: Seth came to visit the set. Through the years, that's what stuck in my mind. But I do remember Johnny Galecki, yeah. He was definitely in the mix. He went on to some good stuff, huh?

Amy Heckerling: I remember Johnny Galecki came in. I liked him a lot. But, you know, I love Breckin.

Breckin Meyer, Travis: I thought Travis could be a cute, scene-stealing role. Not that I think I did, but the potential in the character was that. So I stole a ton from Spicoli and I actually stole a ton from Keanu Reeves in *Bill and Ted's Excellent Adventure*. He was just one of those sweet, kindhearted, dopey guys that when you watch him you kind of go, "Why should I be mean to him?"[7]

Marcia Ross: Leah Remini saw me on 9-22-94. [It] was a general meeting. She would not read per her agent. . . . She was twenty-four at the time. I noted that she was sweet but

7 From the "Class of 1995" featurette on the Blu-ray release of *Clueless*.

played more like nineteen, twenty. Too old to play [high school].

Adam Schroeder: Brittany came in and she was such a standout. She was so bubbly and effervescent. She was young but there was a little bit of a worldliness to her. An innocence and a worldliness, in a weird way. She really got it. She was just naturally funny. She naturally had a funny spirit. Which was great, because Alicia had a different kind of comic spirit. She had a much more, kind of, sardonic thing. And the chemistry between the two of them was really lovely. It was really a lot of fun.

I remember Alanna, who was Seth Green's girlfriend . . . I had known her work at the time, and she was a lot of fun. But it was a much more adult version, I think. She was actually very worldly. Brittany had an innocence about her, I guess was what it was. Just a very bright-eyed, ripe-to-be-made-over [innocence].

Amy Heckerling: I remember Alanna Ubach. She was in a play that we went to see and I really liked her. She read for Tai. This was when she was in the middle of doing a play and her reading was a little theatrical. Then when I met Brittany, I was like: *I love her. I want to take care of her.*

She was just so bouncy and giggly and just so young. This young-girl energy that was so happy. I mean, when you saw her, you just smiled.

Twink Caplan: She was so cute [that] we kept her and she sat on the floor when we auditioned some other people. Because, right away, Amy knew she surely had the part and we kept her for the rest of the afternoon in the room with us.

Adam Schroeder: It was the second time she was coming in and we were doing the mixing and matching. We had her stay in the casting with us and Alicia . . . maybe we were bringing in Dionnes, or maybe Joshes. She stayed and it was exciting for her. She never had been involved in that end of it. I remember there was just a joy. Everything was very exciting to her and it was fun to be around her and to watch her enjoy this. I think she knew it was a really big deal for her. I think all the actors did.

Alicia Silverstone: I remember her audition. When she came in for her audition, it was just like: *Oh my God. Stop the press. This is the girl. This is so clear.* She was so special for that role and just adorable and lovely and brilliant.

Stacey Dash, Dionne: I actually didn't get the whole script at first, I just got the sides. I went in and I mean, just from the sides, I knew it was mine. I knew it was my role. So I went in. I nailed it. They called me back in, again, to read with Alicia. I went back in, read with Alicia. We had great chemistry. So that was in the bag.

As soon as I met [Alicia], she was as sweet as can be. I mean, and so gracious. Of course I was nervous because it's an audition process. But she just made me feel so at ease, and so did Amy . . . she made everything just about having fun.

Amy Heckerling: In my brain, Dionne was like royalty. I wanted someone that felt like they were part of a royal family in some country somewhere. So they weren't acting snotty, they were just in a different realm. [Stacey] had that. She didn't have to act like, "I'm a snotty bitch"—she just had that feeling of power and grace, as though she was ready to wave to the public.

Adam Schroeder: Stacey Dash came in and she was just fantastic: so beautiful and funny and gifted. We knew she was a little older. We were mostly casting eighteen to play the fifteen-to-sixteen[-year-olds].

Donald Faison: This was at the same time the Fugees [were] coming out, and Lauryn Hill was up for the Dionne role. I knew Lauryn Hill, so I called her to see if she would come to my house. And she did. With her busy schedule—but she did. And we rehearsed the freeway scenes and the "lend me five dollars" scene.

Stacey Dash: I went back and read with Terrence Howard and Donald Faison, [who were auditioning] to play Murray. And of course Donald got the role. And then that was it. That was the end of the audition process.

I just knew that Donald was funnier. Donald had great comedic timing and we had great chemistry together. . . . From the moment Donald and I met, even in the waiting room, we just had this great chemistry.

Marcia Ross: We read people. It's not that we didn't read a bunch of people, because we did. But in the end, you know, [Stacey] just was the role. I'm sure we did a chemistry reading. That plays a huge part: they were a great ensemble, these kids. That's part of why, I think, it's as good as it is.

Amy Heckerling: I do remember that I saw Mel Brooks's movie [*Robin Hood*] *Men in Tights*. And I loved Dave Chappelle. I met with him in New York, and I just loved him. In fact, I think I was at the Mayflower Hotel. He came over and we had coffee. Then Wally Shawn came over, because he's my pal. I just thought, *Oh my God, this guy is amazing.*

Donald Faison: I didn't [know that Chappelle was considered for Murray]. That would have been awesome, too.

Amy Heckerling: Donald had a much more kidlike energy. And Dave was like—there was a very cynical, grown-up, funny comic kind of thing that I felt was maybe a little too edgy. As much as I loved him, I felt he was too mature and edgy for what I needed the guy to be doing. Donald was like a puppy.

Donald Faison: I remember walking into the audition with a cell phone. Well, it wasn't a cell phone. It was a fake phone so I could look the part. And I had a bandana on. All I knew about LA was *Boyz n the Hood* and *Menace II Society* and stuff. So I walk into the audition with a bandana on my head and a plaid shirt. Pretty much, I thought if I could look like Ice Cube on this audition, I will have tackled who Murray thinks he is.

And so, I remember going and doing the audition in New York and then them saying, "We're going to fly you out to Los Angeles." I was like, "Well, who else is auditioning in Los Angeles?" And they were like, "Just you. If you don't blow it, you've got the part, pretty much." Twink Caplan told me that. And I was like, "Holy cow, that's awesome."

Adam Schroeder: Donnie Faison came in and became one of our favorites for Murray. And then his cousin, Terrence Howard, also was one of the top contenders, which was kind of funny. Obviously Terrence has gone on to great things and Donnie has gone on to great things, but it's just kind of a small world. A crazy, small world.

Marcia Ross: Terrence Howard was reading for Murray. He was the other choice in the finals. He came down to the end with Donald. Him and Donald.

Donald Faison: We grew up together pretty much. I've known Terrence since . . . I was nine, you know what I mean?

Right before I went to Los Angeles, I don't know what happened. They wanted me, is what I was told. He was like, "Yeah, go get it, man. Go do your thing." You know what I'm saying? But he never told me [earlier] that he was up for the role. I didn't find out he was up for the role until after my final audition in New York, when I was about to go to LA.

Everybody was at that audition [in LA]. Everybody from *90210* and everything like that. I was the only person auditioning for my part. So that was really cool. I met Stacey that day. I met Alicia that day. It was all in this little tiny room but it had this decent-sized waiting area. I remember going and rehearsing with Stacey. We were all paired together and stuff. I think Alicia and I were the only two that really knew we had the role. And everybody else, they were auditioning. I remember being like, *Holy cow, I'm here, dude. Look who's around me! Is that Brian Austin Green that just walked in?* You know what I mean? It was great.

I remember when they called me and told me I got the part, and me telling all my friends that I was going to be kissing Stacey Dash, and them chasing me around the complex that I lived in.

Stacey Dash: I was crossing the street [in LA], I'll never forget it. I got the phone call that I got the job and I almost got hit by a car. I was just jumping up and down in the middle of the street, screaming because I was so excited.

Marcia Ross: What often would happen in the sessions is [Amy] might like somebody but then she wanted to see them again for another role. So somebody I remember, like Jeremy Sisto, might have read easily for three roles. Except for Murray, he probably read for all three [male lead] roles.

Jeremy Sisto, Elton: I could have read for a couple of the different characters and then I decided to read for Elton because I thought he was funny . . . It just seemed like more fun to do the more extreme character, like the worst of the bunch, kind of, as opposed to the romantic guy.

My wife at the time probably liked him, I don't know.[8]

Marcia Ross: [*Reading from her notes*] "Jeremy Sisto—he's a good actor." He read for Josh and Elton that same day and [Amy] said, "No, he's an Elton."

Amy Heckerling: Well, that voice is very distinctive. It felt very entitled. I felt like that would go better with Elton than with a more insecure, angry-at-the-world kind of person [like Josh].

Jeremy Sisto: I remember Amy Heckerling said I reminded her of John Travolta. She liked that because she had worked with John Travolta [before].

Adam Schroeder: I really loved Sarah Michelle Gellar, who was on *All My Children* at the time. She played Erica Kane's daughter and she was just kind of a wicked, beautiful—I think she won the daytime Emmy. I showed Amy tapes of her. She was in New York on *All My Children* but she was just terrific, so we ended up offering her the part of Amber. There became a big negotiation for *All My Children* to let her out. It was just for a couple of weeks and they absolutely stuck their feet in [and] wouldn't let her out.

---

8 Sisto married actress Marisa Ryan in 1993; they later divorced. The actor is currently married to Addie Lane, with whom he has two children.

Amy Heckerling: Just when she would say things with that attitude—it just cracked me up. She could make the rich, entitled, snotty girl funny. She was wonderful.

They wouldn't let us have her. They wouldn't help make it work.

Marcia Ross: Here's a little note: [*Reading*] "To Amy Heckerling from Marcia Ross. Tuesday, October eighteenth. Roles of Amber and Heather . . . Here are the names of the actors to review for these two roles. Amber: Natasha Wagner, Ele Keats . . . Keri Russell . . . For Heather: Natasha Wagner, Susan Mohun, Elisa Donovan, Meredith Scott Lynn, Brooke Langton, Amy Hathaway, Renée Humphrey, and Mia Kirshner."

[Heather] is probably what [Elisa] came in for, yes. Because we probably knew we liked the other one [Gellar], so we were in the midst of hiring her. That deal went on for a long time before it fell apart.

Elisa Donovan, Amber: I had no idea about Sarah being a front-runner for the role of Amber. I do remember reading all of the smaller female roles for Marcia. I also remember Marcia being so great—so encouraging and kind.

Essentially, it was really only the second truly professional job that I had done. I had done a couple of episodes of a soap opera in New York City. And then I had just moved to LA, and gotten a job on the series *Blossom* with Joey Lawrence and Mayim Bialik. So I was doing that show. I just got hired for one episode, and then they had me come back for a couple of episodes, and in the middle of that I got the audition for the movie.

I started at the very beginning. I had what's called a pre-read, where you read just for the casting director. . . . Then I went to the second audition, which was Marcia and I think probably Twink, and I'm not sure if Amy was there the second time or not. The third time it was Amy and Twink and Marcia. I had to go three or four times. And then the final time was at Scott Rudin's office at Paramount. Which was terrifying. It was the first time I had ever been on the Paramount lot, which was so intimidating and so daunting. I remember hallucinating, not really remembering a lot of it, and just being so nervous. But they were super nice. They're such creative people, and such actor-friendly people, it was probably as nice as you could hope for.

Adam Schroeder: [Elisa] was really funny, really beautiful. I remember she reminded us of Ann-Margret. It's an old-school reference, but she had that kind of sexy, ginger, I guess, beauty. She really got it. She got the wit and cynicism of Amber. You want her to be one of those characters you love to hate. But you don't really hate her. She's just—it's comedy. It's funny. And obviously Cher is always going to win. But Elisa was really game and I think she had done very, very little at the time.

Elisa Donovan: I know I was supposed to fly home, and I got the call that I got the job when I was on the way to the airport. And I think I had to not go, or I went for the weekend and I came back, and we started fittings and that kind of thing.

I didn't have what's called a recurring contract [on *Blossom*]; they just kept writing me in. So I had to decide what to do, obviously. I remember my dad saying, "Well, you know, what's this movie thing? Maybe it's not going to go anywhere and who are these people? But the TV show is a real job, you know. They want to hire you and it's on TV and we see it every week." And I was like, "Dad, no, this is a really big deal. It could be a really big movie." So it was a very funny moment of trying to convince [my parents] that it was the right thing to do.

Marcia Ross: The Justin Walker part's a great story because we were really having a tough time casting. A really difficult time. You had to find a person who kind of was gorgeous that she could have the crush on, but you didn't want: "Oh yeah, he's gay." You know what I mean? He had to be different than the other guys, have a different quality than the other guys, but be believable as someone she would absolutely have a great crush on and absolutely go, "Oh, wait a minute: of course." None of it should be a surprise but you shouldn't look at him and go, "Oh yeah, he's gay." You didn't want to do that. You wanted to believe she actually found the guy.

Amy Heckerling: That guy had to be cute, [and] had to be in a different time period from everybody else. He had to have his own style. He had to be reminiscent of another kind of fifties, sixties kind of thing. There's a guy who was Drew Barrymore's boyfriend at the time. He had a rock group. I think he was briefly on one of those TV shows.

Adam Schroeder: Jamie Walters. He came in and we liked him. Yes, he was reading for Christian.

Amy Heckerling: I remember thinking he had an interesting look. He felt like he was from a different time period.

Marcia Ross: I can read a few names here that you would know: Peter Facinelli read for Christian. There are people who I don't even know anymore but—Donovan Leitch, he read for it. I remember him pretty vividly.

Adam Schroeder: I remember the Christian part was hard. It was really challenging and we had to go to New York, actually.

We weren't casting in New York but we did make a trip to New York to see, primarily, Christians at the time. And there was this kid, Justin Walker, who had—I think he had literally just done a Domino's Pizza ad. It was really funny. For some reason, I only remember that he delivers the pizza in his underwear. It was comic, it was funny—it was like a comedy thing. But he just got it. He got the, kind of, old-school Rat Pack thing of Christian.

Justin Walker, Christian: This thing for me was like pulled out of nowhere. My career was really kind of floundering. I was in between agents, I was working with somebody on a freelance basis. I was between apartments. I was sleeping on someone's couch. I got a phone call to come in and read for this film, and I was given the choice to read for Josh or for Christian, and when I looked at the material, the way the rhythm, the vocabulary, and everything else about the part [of] Christian—it was a no-doubter.

Marcia Ross: He read for me in the morning for Josh, when I was in New York. I had Amy in the afternoon for callbacks, so it was a short period of time. I gave him the sides. I said, "When you come back this afternoon, I don't want you to read Josh, I want you to read Christian. Can you prepare it?" That was it. And he came and he did it and that was it.

Justin Walker: I looked at the material and my first reaction was, *I am going to get this*. I really had little doubt. And it was just one of those perfect kinds of serendipitous times of life where I was—all the forces were aligning. I went to the Westway Diner, which is . . . in Hell's Kitchen in New York, and worked on the material. I walked all the way up Eighth Avenue to the Paramount building in Midtown and I went in the room and I owned it. I had it. And they sent me back out of the room.

Amy Heckerling was there, the producers were there, Adam Schroeder was there, who was working with Scott Rudin at the time. They sent me in and out a few times to try some different things. Marcia Ross took a real chance on bringing me in.

Marcia Ross: You knew when he read it. You knew. You felt it. Because we had other people, but nobody was quite it.

Justin Walker: I think it was about a week and a half later, I was flown out to Los Angeles to screen-test [with Alicia]. Donald Faison and I flew out together.

I had never been flown out to do anything like this. This was like being drafted in the NBA lottery for me. This was like, you know, going to the show.

We stayed at the Universal City Hilton. I live right near it. I drive by it all the time and a lot of times, I still look at it and remember.

It went very, very well. We read probably two or three times. It got increasingly better each time we read. My understanding is that Alicia did not particularly feel a connection with me early on, but then as the process went, she saw more and more of what I had to bring and that certainly continued through the rehearsal process for the actual movie. But I felt very, very good about it and I think the impression I had made in New York very much carried over to that particular day, to that particular screen test.

Amy Heckerling: Justin had, not exactly James Dean–y, but there was a kind of late-fifties/early-sixties thing to his look. He seemed to enjoy being in this other world.

Twink Caplan: It was this unique part that somebody had to be so many things and had to have a little bit of a foot in another era. And these were young kids. I don't think they really related that much to, like, Frank Sinatra. . . . We couldn't find it and then we finally found the guy to do it. And he was very sexy.

Justin Walker: I will never forget, I was managing a bar called the Overtime Bar and Grill at the corner of Eighth and Thirty-Fourth, right next to Madison Square Garden, basically. I was speaking to my agent on a pay phone—a pay phone, mind you! And she told me that I got it and I dropped the phone and started sprinting south on Eighth Avenue.

I went up Eighth Avenue when I was auditioning for the part. I went down Eighth Avenue when I found out I got it.

Amy Heckerling: I wanted somebody [for Mel] that would feel like, the normal parts for them to play would be a hit man. And I loved Jerry Orbach in *Prince of the City*. And I also loved Harvey Keitel. I wanted it to be somebody that could be really scary, and anybody else would be scared of him, except Cher. It would never occur to her that he was being anything but funny.

Marcia Ross: Jerry Orbach—we made an offer to him. I remember she really loved and wanted Jerry Orbach to play Mel and he couldn't get off his [TV] show. We couldn't get him.

Amy Heckerling: Jerry Orbach—the dates wouldn't work. Harvey Keitel we couldn't afford. And then there was this series—like *Omnibus*, or whatever—when there's like a TV show that has every week a different story. My friend was working on it and he told me about Dan Hedaya. I forget the name of the show.[9]

9 The show was *Fallen Angels*. It aired on Showtime from 1993 to 1995, and its episodes were directed by some major Hollywood names: Tom Hanks, Steven

So I went to where he was shooting. I don't know if [Dan] was a hit man or what, but it was definitely gangster stuff. My friend Stuart Cornfeld was working on it and he said, "This guy's great." I think at that time he had been in one of the Coen brothers' movies.

So I watched *Blood Simple*. Then I saw that and was like, *Wow. Yeah. That's perfect.*

Dan Hedaya, Mel: I didn't audition for it. Scott Rudin was the producer and I just was offered this job.

I know I liked it. I especially liked the relationship [between Mel and Cher]. I'm an uncle to quite a number of nephews and nieces, and I don't have my own children. But I've been close to children my whole life. I just really liked the relationship very much. I liked how it was written and how the character was written. The tough love.

Amy Heckerling: I wrote [Mr. Hall] for [Wally]. I know that we auditioned people because we had to. I was not allowed to just say, "This person's doing this and that's it."

Wallace Shawn, Mr. Hall: That is Hollywood. The director is far from being the sole decision-maker. Even if she's also the writer, she's not the financial backer, so . . . I think you have to cooperate with a lot of other people. That was made for Paramount Pictures, for a real studio. If all the Paramount executives had said, "We don't like him and we want you to use so-and-so," she would have had to do that.

I don't think I was brought into the process. She was cer-

Soderbergh, Alfonso Cuarón, and—in what is, according to IMDb, his sole directing credit to date—Tom Cruise.

tainly not keeping me posted—she probably did all that and then said, "Come play the part."

Amy Heckerling: I mean, I had Herb Hall read that part because I knew I wanted to put him in somewhere. And I needed to have him on tape to show the people that, yeah, he can act.

Herb Hall, the "real" Mr. Hall and the *Clueless* principal: It came up in conversation one time when she was in my class and we were just talking. I don't remember exactly how it came out but it came up that I was an actor. She went, "Oh, well, you have to audition for this." And that was that. I went and read.

Then later on they called—actually, I think my agent called me and said, "Yeah, they want you to play the part of the principal." And I think it was actually when we were filming that Twink came and told me, she says, "Yeah, you just were too cool to be Mr. Hall." I remember her telling somebody else that at one point. She introduced me to someone and said, "This is Herb Hall. He's a really fine actor and we couldn't use him to be himself because he's not a nerd."

Nicole Bilderback, Summer: When you're reading the script, when you see dialogue on paper, you think, *Oh, okay. This is fun.* But back then, before the movie was released, when you read lines like, "What-*ever*," you're like, *Okay, what is this?* You know?

I actually read for two parts: I read for Summer and for Heather and they liked me for both, but they ended up casting me as Summer.

The girl who ended up getting the role of Heather may have been in the waiting room [when I auditioned].

Susan Mohun, Heather: I think I auditioned over a few months. I had a few different auditions, and I don't think I'm supposed to name names, but my final audition was with Paul Rudd and a famous actress's daughter who seemed to be very good friends with Amy Heckerling. I had a 104 [degree] fever and had gone in the hospital, but decided I was just going to go for the heck of it to the final audition, and was sure that I wasn't going to get it because I was really sick, and this other girl, who looked exactly like her very famous mother, seemed to have it in the bag. So that was a surprise to get the role, and very exciting.

I didn't realize, obviously, that twenty years later we'd be talking about it.

Marcia Ross: I've been a casting director for thirty-five years and . . . when [people] find out I did *Clueless*, it's like—people of all ages, who I don't think were even born when I cast it in 1994 . . . will tell me, oh, I love that movie. I grew up on this movie.

At the end of the day, it's just really, really validating to see how well some of the actors have done professionally. Because that's the kind of thing that, as a casting director, makes you trust your instincts about why you brought an actor in in the first place.

Part Two

MAKING *CLUELESS*

The Joys and Challenges of Making *Clueless*

Clueless is a happy movie to watch, and based on extensive interviews with many of the people who worked behind the scenes to bring it to life, it was a largely happy movie to make as well.

When the project's producers, filmmakers, designers, actors, and artists flashed back to the days in 1994 and 1995 when they were telling the Cher Horowitz story, they expressed feelings often bathed in warmth and nostalgia for a time that not only shaped their careers but, on many days, was just a joy.

"Often I'm asked what movie [I] had the most fun on, and the first one that comes to mind is *Clueless*," says director of photography Bill Pope, a man who has worked in Hollywood for twenty-five years and whose credits include all three *Matrix* movies, two of Sam Raimi's *Spider-Man* films, and *Scott Pilgrim vs. the World*. "Everybody was happy, just like the movie."

When a film is plagued with production troubles or on-set catastrophes, people tend to remember them with as-though-it-happened-yesterday clarity. But *Clueless* was largely calamity-free, which is why Michelle Manning, the Paramount executive who oversaw the production and previously produced teen classics *Sixteen Candles* and *The Breakfast Club*, says she could not extract many book-worthy anecdotes from her memory banks. "Probably the reason I'm not remembering a lot is it was a very well-oiled machine," she told me. "There weren't a lot of problems."

But every movie—even the giddiest, most well-oiled ones in Hollywood—has its challenges. Any endeavor that involves hundreds of individuals working on a tight time frame and, in *Clueless*'s case, a limited budget is going to bump up against some obstacles. As smoothly as things went on *Clueless*, it was still no exception to that rule.

At various moments throughout pre-production and production, there were: crew dismissals and replacements; difficulties with location scouting, particularly for Cher's house; unexpected illnesses and injuries; one instance of eleventh-hour recasting; and that always unpredictable and uncontrollable force known as messy weather. Those standard and relatively minor moviemaking problems tossed occasional monkey wrenches into meticulously arranged shooting schedules and carefully laid plans. In spite of those glitches, *Clueless* still managed to come in just under its roughly $13 million production budget and behind schedule by only a few days. (Originally, it was slated to finish filming in forty-seven days; according to the official production report, it took fifty-three.)

While there were certainly some stressful moments during the making of *Clueless*, most remember the set as a harmonious, low-key environment. It probably helped that several members of Team *Clueless* had worked together before. Writer-director Amy Heckerling and associate producer Twink Caplan, who also played Miss Geist, had been friends and colleagues for many years. Heckerling also had previously collaborated with costume designer Mona May on a TV pilot that never went to series. Several others—including producer and unit production manager Barry Berg, production designer Steven Jordan, assistant directors Richard Graves and Danny Silverberg, and makeup supervisor Alan Friedman—had just finished working together on Paramount's *The Brady Bunch Movie*, which was released in February of 1995, ten days after *Clueless* wrapped. But the laid-back, let's-have-fun tone may have been set most definitively by Heckerling. "Usually that's where the tone comes from," says Graves, who acted as the first assistant director, or AD, a role that made him responsible for drafting the shooting schedule. "If she had been a super-uptight personality or something like that, it might have been completely different . . . but she was very relaxed and enjoyed the confidence of her actors."

"I think the cast and the crew adored her," says Berg.

Producer Scott Rudin, the man who finally got *Clueless* the green light it needed, has a reputation for being many things, including an exceptionally astute and prolific producer. But being low-key and relaxed is not one of them. More than one source recalled that the tension thermostat tended to rise a bit when Rudin was on set. Still, others said Rudin struck a good balance between leaving Heckerling and her crew alone to do their thing and providing detailed, often helpful input. Essentially, Heckerling needed a bulldog in her corner. And in Rudin, she found one. (Rudin decided not to be interviewed for this book.)

"He was also very good at knowing what was needed, because my tendency is to go, 'Please, sir, may I have something?' and if I get anything, I'm happy," Heckerling says. "But he was like: 'No. You need this, you need that: get 'em.' So he was very good at protecting me."

The filming of *Clueless* began on November 21, 1994, the Monday before Thanksgiving, and wrapped on Tuesday, February 7, 1995, one week before Valentine's Day. What happened during that period was . . . well, it was like that book we all read in ninth grade that said, "It was the best of times, it was the worst of times." But as many members of the *Clueless* crew tell it, it was mostly the best of times.

Sherry Lansing, former chair and CEO of Paramount Pictures: It was one of those movies: We didn't argue about the budget, we didn't argue about who should be in it. We didn't argue about anything. We just went ahead and made it. *Mean Girls* was the same way . . . there was no drama associated with either of those pictures. I kind of think of them together, even though they're completely different.

Adam Schroeder, coproducer: We were very left alone in a wonderful way. We didn't really get visits from the studio. . . . We were doing very well coming in on budget and there weren't big stars in the movie for the studio to have to worry about. Not that these weren't—the actors are always important. But we were very off the grid, which was really nice.

Richard Graves, first assistant director: As I recall, it was pretty pleasant. Amy [Heckerling]'s super sweet. I love Amy.

Amy Wells, set dresser: She's very soft-spoken, so in that sense it was pretty low-key. Richard was a very good AD, so he was never yelling and screaming. I guess it was pretty low-key if you compare it to a lot of other shows.

Paul Rudd, Josh: I was just so psyched that I was working with the woman who directed *Fast Times*. I got to ask her questions about it. I got to be directed by her. It was great.

Stacey Dash, Dionne: Every day was a joy. I mean, you did not mind waking up at five a.m., six a.m., whatever the call time was. We were just all excited. It was like going to play, you know? It was like kids going to play all day.

As much fun as you see on-screen is as much fun as we had every single day.

Alicia Silverstone, Cher: I felt like it gave me so much creativity as an actress—I could always be playful and free. It was so silly and lovely. There were many little moments that I loved, like the one scene where I was shopping, and I flipped my hair while looking in the mirror. It was so obnoxious, but it was just playing in the moment. I loved embracing her innocence.

Jeremy Sisto, Elton: I was young, so I kind of had a feeling of failure after every scene I did. *[Laughs] Aw, I missed something there.* I was young, neurotic. But my best memories were of just hanging with Donald and Breckin. Those guys were really funny, so that was a good time.

I remember me and Donald and Breckin sitting around being like, "You think anybody's going to see this?" And being like, "Yeah, maybe a *few* people."

Steven Jordan, production designer: Everyone respected one another, I think, and that's not always the case. Amy was clearly a leader, and a very good one at that, and I think if you're working with someone with a point of view who knows what she wants, it makes everyone else able to do their jobs.

Bill Pope, director of photography: Amy is funny as hell on the set. There's no anxiety. You're surrounded by kids. Everybody's happy to be there. Nobody goes back to their trailer. Everybody just hangs out and has a good time.

Paul Rudd: I remember shooting that scene in the Jeep, where it's like James Bond. That was one of the first things we shot and I remember thinking: *Wow, this is really cool.* We were just on some side street in LA [and I'm] going, *Oh my God. I can't believe we're shooting a* movie. You know, it's just that thrill of: *This is all brand-new and unfamiliar, and it's really happening, and I went to school to study this kind of stuff, and now I'm* doing *this kind of thing?* It was very exciting.

David Kitay, composer: It was just this awesome haze of fun. Some movies have a funny cloud over them and they're always kind of icky. Some movies are just like that. Often with her movies, there's just a flow. You just feel like you have this nice glow of sunshine on you all the time.

Richard Graves: I've had other shows where there have been huge issues with people not knowing the script and stuff like that. But as I recall, [the actors] were pretty well prepared. People didn't go missing or anything. There were no issues that I remember with drugs or anything like that . . . no good scandal stories that I can remember. It was kind of dull as far as that goes.

Alicia Silverstone: The challenge was being in a movie when you're a little girl and working so many hours. It was very tiring, certainly after doing so many movies in a row. Aside from that, being [Cher] was just a sheer joy.

Twink Caplan, associate producer and Miss Geist: I remember walking through Paramount with Alicia, sitting on the grass, talking about the scenes and stuff. Or going into her trailer and telling her her dog was shitting in the makeup trailer, we've got to get him a leash [*laughs*], you know, because people are stepping in it. But she was so pure, Alicia, so sweet and just a joy, just really a joy, you know. I really loved her. And I mean, Stacey Dash and I became very, very good friends and we're still good friends today.

Paul Rudd: I remember . . . doing little things that I knew my friends would get a kick out of.

When we all go to get food for Mel and the guys, when we're all handing out [sandwiches]: you don't see me, but I just go, "Mmm. Meat." I remember saying, "Meat," and I remember saying that specifically thinking, *I can't wait until my friend Greg hears that*. Because I know he would laugh at that. I remember thinking, *That's what people must do when they make movies. They put in little things that only friends of theirs are going to get.*

I remember being kind of blown away by the production of it all. And I remember thinking, *God, the guy who is shooting this movie is so* cool. I really liked him, the DP, Bill Pope. I remember just thinking: *God, he's just such a chill guy and he seems like he's really good.*

Bill Pope: I can't remember what our budget was. Like $10 million, maybe? Our offices were right next door to a set they were building for *Waterworld* on the back lot. The set cost $10 million and our entire movie cost $10 million. Every day, I'd leave and go look at that set and go: *Wow. That's amazing.*

Steven Jordan: The art department budget was—I don't know [how much]. It was a real struggle at times. A lot of the things that cost money, like fabrics—it's very hard to convey to a producer that you need this, you know, $80-a-yard fabric for drapes. But it does make a difference, and in some cases we were able to go for that. I know my set decorator put miles and miles of dupioni silk in the windows. It did make a difference.

Amy Wells: It was definitely a [budgetary] challenge and Barry Berg was a very tough line producer. I remember you'd come and ask for stuff and you'd just feel like they'd really rake you over the coals. Constantly.

Bill Pope: When I first went to meet Barry Berg, in his office, on a pedestal, was a television set playing on a loop the movie *Ed Wood*. I'd say, "Can I have some more money to do this?" And he'd say: "How would Ed Wood do this?" That was his token response. I'd say: "You mean no, right?" He'd say: "Yes. No is my answer. You don't get any more money for this. You can't have a crane, you can't have this. Just don't ask."

How would Ed Wood do it? [*Laughs*] That was always what his response was.

Barry Berg, coproducer and unit production manager, after hearing Pope's *Ed Wood* story: [*Laughing*] That sounds right to me.

Steven Jordan: I know it was brutal. I've always believed that sometimes that's a good thing. Because it really forces you to be creative.

Bill Pope: If we'd made that movie for $25 million . . . it wouldn't have been as good a movie. We would have just shot ourselves in the foot somehow.

Adam Schroeder: This is a movie that takes place in Beverly Hills, but we shot most of it in the Valley. Cher's house was in Encino, actually next door to John Goodman's, the actor John Goodman, which was funny. And the mall we shot in was in the Valley. We shot a lot in the Valley because it was cheaper.

Jeffrey T. Spellman, locations supervisor: It wasn't a huge location budget, but it had to be well over half a million dollars. Oh yeah: we spent a ton of money with the house and filming at the college and all that stuff.[10]

The toughest part was finding [Cher's] house. That was a big one that we all had to really search high and low for.

10 *Clueless* spent more than two weeks shooting at Occidental College in Los Angeles, where all of the exterior, and a few interior, scenes at Bronson Alcott High School take place.

Steven Jordan: That was clearly the most challenging [location to find].

Jeffrey Spellman: I think early on we had another production designer and for whatever reason, they changed courses midway through the prep and Steve [Jordan] came on and brought it all together. That's when we decided on a new house and all that good stuff.

Barry Berg: I'm the one that had to do the replacing [of the production designer]. It wasn't a question so much of talent as that his vision just wasn't Amy's vision. I was obviously intimately involved in all of that, being at every meeting and every location and so on, and very quickly realized that he just didn't see—he didn't understand what she was saying. He didn't get her vision. It wasn't a bad thing. It was just a creative issue. So we immediately made a change, and to Scott Rudin's credit, when I told him that this had to happen, he just said to me: "Okay. Do it. Bring in who you think is best." Scott is very hands-on, but he gave me everything I needed in the way of support to make that change, make it quickly. And Steven came in and just did a wonderful job.

Amy Wells: It was my first real venture into doing a feature. I had done some really small things, but this was like my first, you know, Paramount, big feature. I think I was very insecure, and then I was even more insecure when they fired the designer who hired me because I didn't feel like I was the one chosen by [the new] designer.

It was not the easiest situation. I think [Steve] probably thought I was very inexperienced. Which I was. Because I wasn't his choice, that was exacerbated. I've gone on to do some pretty big stuff, like *Mad Men* and lots of other things. So I can look back on it and say, yeah, it was an irritating experience. And guess what? That's fine. When we were starting [*Clueless*], it wasn't a big deal. It wasn't considered a really big movie and it was kind of fun. Being a first-time decorator, to have the person that brought you in fired, and then I'm kind of out there going: *What are they going to do to me? Am I next?* It wasn't very good for my creativity.

Steven Jordan: They had done some preliminary scouting [for Cher's house] before I started and then they took me up to this house that people liked, and it literally had rooms that were so large, I couldn't find furniture to fill them in the right scale.

It was like you could land an airplane in the living room. I mean, literally, it would be very difficult to shoot a scene with two people in it and keep them in the frame. . . . So I just said, you know what? I think we can do better.

So at that point I went back to Amy [Heckerling] and I said, "Look, this house is magnificent in scale, but I'm going to have to make the rooms smaller with false walls." So that's when I started my search.

Jeffrey Spellman: We were really, really that close to "this is it," kind of a thing. . . . Not signing anything yet, but really close, so close that when we found out we had to go out and get a new house, it was like, *Oh my God. You've got to be kidding.*

I work in television mostly nowadays, and you look for something for a week and then that's it. Here, you're looking for stuff for three or four months. It's like putting needles in your eyes after a while.

Steven Jordan: I remember one time being out with the location manager, looking for Cher's house and driving up this enormous driveway. We rang the doorbell and the door opened automatically, electronically, and there was a pug in a sweater at the front door. Then a few minutes later, a housekeeper came to the door and said: "How can I help you?"

Jeffrey Spellman: We went back to the drawing board and looked some more and ended up with the house in Encino that we settled on.

Steven Jordan: It looked promising. Once the front door opened and we saw that staircase, it was like, "Oh my God. This is pretty great." It turns out the people that owned the home were getting ready to move out because they were in the process of getting ready to do six months of repairs from the '94 earthquake. And they said, "Well, it's kind of bad timing. We're moving out right now." I said, "Well, how about this?" We made them an offer. They accepted.

I remember the day that I came back and found this house and showed pictures to Amy, Scott, and everybody: they were interested. And I'm like, "All right, let's get in a van." It was Friday afternoon. I'll never forget it. We left Paramount and we were driving to the Valley in this horrendous rainstorm. I think the traffic was at an absolute standstill. People were getting really frustrated. I think a twenty-minute trip took us probably close to two hours. And I'm thinking, *They're going to hate this place just because everyone is going to be in such a foul mood.* Happily, it didn't turn out that way. But it was quite a trip.

Amy Heckerling, writer-director: The house, I think, [belonged to] a meat supplier, somebody that supplied meat to fast-food places.

Jeffrey Spellman: It was a family that, fortunately, had some knowledge of filming. They'd had a little bit of it in the past, so they kind of knew what it all entailed. For a project like this, we ended up moving them out of the house, bringing in the moving trucks and all that, moving their furniture out and repainting the house for tones that were a little more realistic for our character. Then bringing our furniture in and then doing the reverse at the end. It was almost six weeks to two months of work there at that house. That's quite a long time in a neighborhood.

We had an El Niño that year that was huge and you'd get three inches of rain in a day or something like that. And it was *every day*. We parked our crew and trucks probably about a mile away in a city park. It's in the flood basin, the Sepulveda basin, a big popular park out there. Come midday . . . the park rangers came over, "Well, we're gonna have to move your stuff out, you know. The park has been flooded."

Richard Graves: We had to let the crew go and get their cars out of the lot because they were going to be trapped and flooded.

Steven Jordan: Just the rain on the movie that year, in January, was just phenomenal.

Jeffrey Spellman: And then that kind of rain, no matter what you do to protect the house [we were shooting in], there's going to be damage. You've got people coming in and out with equipment and all that. So at the end there was quite a bit of damage, a lot of it from the rain itself.

Steven Jordan: You had to figure, the company's out there, which is probably anywhere between eighty and one hundred people, and it's pouring rain, and you're inside but all the equipment's outside so all the cables have to get dragged in. The crew can't be in the house at the same time that they're shooting, at least the majority of them. So they need a place to go and that's generally outside. That's how, within a day, the lawn can turn into mud.

Jeffrey Spellman: Oh my gosh, we put down board—layout board, we call it. It's a real thick cardboard. We put that down over all the floor where we shoot on location. That stuff only holds up for a minute or so after we start bringing wet equipment through. So we're constantly trying to change it out but it was a futile task. Floor damage—you name it. When they were finished, I'm sure Paramount looked at the bill and were quite puzzled by it. But it was quite an extraordinary circumstance.

Danny Silverberg, second assistant director: Whenever you do a schedule you always have a backup plan. Like, okay, you can go inside and do something or other as a cover set. On *Clueless*, because most of the cover was shot out by the last couple of weeks of the schedule, the Bosstones scene, which was scripted as an exterior of a frat house, had to be restaged as an interior warehouse, because of weather. You get to a point in production where you start running out of things to shoot if it rains.

Before production—and the rains—began, another issue arose regarding the process of casting the hundreds of extras who would appear throughout the film.

Barry Berg: I think we were having a meeting of some sort, a production meeting. And the extras casting people were supposed to be there, and they weren't there for whatever reason. I don't remember why anymore. Scott felt that if they couldn't show up on time, there's no reason to give them the job. Again, we made the change instantly in that regard.

Adam Schroeder: I do think that [the extras] were seeming much older and would potentially take you out of the high school environment. But we found them, again, with the replacement.

Danny Silverberg: We brought in Charlie Messenger, literally, maybe about a week and a half out from shooting, in a very extras-heavy show.

Charlie Messenger, head of extras casting: I received a call from Scott Rudin. I met with him in the middle of the week. He said they had dismissed who had been casting the film and that the greatest need was this age group: could I do it? And I said, "Sure." He said, "Yeah, well you go to work on Monday. Sunday we want to see an open call." We scrambled and we had three hundred kids on Sunday. From that they chose a core group of athletes, jocks, cheerleaders, nerds, regular kids, kids of diverse ethnicity—all the types that make up a high school student body. That remained the core group but there was some attrition. I would say over the course of the three months, two months, that it took to film, we ran through six or seven hundred kids.

Usually when you're hired to cast a movie, you know a month or so ahead of time. You're given the parameters. You get a script. You get the breakdown, what they think the actors' breakdown will be, and you have time to work on it. This was short, yes. Particularly dealing with the kind of extras you have to deal with on that one: the young-looking extras.

Danny Silverberg: When we spoke to Charlie Messenger, we said, "Look, Charlie, this is a very specific look. And Amy's very hands-on when it comes to the casting of the extras." He was fine with doing that and he delivered great people. They did a really great job.

Richard Graves: [Scott Rudin] got involved with extra casting and insisted on this pre-production extras call and looked at every face and preapproved every face that was going to be in the high school. Not that it really made that much of a difference in the long run, but it was important to him. . . . That's actually something that happens a lot on movies. I mean, it wasn't that far out of the realm. I was just surprised. Usually, someone like him is not that involved with something like that.

Barry Berg: He is very hands-on and has incredible taste and he wanted things to be just right. And that's what we did: we made them just right.

Charlie Messenger: It was a little stressful, because of the short prep time and because of the age group . . . Within two or three hours we could have cast *Clueless* today, with the Internet capabilities. Within a few minutes, you can reach thousands of the type of people you need. That didn't exist then. But it's still a stressful job.

Amy Wells: I remember the food drive. I remember I had some signs made for the food drive and it turned out Scott Rudin came in and wanted them to be much more upscale, so over the weekend we had to rush and get new signs made.

It was one of my first movies, so for me, everything was high-stress.

In case you're wondering, the real Pismo Beach never experienced a disaster of the sort described in the movie. Heckerling explains why she chose to make the coastal town north of LA the focus of Cher's effort: "I wanted to make her be doing something good for others, but I didn't want to make the others' [situation] sound too dire. The word *Pismo*, also—I think it was in a W. C. Fields movie."

The pressure also took a toll on the film's star, Alicia Silverstone, who racked up a lot of what the Screen Actors Guild refers to as "forced calls" during the shoot, meaning that she was frequently asked to arrive on set with less than the guild's requisite twelve hours of time off following the previous day's work. Silverstone got sick twice during filming, illnesses that, because of the meatiness of Cher's role, impacted the whole production.

Alicia Silverstone: I was in every scene of the movie and had just come off doing eight movies back-to-back. I love my job, but filming means fourteen-hour days every day, on any movie. So as a young girl who didn't know how to take care of herself, that took its toll.

Amy Heckerling: I remember, yeah, she got sick a couple of times. It was nothing unusual, just—if you look at the movie, you see that's all her, all the time. And on top of all that, there's costume fittings. So she was worked pretty hard for a young girl.

Richard Graves: We ended up having to do something that we almost never do, which is shut production down, because we didn't have anything to shoot without Alicia.

From the Clueless *production report for December 22, 1994, a day when exteriors at Occidental College were being shot: "A. SILVERSTONE WAS TOO ILL TO REPORT FOR WORK. COMPANY MOVED UP SCENES TO MAKE A DAYS [SIC] WORK WITHOUT HER . . . B. MURPHY [SAG] AND B. MEYER [SAG] WERE NOT ON CALL SHEET BUT WERE CALLED IN TO WORK."*

The next day, Friday, December 23, 1994, the company took an insurance day and shut down production, resuming work on Tuesday, December 27, after the Christmas holiday. Three weeks later, on January 12, 1994, Silverstone had to take sick time again, due to a stomach ailment.

From the Clueless *production notes for January 12, 1995: "THE DOCTOR WHO TREATED [Ms. Silverstone] DEEMED IT NECESSARY FOR HER TO GO HOME & REST FOR THE REMAINDER OF THE DAY. THIS LEFT THE COMPANY WITH SC. 34 PT & 35 PT. (ELTON'S PHONE CALL 3/8 PAGE) TO SHOOT AFTER WHICH THE COMPANY WAS FORCED TO SHUT DOWN FOR THE REST OF DAY. THIS PUTS US ONE DAY BEHIND AT 'CHER'S HOUSE' AND FOUR DAYS BEHIND OUR ORIGINAL SHOOTING SCHEDULE."*

Silverstone returned to work the following day, according to the production notes, after a doctor confirmed she was well enough to resume filming.

Richard Graves: I'm not sure I should tell this part of it, but I just remember [a] producer telling the doctor to give her a very, very, very thorough examination. He said, as long as we're shutting down, he wanted every nook and cranny examined.

Barry Berg, who signed off on all the production reports, did not recall much about Silverstone's illnesses when he was asked about them. "I think she had a day where she was ill and we had something else to do," he told me. "So it was no big deal."

Alicia Silverstone: I remember on the set of *Clueless* I was always so sick and always had ulcers, and would ask my driver to go get frozen yogurt because that's all I felt I could eat. I would get allergy shots. I was totally out of touch with my body.[11]

11 *New York Times* interview, March 9, 2010.

Adam Schroeder: She's the star of the movie, so you're kind of worried about the actors and you hope that she's going to be okay and all. Again, it's what happens in life. I don't think I've worked on a film where somebody hasn't gotten sick one day and it's juggled us around a bit. But thank God it wasn't anything serious and I think she was fine after a day or so. It's like a chicken with your head cut off—what are we going to do? But you figure it out and you move things around. We did shoot some stuff around her and I think we may have just, when she came back, shot her side of some of the scenes.

From the Clueless *production report for December 7, 1994, when the skate park competition was staged at a park on Shoreline Drive in Long Beach:* "B. MEYER (SAG) INJURED ON SKATE RAMP DURING REHEARSAL OF SC. 140. SEEN BY MEDIC AND TRANSPORTED TO ST. MARY'S MEDICAL CENTER EMERGENCY. DIAGNOSED WITH SPRAINED RT. ANKLE AND PERMITTED TO RETURN TO WORK ON CRUTCHES UNDER PROVISION OF NOT WALKING . . . *(1 day behind due to injury.)*"

Breckin Meyer, Travis: I did not get injured [during the Val party scene]. I got injured on the half pipe.

Adam Schroeder: Breckin was doing a lot of his own stunts on the skateboard, and he did twist his ankle a little bit. I remember he got a little injured. Most of the stuff we had shot already, but then I think we had to maybe shoot some of it later on. . . . I think we had to come back and just finish it up. He wasn't majorly hurt but hurt enough that we didn't want to take a chance.

Amy Heckerling: Yeah, he did sprain his ankle. I mean, we were really worried. A lot of that stuff is actually him skating on that ramp, and the big tricks flying in the air are those professional guys. . . . I don't remember going back [to film] anything else, but possibly we did.

The remainder of the scene was shot on an additional day: Tuesday, January 31, 1995, at the same park on Shoreline Drive.

Another cast member, Brittany Murphy, also had to contend with an illness during filming. But it was not her own: Murphy's mother, Sharon Murphy, was diagnosed with breast cancer. She would eventually beat the disease, but it would take time. According to a 2006 People *magazine interview with Brittany Murphy, after going into remission post-*Clueless*, Sharon Murphy's cancer recurred in 2003, then went into remission following a double mastectomy in 2004. So when the illness first struck, while Murphy was filming her breakout movie role, it was only the beginning of a long road. Nevertheless, according to Heckerling, that personal setback did not adversely impact the young actress's ability to become Tai.*

Amy Heckerling: As far as showing up and being totally prepared, it had no impact. But I knew that was going on with her, and her mom was on set and they were very close. She was being a very wonderful, supportive daughter.

Twink Caplan: She was always with her mother, Sharon. Always. If we had a party or we did anything she would come up and say, "Twink, can my mother come?" And I'd say, "Of course," you know. But she and Sharon were so close. I remember years later she had a big birthday party when she was dating Ashton Kutcher. She had a big birthday party for her mom with, like, slides and everything. I mean, the two of them were like the closest I've ever seen two people.

Adam Schroeder: Since Brittany was the only cast member who was underage, Sharon was there, because those are the rules of SAG. Sharon really became part of the crew. She was such a lovely—she is such a lovely woman. And they were so close. I remember, I guess we really did think of her as part of the family. We made up a crew jacket for her as well, at the time. She really was a big part of it and there for everything.

Steven Jordan: It was such an enjoyable project. The flashbacks are all good. I think at the end of the day, sometimes you're on jobs that are so miserable it takes a year to sort of get over the toxic environment you were in. Thankfully and happily, *Clueless* was not one of those projects.

Danny Silverberg: I remember Paul Rudd being, particularly, a sweetheart of a guy. He gave out these really thoughtful wrap gifts to us, of these—they were little tiny kernels of rice with our initials on each one, put together in a necklace. . . . I thought that was really nice and personal of him. I just remember him being a really nice and down-to-earth guy.

Paul Rudd: When the movie's ending, my manager had said, "You get people gifts when a movie ends." And I said, "Oh, you do?" And he said, "Yep. That's a tradition. And I know what we're going to get them." So he kind of helped me get gifts for everybody. What I got everybody was a necklace with—each person had their name written on a grain of rice. It was like the dumbest [gift]. *[Laughs]*

I like to think that somewhere in the world, Bill Pope is walking around with his name written on a grain of rice. It kinda just makes me laugh a little bit.

Barry Berg: I have absolutely no bad memories of that show. It was just a great piece of film to work on.

Paul Rudd: After the table read we all went and got a bite to eat.

We went to a place not far, around the corner, that I used to go to, which was kind of a bar. They probably should not have let some of those kids in—it was actually a bar. I won't out the place because I think it's still there. But it was just some little dive bar, and I do remember all of us sitting around saying, "How cool is it that we're all going to do a movie about kids our own age?" And having that conversation about the John Hughes movies to our generation. It had been a while since there was one of [those]—"How cool would it be if this thing had legs?" But in that way that you have that conversation, I'm guessing, every single time you do anything, especially when you're that age.

Then it kind of did [have legs].

The Bright Sunshine of *Clueless*: Establishing the Film's Visual Aesthetic

The world of *Clueless* is a place where a Val party's Christmas lights glow in vivid jewel tones; where feathers reminiscent of Truffula trees poof off of purses and pens; and where the California sun frequently creates a halo of light around our heroine, Cher Horowitz, even though in real life, the sun often failed to shine while the cameras were rolling.

The gloss and brightness of *Clueless*'s imagery may seem perfectly natural. But there was a great deal of effort, technical skill, creativity, and collaboration involved in making the film look as radiant and inviting as it does, as Amy Heckerling, the visionary behind the film's aesthetic, and several of its key architects—including director of photography Bill Pope, production designer Steven Jordan, and costume designer Mona May—explain.

Bill Pope, director of photography: [Amy Heckerling is] this mixture of super sophisticated and super naive. I don't know how to describe her. It's almost like Cher is the same, actually, now that I think about it.

Steven Jordan, production designer: I think one of the things about Amy's work is that she's a wonderful observer of culture. It's really her strong suit. And I think I was able to do [that] successfully on a visual level.

Bill Pope: Our conversations were from her slant. I remember I said, "Look, you've got to tell me what you want this [movie] to look like. Can you describe it? Give me the descriptive words." So we went through it, we went around, and at the end of the conversation, she said, "You know what? The word is *happy*. I want this thing to be happy. I don't want any sadness. I want complete happiness throughout this whole movie. I want it to be suffused with happiness." I said, "Well, what's happy to you? What does happiness look like?" She said, "I have no idea. But I know it when I see it." I said, "Well, okay. I'll be back tomorrow and I'll show you choices."

I had a laser disc printer. I wish I still had it. It was a really beautiful printer. I went back and got fifty laser discs, or rented them, and started printing out pictures: from comedies, from all sorts of movies, of every type. They were like eight-by-tens.[12]

Amy Heckerling, writer-director: I think he had something where he could print pictures off of his TV.

Bill Pope: I went into her office the next day and we laid them out on the floor and we just walked around. And I said, "Point to the ones that are happy."

12 The director of photography is synonymous with the cinematographer. He, in concert with the director, designs the film's visual aesthetic, making sure that the lighting, camera angles, and film quality tell the story in a way that achieves the director's vision.

Even though all the images had—somebody else could have described them as happy. To her: "That one's sad. That's sad." Because there was some sort of conflict, or some bad dress, or some bad expression, or the wrong emotion in the person's eyes, or a bad hairdo. She said, "These, this pile over here is happy." I said, "Okay. This is what the movie is going to look like." Then I knew how to make the movie.

Amy Heckerling: One of the movies that looked like it was California rich people and funny and happy was *Shampoo*. And the Sylberts, you know, the decorators and costume people: they're geniuses. And it had that feeling of classical old stuff that's new and California.[13]

Bill Pope: I didn't save [the pile]. I probably didn't even save it at the time. I just sort of knew from looking at it—I knew how close she wanted to be to the actors physically, that she wanted to see the environment, that she wanted to see the actors play within the environment. It's a very Hawksian approach to cinema, to see the people playing off each other in the same frame and see the environment and the clothing. The milieu of Cher is as important as Cher. She's nobody without her place. So I understood the desire to stay back and to sort of roam around with the camera, sort of effortlessly follow the people and to not call attention to the cinema, the making of it. The sort of bright colors and the lovely soft light. It's sunlit, always sunstruck.[14]

---

13 Richard Sylbert was a noted production designer whose work can be seen in a number of classic films, including *The Manchurian Candidate*, *The Graduate*, and *Shampoo*. His twin brother, Paul Sylbert, also a production designer, was married to Anthea Sylbert, who worked as a costume designer alongside Richard on several projects in the late 1960s and '70s, including *Rosemary's Baby*, *Chinatown*, and *Shampoo*.

14 When Pope uses the term *Hawksian*, he's referring to the work of director Howard Hawks, who was responsible for such classics as *Bringing Up Baby*, *His*

Steven Jordan: I think the one instruction [Amy] gave to all of us was "bright and happy." Those are the two sort of guidelines that all of us worked with.

Amy Heckerling: Whenever you say that you like things light and you want faces lit, people go, "Oh, that's TV." A lot of cameramen go around priding themselves by going, "I'm the prince of darkness." Well, you know, why don't you just call yourself the killer of comedy?

[Bill] knew how to understand my fears. I'd go, "You know what? I don't like being outside. I can't control the light." And he'd yank me over to a tree and show me the light coming through leaves and he goes, "You don't like it?" And I'd go, "Oh, yeah. Well, *that*." So he knew what I liked and what I thought I was afraid of and how to make that pretty.

Bill Pope: We shot it over Christmas. We used Christmas vacation, because that's when we could get Occidental College and the high school up in the Valley that we worked in, and the month of January. Both were record rainfalls. Most of it was shot in the rain, so I remember looking out the windows of the houses we were shooting in and seeing my crew, who called themselves Team Gore-Tex, standing out in the rain with the lights shining through the windows to make it look sunny at all times.

We had to really wait sometimes for a week for a sunny day so we could go shoot on the campus. It was a conscious choice to make it sunlit and sunstruck and happy. You waited for your time. It was a major effort to make it sunny and happy. It wasn't

---

Girl Friday, *The Big Sleep*, and *Gentlemen Prefer Blondes*, the last starring Marilyn Monroe and Jane Russell.

by chance that we happened to be filming in Beverly Hills and it was sunny. It was anything but.

Amy Heckerling: The window of when things would look right was so tiny. We didn't have a big shooting schedule, so I know that it was really hard on him.

Bill Pope: We chose a large amount of fill light and really soft light wrapping around the actors. Not that they needed it. They were all twelve years old and full of collagen and so on. I could have hit them with anything. But it's a warm, welcoming feeling to be surrounded by soft light like that, with some splashes of sunlight.

You push [the light] through large, white pieces of cloth that soften it, like in the shadows, when you're standing in the shade on a sunny day and there's sunlight splashing all around you but you're standing in the shade. The light's soft on you. There's no harsh light hitting you. The way I did [Alicia's] blond hair—I think I always hit her with a blond backlight.

What's funny, what you can't take your eyes off in this movie is Alicia. I mean, her face and her acting is just beyond. It's one of a kind. It ranks up there with *Born Yesterday* or *Singin' in the Rain*. It's one of the great comic performances. You want to choose your close-ups judiciously, but the things that she does with her face are so—my high school English teacher would yell at me for saying "so unique." But that's what it is. She's utterly unique. There's nobody like her.

Danny Silverberg, second assistant director: There's a shot I remember specifically where she's looking up toward Christian when he first comes into the room and she's gazing at him longingly. It's like, we had every light imaginable in that room and every flag, just sculpting her face into this angelic, beautifully lit—it took a long time to set up and it was really hot in the room because of it. But she looked fabulous.

Bill Pope: You're drawn to take her close-up somewhere in there so you can judiciously put it in and bring the audience close to her. You don't have to have close-ups of everybody else, but you're kind of looking and trying to discover Alicia's point of view. That's what's so unusual about it: this girl has this amazing point of view, which she takes as obvious and we take as miraculous. You're sort of drawn to that face. That halo of blond hair and those crazy lips, that amazing jaw of hers. You can't take your eyes off her.

You know, there were great faces in that movie. There was Stacey and Paul and Dan Hedaya, for that matter. Donald Faison. Breckin. Jeremy Sisto. Wally Shawn, for crying out loud. Amy picked some great, great faces. You can't stop looking at any of them.

Steven Jordan, production designer: When you do comedy you want to put the audience in a place that they want to be. You don't want these dull, drab sets and locations. Which is one of the reasons I use color so much. My job as a designer, basically, is to enable the company. I have to create environments that the DP can light, a palette that Mona can work with. If I don't do my job well, it makes it impossible for other people to do their jobs well.[15]

15 The production designer is a department head who oversees the art department, sets, scenery, and props. Essentially he and his team are responsible for the way the environments look in a movie, including the locations and everything in them: artwork, furniture, and any objects—pens, books, computers—that the characters hold or touch.

Amy Heckerling: I had told [Steve Jordan], I wanted that sense of fake Europe. . . . Stylistically there was the prewar, where there were details on things. But California's not big with that because it's a newer city. So in the eighties when they started building not modern-looking stuff, but things that were McMansions looking more toward the past and the columns and styles that were more old-fashioned, they would look toward Europe or different countries.

There's this place on Rodeo [Drive] that goes up a hill and has stores. It's where [Cher]'s first coming down and she pulls the shopping bags over her shoulders. That's the sort of style I wanted. It's not Europe. It's new. It's like Disneyland Europe. But it photographs as pretty and fun. It doesn't have the falling-apartness of ancient stuff. When I tell [Steve] that, he gets it and he runs with it and he embellishes it and he made it perfectly, exactly wonderful.

Steven Jordan: In my scouting and research, I was impressed with how many people in that world buy new antiques. It was kind of a phenomenon to me. I remember scouting in one home and they had a treadmill that was completely encased in the Chippendale-style cabinet. It was hysterical. Imagine being on a mahogany treadmill.

Amy Wells, set dresser: We wanted it to be very upscale, very much of that time, in the Valley. [Cher] didn't have a mom—it was just that kind of thing. Probably a decorator would have come in and done [the house] for them.

Steven Jordan: Amy [Wells] did an awful lot of stuff at a place called Diamond Foam out here, which is one of the better fabric outlets. [She] really got some great stuff. But a lot of it came from Warner Bros. and Paramount and Universal shops as well. Because again, we just did not have the budget to fabricate everything.

Amy Heckerling: The house had to be a background, so the fact that it was black and white, but happy black and white, that worked really well for whatever color scheme they were going to have.

Mona May, costume designer: What was great with Amy, and that really taught me something for the rest of my career, was how to balance things in a scene. How to balance the character, how to balance the color, how to balance the looks. It's a lot of work because you have to really physically print the picture, put the pictures on the board for each scene, look at it—it's like a puzzle where you have to move things around if they don't work. *Okay, where is that outfit going to go? Because it's not going to go well here*. You know what? It made me a better designer. It changed the way I look at things.

Amy Heckerling: A lot of times people think, *What I'm doing is the most important thing*. So: "I don't care about what you think the shot should be, you have to show the shoes." Or: "Screw you and your costume, I want that light." But [Bill and Mona] were respectful of each other and appreciated what the other was doing.

Mona May: It takes a certain kind of artist to shoot film from a fashion point of view as well. Of course, it's about characters and we talked about it, we really planned it. We made sure that when there's a great outfit, we see it head to toe, that there are long shots, that there are close-ups of the backpacks or close-ups of the cuffs. That you see it . . . [Bill] was really, really cool because he got it. He understood Amy, he understood my point of view, and he was totally game. A lot of DPs are kind of in their own world, and they kind of have their own agenda. But Bill's such a collaborative person and really, it added to the film tremendously, with his way of shooting it.

Bill Pope: I have three sisters. I'm the only boy in this house full of women growing up and my mother owned a dress store, so I was surrounded by fashion all the time. So it just came to me naturally. I understood people's interest in fashion and the importance of it. At that time, I probably spent too much money on clothes myself.

Mona May: I can do my work to a certain point but if we don't see the right detail, it's gone. . . . I cannot credit Bill Pope enough, how genius his eye was and how much he has elevated all the fashion in the film because we're able to see the detail.

Steven Jordan: I think that's probably what a lot of the success of that film is. I think Mona, Bill, and myself were all able to bring our two cents to it, and I think Amy was [the] one that could work in that fashion, embrace those ideas.

The Fashion and Beauty of *Clueless*

When Amy Heckerling tapped Mona May to create the clothes for *Clueless*, May—a designer who then had only three feature films on her résumé, including such blatantly ungirly movies as *3 Ninjas* and the martial arts action sequel *Best of the Best II*—was more than ready to try something bold. And Heckerling was happy to let her.

With Heckerling's input and support, May looked to the high fashion on display on European runways, then twisted it in ways that suited the *Clueless* characters and matched the visual aesthetic of the film. But given the limited costume budget and the breadth of apparel that needed to be gathered—including clothes, hats, shoes, and other accessories from designers such as Anna Sui, Dolce & Gabbana, and then-up-and-comer Jill Stuart, as well as vintage shops, production houses, and regular stores—the approach had to be strategic. It also had to be complemented by the work of her partners in prettifying: makeup supervisor Alan Friedman and hairstylist Nina Paskowitz, who also played key roles in sculpting the beauty and style of *Clueless*.

Mona May, costume designer: When we started with this movie, read the script, and talked about it, it wasn't about going to high school—American or LA high schools—and looking at what the kids wore. At the time, it was Kurt Cobain. It was very much the grunge time. Amy really wanted to have me invent something completely fresh and different, so it was cool. And she really appreciated that I came from Europe, where I could bring a little bit of that point of view to everything.

That's what's so great about Amy. She understands fashion, knows fashion, lives fashion, gets it completely. Which is very rare for a director. Most directors are men and they don't really understand what an A-line skirt is or, you know, all the kinds of nuances and details of fashion that Amy and I can talk about for hours.

Mona May actually makes a brief cameo appearance in *Clueless*; she's Fabian, the masseuse who attempts to relieve the tension in Cher's back.

Alicia Silverstone, Cher: I've worked with Amy and Mona again, as a team. I didn't remember this about *Clueless* until I did it with them all over again in *Vamps*—they work together so beautifully. Amy will have all these ideas and Mona will have her ideas. And Amy will come in and she just sort of—like on *Vamps*, she took her shirt off and put it on me. She's standing there in her bra, going, like, "More of this!" She was just in there on the floor with me, figuring it all out. She's just really, really detailed and involved in the costumes in such a brilliant way that they work so well together.

Mona May: At that time, I had to come up with things, completely come up with, like a fashion designer really comes up with future fashion. Because nothing existed, so it was interpreting what was happening in fashion—what's on the runway shows—but then taking that back to the script and filtering that through the characters.

Amy Heckerling, writer-director: Plaid had made a comeback obviously because of grunge. You know, these things are always coming and going: stripes, polka dot, plaid. We're good, we're bad, we're out, we're in.

My main concern was making [the characters] look good, of course, and having fun . . . with the whole rave stuff, with the Dr. Seuss hats. There was that sense of crazy whimsy coming back.

Mona May: To Amy, it was very important that they're not [in] runway shows, they're not models. They're real teenagers and we have to bring that fashion to the reality of their environment: who they are, where they are, how old they are.

When we were doing fittings, it was really interesting how we had to kind of make sure: what kind of shoes would make this outfit younger? We came up with Mary Janes because it really looked youthful. They were not running around in stilettos, looking like little hooker girls. It was very important that it is youthful and charming and sweet.

Amy Heckerling: Slutty was not part of it. They were teenage girls that couldn't drive yet. The one that had had sex was—well, I guess also, you might say she was the most grungy, Tai. There were skateboards, druggie stuff. But nobody was wearing bondage-y shit or overtly cleavage-y things.

Mona May: We actually used very little black in the movie. That was a very conscious thing Amy wanted to do. She wanted the palette to be really happy, very vibrant. I think there are maybe two or three, maybe four things, that are black. I think there's a black leather skirt. But very, very few things that Cher wears are black. Even for most of the girls, you didn't see much black on them.

Amy Heckerling: I had the sense that I wanted the different color schemes going throughout. So Cher was wearing the fall colors when school starts, and she's wearing the Alaïa, the Christmas-red dress, when it's Christmas. Then she's in the pinks when it's springtime.

Mona May: I think [the budget] was like $200,000. Which was nothing. To have the main character have sixty-three changes, and you'd have all the big female characters have that many changes in the film, plus all the supporting cast and the background that I had to dress head to toe: that was really not a lot of money.

I didn't have a lot of time as well. I think I only had six to eight weeks of prep, which includes the research, all the European research that I had to do—the magazines, the runways, and creating visual boards, discussing with Amy and trying to figure out what are the links that are between the characters and the fashion: what's going to work, what won't work. And then the next step was pulling everything, making stuff, assembling stuff from high-end boutiques to thrift stores to secondhand shops.

It's a lengthy process.

Alan Friedman, makeup supervisor: Mona May had done tons of research and she had tons of tears and cutouts and pictures and that sort of thing, of what she was going for with either each look or each character.

I really very much relied on . . . the research she was able to do. I don't know how many months she was on it beforehand, but she was always very generous about helping you out. We're all working in essence toward the same goal and we're all working, really, toward Amy's vision.

Nina Paskowitz, lead hairstylist: It's an interesting thing because on the one hand, there was a lot that we were able to arrange in advance, like the Pippi Longstocking [hair] on Elisa [Donovan] and a lot of the background. . . . When I say *advance*, sometimes that means just the day before. That's how "advance."

We had to do a lot on the fly on *Clueless*, so we would literally bring a whole bag of hair ornaments to the set, see what worked once [the actors] were placed in their position and had the clothes on, and go, "Ooh, what can we throw in here and here and here?"

Mona May: I can probably guess [how many costumes we had overall]. Hundreds. Probably a thousand costumes. By the time you dress all the kids in high school, by the time you do all the different groups, the parties—oh my God.

Stacey Dash, Dionne: We did a week of fittings before the movie started and it was about eight to ten hours a day of trying on thousands and thousands of clothes. And Mona's genius was, she was able to not only have each costume exclusive to each character, she was able to meld it all together with everyone else so we all complemented each other. That takes a lot of talent, which is what Mona May has. So it was a pleasure to do.

Mona May: Every extra has been touched by my department. In some cases, head to toe. I think that's where also the success is from, because everyone was touched. It's not like "Extras: come in, line up, go." It was to the smallest little detail.

I'm like a crazy artist who is checking every extra, you know. I mean, Amy, too. She would come down, too, and double-check everybody. . . . She really wanted to make sure that everybody who was in front of the camera was perfect. So not just the wardrobe, it's the hair and makeup.

Nina Paskowitz: Everybody went through the works. And the thing is that we had an A-list group of background [actors] that worked all the time. Then we had secondary players that worked all the time but didn't have lines. But they were seen every day. How we got it done is amazing.

Alan Friedman: So often [in a movie] you get a school full of people or an auditorium full of people and then they're just moving scenery, they're moving props, and nobody really cares what they look like . . . We specifically would try to attend to everybody, make them look the part.

Mona May: Imagine if just Cher and the girls and everybody looked great and then everything else was boring and everybody else was just walking around in their baggy jeans. . . . It just would not feel as rich. It wouldn't be the feast for the eyes that everything was.

What was fun about this movie and maybe not having a lot

of money, it made me more creative. I had to go to the thrift store. I had to go to high-end stores. I had to make some stuff and create things because they were not even in the stores, because they were just being thought out and dreamed up by the designers on the runway shows. It was really a mixture of high and low [fashion], which, interestingly enough, now is so in and so cool. But then it really wasn't happening yet.

I had maybe twenty bins, like laundry baskets, full of hats.

I come from Europe and I myself in my own wardrobe and my style, I wear a lot of hats. I find hats super sexy, very, very fashionable. . . . Here we created a whole new fashion, which was like going back to London to Philip Treacy, who was one of my idols: a hatmaker who's just a genius. To this day, [he] creates these unbelievable hats that the royals wear and all the ladies that go to the horse races and society ladies all over the world, as well as fashion shows. He was my inspiration for that, to bring the hats that were really cool and fun and street fashion to our film, and add to each outfit even more. I think it's so much more complete when you have the schoolgirl outfit and then you have the hat [with] that, right? It's just at another level.

Kokin, hat designer and maker: What was interesting was it was these young high school girls, in couture hats, worn in this very offhanded way. Like, "Oh, I put a hat on."

Mona May: That's why I'm so proud of this film. Because I didn't go shopping. I didn't go to Macy's and pull something off the rack and go, "Oh, put that on." It was such an effort, a creative effort, to really invent the fashion, to create something that a year later was going to stand on the screen and be new and fresh and set the trend. That was the first, foremost goal. It wasn't like: "Oh my God, twenty years from now this movie is going to be cool." It was really: the first goal was to make the movie cool once it comes out.

All That Plaid

Amy Heckerling, writer-director: I've got to give props to Mona May because we had worked out what styles and, sort of, the plaid based on the whole grunge movement, but in a cool, fun, more expensive way. And then she had a sort of black-and-white outfit for Cher, which was really cute. I said, "Oh, that's really great looking." She went: "Mmm." She was losing sleep. She didn't see Cher wearing that the first day of school. I wanted a sort of autumn palette. We were going for different color schemes and different seasons [throughout the movie]. I said I want the feeling that the leaves were changing and everyone's dressed like that. Then she came up with the yellow—and not many people can pull off yellow, you know—and [Mona] just was like, "Ah, I got it!"

Mona May, costume designer: For that scene, we probably tried ten or fifteen different outfits. They were all plaid. Different colors: little dresses, little jumpers, or just different things. Once we put the yellow on—I don't remember if it was number five or number ten or whatever—but it was like, "Wow. Here it is." Other things just immediately fell away and didn't really make the cut. Then, of course, once we were looking at all the pictures, it was like, "Hey, this has got to be the first outfit. This is it. This really: it defines the moment. It's right to introduce her in that. It really is Cher, completely."

That's an original Jean Paul Gaultier. That was one of the few pieces that we splurged on at the time.

I think we wanted to make something very fresh and

coming-back-to-school, so plaid was kind of the obvious choice. It's quintessential.

When we put it on [Alicia] in the fitting, it just was absolutely fantastic. We didn't want to do red. We wanted to take that basic and spin it. So if you had that regular red and blue plaid, it wouldn't be something as fabulous and fresh and interesting as the yellow and black that we found. And I think it popped on her. She had to be like the butterfly.

I think that Dionne was always better in the primary colors. All of the palette was pretty much jewel tones with primary splashes, and red looked so good on Dionne, on Stacey. It was such a fabulous color. And I think that sometimes—again, I think the red would be too much on Alicia. The blond and the red lipstick; it's a lot. So we always had to find the balance between the girls.

Amy Heckerling: The over-the-knee socks have just been an obsession of mine my whole life. You know, because of *Cabaret*, and movies from the twenties where they have the roll-down stockings. You know, garters. I just always thought that was such a sexy thing, to have a thing over your knee and then your thigh showing.

It had a little glint of being in style for a second and went away. When I wanted to use it, it was gone. But I was like, I don't care. I like it. When Liza Minnelli is singing "Mein Herr" [in *Cabaret*] with the short black shorts with the over-the-knee stockings, I go, *Well, that's the best outfit a girl could wear, ever*. I just wish we could all walk around like that.

Mona May: It was Amy. We were talking about it and she really wanted to do something fun. We were talking about the quintessential schoolgirl outfit and what the pieces were, and knee-highs, and where can we take it? Again, it was her brilliance: what about if we try it over the knee? I said, "Let's bring them to the fitting. Let's see what happens."

I wasn't really sure it was going to work until we saw it on Alicia. And again, it looked great on her leg, it really made sense with the outfit, it looked cute, it looked sweet. And it was fresh.

Stacey Dash, Dionne: I thought [my plaid outfit] was fantastic. [Mona] created it, she designed it.

Mona May: [Dionne's hat] was my favorite hat. It was by a really cool designer that I befriended in New York at the time, Kokin, who ended up helping us on this film and creating some of the hats for the film. My relationship with him started many years ago, and he is just super, super creative. He totally got it: what we were looking for, and how kind of wild and fashion-forward we wanted things without looking like you're going to the races. And he understood textures that would complement this: the vinyl bow and just enough of the brim not being too big.

Kokin, hat designer and maker: It was my design. . . . It was my work fitting into her scheme and her characters. So I think we worked with pictures and things that I had, and they just ordered or we changed colors or whatever.

Mona May: I gave him some pictures of things that I'd seen, some ideas—kind of a small sketch, something that we'd already talked with Amy [about] as well. Because those were, again, expenses that were to us quite big. It's not cheap to design a hat and have it made by a hatmaker. So we wanted to make sure that the guidelines and ideas [were] already there, that we're not going on a wild-goose chase. We just didn't have the time or money to do that.

He was really clever. He had a lot of hats in his collection at the time that I could say, "Okay, this is the shape, add it like this, keep the big bow, I definitely want something red in there to complement the red in the outfit and the black and white." Then you let him go, kind of like Amy lets me go. You give the picture. He did a fantastic job. He got it immediately, which was wonderful. He really understood that it has to be fun and youthful, not church lady.

Kokin: It's [made out of] lacquered straw. It was very structured. That's the hat people remember the most from the movie, I think. . . . But it was like a couture piece. It was expensive and difficult to produce, and it was expensive and difficult to sell. But I made it a certain price for a certain woman who's got to have that look. I don't remember [how much it cost]. Whatever it is, now it's pennies.

Mona May: The hat was at least eight or nine inches tall, and I think the brim in front was at least ten or eleven inches. It was a pretty big hat, yeah. The bow itself was probably like seven inches [wide]. We definitely pushed it with her.

Kokin: The other problem was when you put the bow on, it's a very stiff material. And so when you put it onto this hat . . . the front, which is where the bow and the flower and all that stuff was, you'd get this lump, that if you wore it for twenty minutes, it hurt. So we had to figure out how, after applying the whole thing, if we steamed it and pressed the lump out by hand, so that you didn't feel it after a while.

And then the crown is deep, so we had to put a lining in it that was a little shorter. So you got the look with the height but it didn't go down to your nose. These are all technical things that nobody thinks about. And it was something that was done, like I say, before Mona even called me. But not long before. It was [in] the spring collection.

Mona May: Oh, [Stacey] loved it immediately.

Stacey Dash: The hat I thought was genius. My Dr. Seuss hat, I thought was brilliant.

Mona May: The Cat in the Hat, but fashionable! You know: wow, this is a crazy hat but how cool was that? It worked with the outfit, it worked with her. Again, it wasn't right for Alicia but it was right for Dionne.

Stacey Dash: I had to hold on to it when we were driving because it could have blown away. But it was fine. It was comfortable.

Kokin: I don't how many of [those hats] we sold—not many—and there it is in the movie. And everybody remembers that hat. Do you know how many people have dug that up and they want that hat again?

Mona May: When I look at the outfits they are endearing. They really are schoolgirl, even though they are high fashion. There's so much plaid in the film, there's so much skirt, there's so much vest. I think that's part of, maybe, the staying power, too, of the film. It just is innocent. It is something quintessentially timeless. It is the schoolgirl in the plaid skirt—you know, added with the stockings, of course, and all the fashionable hats and berets, making it more high fashion. It will never go out of style.

Ensembly Challenged? Hardly: Dressing the Girls

Alicia Silverstone as Cher

Mona May, costume designer: Alicia, she was at the beginning of her career and I think she had to learn how to really become this character: how to walk, how to talk, how to flip her hair, how to wear fashion. She was completely, kind of, a tomboy, running around with the animals. She's still now kind of a hippie. You really had to, in the room, teach her how it all should come together.

Alicia Silverstone, Cher: At the time, I didn't really understand fashion or costumes at all. I was young. I think I was seventeen, or eighteen at the most. I was much more of a tomboy and just sort of wore—dress it all down, not make any effort, that sort of thing.

Mona May: High fashion is something not everybody is comfortable in. It can be uncomfortable or binding—you have to kind of embody it and know how to just go with it.

Alicia Silverstone: The idea of spending so much time figuring out all the clothes: it was a chore. But when I saw the film—and I remember even on set [with] Mona May, the brilliant, brilliant costume designer, I would be like, *Oh*, Mona. *All this fuss!* When I saw the movie, I was like, "Oh my God." She did such an amazing job. And I knew that as I was going along as well, it's just one of those things—when you're going to have sixty-three costume changes, that's a lot of fittings and a lot of tailoring and trying on clothes and just a lot goes into that. So it's no joke in terms of your time. But my goodness, she did an amazing job. The clothes are so brilliant and ridiculous.

Amy Heckerling, writer-director: It was hard on Alicia because first of all, she was young. She was a kid. And she had been in some movies, but this was all her. . . . She had to wear different clothes constantly, and know all the lines, and get enough rest to look cute. So it was a lot. It was a *lot*-lot, for somebody so young.

Mona May: To do these sixty-three changes [that Alicia had], we had a minimum of twelve or more fittings, at least two hours each, where we were trying things on and putting things together. It has to work for the actor's body, and it has to be right . . . for the character, and it has to be right for the scene.

We had really simple lines on her. And I also thought that looked the best on Alicia's body, that it wasn't fussy. . . . There's not crazy details on her.

Her body was still almost childlike. How do we deal with that? How do we make her not too childish, [but not] too grown-up, too sexy? What are the right colors? What is the right shape? That's why she looked great in all the A-line skirts, why she looked great in the shift empire dresses with the little cap sleeves. Because that made her like a little girl. That's why we put little bows. That's why we used the headband, to kind of even accentuate more of that.

Nina Paskowitz, lead hairstylist: Mona would have maybe three options of what she's going to do for [Alicia] and then suddenly she'd change her mind, or suddenly it was like, "No, let's go with this one." So what Alicia and I would do is kind of set up, "Okay, if we go this direction, what should we do? If we go *this* direction, what should we do?" I'd have a concept of varying hairstyles. Unlike all the other girls that were a bit over-the-top, I always wanted Alicia to look really sleek and pretty and sassy, but without being too cutesy. I didn't want her being too affected by it and to take away from the fact that her clothes were pretty substantial in terms of, you know, making a statement. A lot of times it was just: let's keep it down, let's keep it really sleek. And let's put a clip on it or let's put a little hair ornament or something to dress it up a little.

A lot of it was literally when she was dressed, we'd figure it out at the last minute. I probably would have three minutes to do that, if that. It was a pretty fast-and-furious-paced show.

Alan Friedman, makeup supervisor: She had what I called the number one look, pretty much the same through the whole movie. And a lot of that, honestly, is by design, from an expediency standpoint. So often [in a movie], you start with scene twenty-seven this morning and: "Oh no, no, no, we're not going to do twenty-seven, so-and-so isn't here. Let's do scene thirty-eight." All right, the hair comes down and you do scene thirty-eight. "Oh no, no, no, wait, we can't. There's something going on next door today. Let's go do scene fifty-two." Okay, the hair goes back up and the makeup comes off and the wardrobe changes. So I guess what I'm saying is if I didn't have to keep changing makeup, that was going to be expedient from a scheduling standpoint.

I don't think we had any divas. Alicia: the only conflict I ever remember was she had—on the one hand, she wasn't a party girl. But somewhere, I guess she had an active lifestyle, shall we say? But you know, it's like school. You're there to work but you can't wait to get out of there and go do whatever it is you do. And we had an issue—early on, when I start working with people, I will give them their own little set of makeup remover, cleanser, toner, moisturizer in their trailer. If they'd like one sent home, too, I can do that, too. So on the second or third week, the producers brought me to the dailies and said, "Look, she's getting pimples." And I said, "Well of course she's getting pimples." They said,

"Well, what do you mean, 'Of course she's getting pimples'?" I said, "Well, she won't take her makeup off." You know: "Well, you take her and you tell her." I said, "No, no, I'm not her mother. You know, I gave her the—she has a set of stuff in her trailer and she has a set of stuff at home." "Then you make her take everything off before you go home." All right, fine. So that lasted a day.

Nina Paskowitz: For me, it was using essential oils, running them through her hair, not overprocessing it in terms of heat or blow-drying. She'd come in and [her hair] would usually be damp, and it was trying to air-dry it, and then flatiron it a little bit, blow-dry it a little bit. But she kept it in really good condition, whatever she was doing on her own, separately from what I was doing as well. . . . I was very lucky that I had a great palette to work with.

Adam Schroeder: We gave [Alicia] all her clothes at the end.

Mona May: I was under the impression that she did keep most of her wardrobe. The rest, who knows what happened to it? Paramount used to have a wardrobe department, which is nonexistent now. That could have been sold or just dismantled.

In online outtakes from the Clueless *reunion story published in* Entertainment Weekly *in 2012, Silverstone said that—by the way, you may need to sit down for this—she gave most of the ensembles away.*

Alicia Silverstone: I thought the clothes were so wonderful, by the end I wanted all of them. I took a few things here and there. I didn't do a very good job at saving any of them. I was stupid about that whole thing. I think I gave them all away.[16]

---

16 *Entertainment Weekly* online article, October 5, 2012.

According to a report in London's Evening Standard, *Cher's red Alaïa dress was scheduled to be auctioned by the Phillips auction house in London in September of 2000. It was expected to sell for £200 to £400. Attempts to confirm exactly when it sold and for how much were unsuccessful; according to Alex Godwin-Brown, head of press and events for Phillips, the auction house no longer has records of it sales prior to 2006. Hopefully Silverstone at least kept the plaid Gaultier ensemble.*

Stacey Dash as Dionne

Mona May: Where Alicia had to kind of be coached to understand fashion, Stacey knew immediately: how to wear it, how to turn it, how she wanted to wear it. That girl, she gave *us* lessons. She was unbelievable, truly. She was such a joy to work with because she completely got fashion. She loves fashion. . . . She was older, a little bit older than Alicia, and she already had that kind of inner knowledge: exactly how to put the first foot in front of the other and how to turn the hip.

Stacey Dash, Dionne: The clothes were really a character in the film. So when you got dressed in the morning, you knew you were going to feel, do, and be what your clothes were saying. It was great.

Mona May: She probably could wear a water basket or those things that women wear in Bali and be the most glamorous girl ever. She seriously could have one of those towers of five books [on her head] and walk perfectly straight and they would never fall. And would do it in ten-inch stilettos. That's just Stacey.

Nina Paskowitz: One of my favorite looks on Stacey: when she goes to that party [in the Valley] and she's got those little flowers in her hair. Her hair was—they were braids. She was really fun and she always looked really cute.

Stacey Dash: I loved when they put the ribbons in my braids. But it took a long time, that's the only problem.

That was one of the things that I did not like. Because I wash my hair every day and so the braids would just slip out of my hair and I had to get them done a lot more often than most girls who get braids have to . . . my hair's very fine. The braids would just slip out, so I'd be getting my braids done, as opposed to every two months, I was getting them done every two weeks. And I was having to sit for seven hours and get my hair braided. But it was worth it.

Alan Friedman: This was the beginning of the elite getting tattooed and pierced. So Stacey's character had a few tattoos. . . . We had art drawn up and tattoo transfers made and that sort of thing. Most all of the tattoos were stock transfers from two different companies—alcohol transfers from rice paper—made in two different-color inks. Stacey's nose rings were just jewelry. Her nose was not pierced.

Mona May: On Dionne we went more racy and gave her the short, short skirts. But then you know, also, [her tops weren't] so low-cut. We did a high neck with a big cuff with a white collar, always kind of offsetting it. She could have gone raunchy mama very easily.

She kind of had that very street, funky, very cool, African-American style that can totally pull it off. And it was fun, even to the point of the silly crochet white cap that I made for her during that [scene] where they're driving. I mean, it was hilarious. It was like somebody just took a doily from their grandmother's house and made the hat. But she truly could wear anything.

Brittany Murphy as Tai

Mona May: Amy kind of wanted to show that she was artistic. She drew and [she had] her little graphic T-shirt. Kind of funky, down-to-earth. That was very important, to make her look as kids were dressing then and have somewhere to go for the contrast of the makeover, of kind of her changing through the film.

Alan Friedman: It's more dressing somebody down. It's going way the other way. It's like shooting that "before picture," as I call it.

If you look on television when they're selling you, whether it's makeup or face cream or whatever, that before picture: everybody has dark circles under their eyes and the patchy complexion, probably no makeup, and they always look very unhappy. Suddenly now you clean up the dark circles, and you put a little color on their face, and you've got this little makeup base, and some lipstick or lip color, and a little smile on their face, and suddenly, isn't it amazing how fabulous they look? It's that kind of thing. It's taking somebody back the other way. You don't start from zero. You start from negative ten and then you can then take them to positive twenty and so you can show a transition or indicate a transition that way.

Mona May: I think what was interesting was when the girls did the makeover for her. There's this whole scene of her getting dressed in Cher's closet and she's trying all the things on and she's shy. She's kind of like, "I don't know, is this too much? Or is this too short?" Remember when they cut her T-shirt and—"No, I don't want to show it." It was very interesting how they were trying to make her something she wasn't. So we pushed the clothes to look like the girls dressed her. It was the Mini-Me. Mini-Cher. There was the plaid little vest. There was the little skirt. But again, it was her. It wasn't like the high end. So let's say if Cher wore the Dolce & Gabbana version, she wore the Contempo Casuals version.

Amy Heckerling: She looked good with little cropped jackets. Those were big then. They looked good on her. You had to work the proportions smaller because she was a tiny little girl. Alicia: she's only my height. They're not tall girls.

Nina Paskowitz: That thing with [Brittany's] hair changing color from maroon, from her being all that, kind of, grunge in the beginning—what we actually did was we had her natural color that was that kind of reddish color that it was later on. Every time they wanted her hair maroon, we sprayed it with hairspray that was a maroon color. We couldn't do anything more permanent than that because we were always switching scenes. I think I ended up ordering a case of that color, which was made by Color Moments, and just sprayed her hair every time they wanted it to be that color. And then we had to wash it out when it wasn't supposed to be there.

Alan Friedman: I know Brittany, we had a couple of tattoos on, like, a little flowered bracelet.

Mona May: I think what was wonderful through the film, too, as Cher takes her under her wing, at first she's just so enamored with the girls and so happy to be part of this group. But then she kind of finds her own voice. When this whole incident happens in the mall and she kind of falls over [the railing], and she becomes popular because something happened and people listen to her, she's like: *Wow. I have my own voice*. I think from then on, a little bit of a change happened in her look where I tried to make it more real for who she is. All the way to the end when she goes to see Breckin's skateboard competition, you kind of see a different girl. She has a little bit of a skateboard influence. It's more casual. It's still stylish. She kind of found herself, but she's not trying to be Cher anymore.

Elisa Donovan as Amber

Mona May: She's kind of the quintessential bitchy girl in school. She's very, very rich, probably as rich as Cher. She is very ostentatious and really doesn't give a damn about anybody or anything but herself. So I think that was important to show through the clothes, that she's in her own world—she doesn't care at *all* what people say. It's the opposite of Tai, because she's so sure of herself. . . . It really had to play loud.

Elisa Donovan, Amber: I, generally speaking, hate going to wardrobe. I hate fittings, I hate the whole thing. But doing the movie, it was just so much fun because it was such a part of the character. I would go in for fittings and they would pull out these hilarious elements or additions to the wardrobe, like a certain kind of pin or a kind of weird purse or something that they were creating. Mona and Lisa Evans, [she] was the assistant. The two of them were just always going and always thinking about Amber and then making, sometimes, her wardrobe in comparison to Cher's, and things that were similar would be something extrapolated from hers that Amber would make jump off the screen. I remember them saying, she's in a couture show all the time. So like, she's going to English class in a couture outfit. Which no one wears. Nobody wears that clothing in the real world. It's strictly for the runway. But in her mind, that's how you roll.

We had a hair and makeup test before we started rehearsing. . . . I went in there with very long hair. I had hair down to my shoulders, probably. Very, like, girly long hair. In the hair and makeup test, they cut it. They gave me these heavy bangs that started in the middle of my head, and where it was like a bob, almost. I looked like a completely different person.

Nina Paskowitz: I was like, "We should give you some really hot, sassy bangs." She was so into it once I started doing it, it was really cool. She came in and her hair was more like she wears it now, where it's just loose and longer. I think she came in with that bright red color, that orangey red.

Elisa Donovan: It was like, oh, let's do something really fun because she's the fashion-conscious one and she's going to be really outlandish. I remember not having much of a say, no. Or if I did, I wasn't exercising that because I was like: "Sure, great, okay."

Nina Paskowitz: Yeah, she was totally nervous. Definitely.

Elisa Donovan: It made her more distinct in terms of the other girls and it was more versatile, that kind of haircut, where they could put in different hairpieces and do a lot with my bangs. It was a more creative and edgy sort of haircut than what I had before.

Mona May: The Pippi Longstocking theme, it went all the way from making the whole outfit from a knit so it all matched, with the little scrunchy over-the-knee leggy things, with her arm-warmer glove things, putting the wire in her hair . . . it's obsessive-compulsive fashionista.

Elisa Donovan: That's my hair. That's actually my hair. So they attached pipe cleaners somehow to my head, or maybe she braided it—that was it. Nina, the hairdresser, who was also amazing, did the braid around a pipe cleaner and then bent it into that shape, and teased the top of my hair also.

For a multitude of reasons, Amber was always taking up more space than she should. That [hair] was certainly one of the main reasons.

Mona May: I made [the Pippi Longstocking outfit]. All of her outfits were [partially] made. . . . Even the sailor outfit was buying the red pants, getting the jacket, changing the buttons, decorating the hat, getting the right purse, getting the right shoes. You could just imagine her having a whole sewing studio at her house and she's just ordering people what to do. . . . She was like the pre–Lady Gaga.

Alan Friedman: With Elisa, certainly, it was: "Go put on your outfit." Elisa had a favorite lipstick. Other than that, she was game for about anything. I mean, she generally wore the same lipstick for every scene, but she would let me sort of go at it. She'd sit down in a baby-blue outfit with purple feathers and I could do baby-blue eye shadow with purple definitions and she was fine with that. And purple cheek color. The next scene was something [where] she'd be dressed in yellow and hot pink and she was game for that. Yellow and hot pink went on her eyes.

Elisa Donovan: It was one of my first jobs, so it made such an enormous impression on me. But in that moment, I felt like this is what you do when you work in movies. You spend three hours to four hours in hair and makeup, and you wear clothing that is never comfortable. It's just not always that way. It was that way for that character. When I moved on from [*Clueless*], I went: *Oh my gosh, I can get in and out of hair and makeup in an hour?*

All the Young Dudes: Dressing the Boys

More fashion fuss may have been made over the *Clueless* ensembles worn by Cher and her girlfriends, both during the making of the movie and afterward. But that doesn't mean the young men in *Clueless* were stylistically neglected.

Just as they did with the female members of the cast, the costume, hair, and makeup departments developed the looks of the male members of Cher's social crew—Josh, Murray, Travis, Elton, and Christian—to make sure they popped on-screen in ways that established their individuality. The guys may not have been dressed in Alaïa. But the *Clueless* team made sure they all looked good . . . unless, of course, they were dudes in baggy pants who were supposed to look bad.

Mona May, costume designer: I think it was really fun to do the boys. . . . You don't see a lot of the boys in the film [in terms of fashion]. You don't really put a lot of attention to them, and Amy wanted to make sure we don't lose them, that they don't just become wallpaper. They are more than just something on the scripted page.

Nina Paskowitz, lead hairstylist: The guys were really important to the whole film, and [it was important] to keep them feeling real and natural. But at the same time, each one had their own little quality that made them stand out.

Mona May: Paul [Rudd] is really cool because he is a very intellectual person. He really thinks about stuff and it was great working with him because he brought a lot of plot into the process. He got it. He thought about it. He talked with Amy about it, he talked with me about it. When we tried the stuff on, there was always discussion about, you know: is it right? When we did the breast cancer [T-shirt] thing, it was kind of the beginning of all the pink ribbon stuff that now is so popular. Would [Josh] do it? Yes, he would. He's that secure in himself. He really is a feminist, in a sense.

Paul Rudd, Josh: I had only gotten out of college a few years before. I think they just kind of wanted it to be like what I would wear. You know, like that Amnesty International shirt—that was my shirt. I remember wearing a lot of my own clothes.

In one of the scenes, I was wearing a T-shirt from this band called Trip Shakespeare, that was a band that I *loved* from Minneapolis. That I was wearing one of their shirts, that was the coolest thing in the world to me. It's like: *They might* see *this*.

Alan Friedman, makeup supervisor: I can't remember if we actually rolled film on it, but we did a test on Paul Rudd where I laid a little sort of stubble chin beard, little goatee on him. When [the producers] saw it, they all just went, "That's the dumbest thing we've ever seen."

Adam Schroeder, coproducer: We wanted him to have this goatee thing happening in the beginning of the movie and he was clean-shaven and we didn't have enough time for him to grow it. We looked into makeupping the stubble, but it just wasn't perfected at that time.

I think we pushed the scene [where he's reading Nietzsche] a couple of days just so we could get a little chin-pube action out of him.

The club on one of Rudd's T-shirts is the 688 Club, a now-defunct Atlanta music venue where alternative bands like R.E.M., 10,000 Maniacs, and the Replacements performed in the eighties.

Paul Rudd: I'd had many goatees in my life up to that point and I remember being annoyed, like, *I wish I had a little more time to grow this thing in*.

Nina Paskowitz: They wanted Paul Rudd's hair longer, and it wasn't longer. So they said, "Well, we want to see what it looks like longer." So they did a test with him, adding some kind of hairpiece-wig thing. I can't remember if it was a full [wig], or if it was something like pieces. . . . They wanted to see something where they had more length. So we did this thing, and it was to the bottom of his neck and it was ridiculous. Thank God they just let it grow out.

Paul Rudd: I remember thinking: *It looks kind of like a wig*.

Mona May: [In one scene] he's wearing a T-shirt from a club in [Atlanta] or something. [We were] making sure that we showed who he is, because it's very hard with boys through fashion.

Paul Rudd: People have asked me about that shirt and said, "Dude, that was so cool that you wore that shirt!" I wish I could take credit for it. That one was wardrobe. But the Amnesty International shirt was mine. And by the way, I had two of them. That's how crunchy I was.

Mona May: As simple as he was with jeans and a T-shirt, it was always very clean. I think that we wanted to not make him in any way clowny or edgy. . . . If we had him in more trendy clothes, in a way, then that wouldn't make sense.

Murray . . . [wore] much more of the hip-hop [style] at the

time. You know, kind of more sport dressing in a sense, with the Adidas suits and of course baggier clothes. A lot of caps. A lot of color. I think that was really nice to be able to use, and go with the outfits that Dionne wore.

Donald Faison, Murray: I did not have braces. I never had braces in my life.

[The braces in the movie] are fake because I had an extra tooth and they wanted to hide that because it kind of looked weird when I smiled. So they put braces on me.

What happened was [when I was younger], one of my teeth didn't fall out. So because of that, I had an extra tooth.

Alan Friedman: The fake braces were made by Gary Archer at GA Enterprises, a regular dental lab that also does "showbiz" stuff—vampire fangs, gold teeth, blackouts, fake braces, veneers, etc. They were only for the top. Donald was very good at managing them. A few years ago I gave them to him—there were two sets for shooting, in case one turned up missing—as a keepsake.

Mona May: With Breckin, I think we had to kind of go with the old Spicoli look. We laughed with Amy that it's really the quintessential kind of stoner, skateboarder kid. He also represented, in a way, the time of the nineties, kind of the baggier, looser clothes.

Nina Paskowitz: She kind of wanted his look based on Sean Penn from *Fast Times*. I can't remember if his hair was a lot longer. But she wanted that kind of bob thing, where it's kind of surfer-ish.

Mona May: Everything he wore and that group of people [wore] was aged and washed. As opposed to our girls, where everything was very pristine and pressed.

Alan Friedman: I remember Breckin had an anarchy sign [tattoo] below one of his knees and he generally was in baggy shorts. But it's not often your frame is wide enough, unless he's on a skateboard, to see it.

Mona May: For the Jeremy Sisto character—he had the best shirts. Everything was Armani. Everything was the beautiful Missoni sweaters. He really was on par with Cher. He knew what was good. He had the money, he traveled. He was a snob. . . . He was the male version of Cher.

Jeremy Sisto, Elton: The weirder versions of trendy that we could find were the things that we were kind of excited about. I remember doing some weird thing with my hair where we were pushing it all forward.

Nina Paskowitz: I don't like people in my films to look like they just got a haircut unless it's a military thing. So I just had to chip into his haircut, probably a couple times a week, just so it wouldn't get full and bushy, because he's got a lot of hair. We wanted it to look cute and different from the other guys.

Mona May: [Christian's] costumes are completely vintage. Those are true 1940s pants, 1940s jackets, 1950s-inspired stuff. I mean, everything came from a costume house where they have authentic, real clothes from the period. What was great, too, was that his body suited that very well. Then we can kind of modernize it with the black, sexy, tight Calvin Klein T-shirt underneath. You know, very James Dean. Very kind of hot, masculine, James Dean but still with a lot of flair.

Justin Walker, Christian: I remember that this extremely cool and talented woman, everything she put on me I liked and worked and in my mind, fit the character. So it was like, a no-brainer. I mean, that's not always the case. I also think certainly in a very highly stylized movie, there's a thin line between it being cool and working and it being purposefully over-the-top. . . . Mona May and her design clearly nailed it. Clearly.

Mona May: I think that we never wanted him to be a flamboyant character. The vintage [clothes] gave him a separation from everybody else. He was unique. I think that's what made him stand out from everybody else and gave him some kind of a classiness above everybody else. He comes from another school, you don't really know where he's from. There was never a suggestion at all that he was gay. And the clothes . . . they really did have a feel of the Rat Pack, as the father called him.

The opposite extreme of what Christian wears in Clueless *could be found on the extras who played the baggy-pants guys in the "All the Young Dudes" montage. As May explains, the movie's disdain for boys in droopy drawers is one she shares.*

Mona May: I hate the low-riding pants. To this day, when I see people on the street I just want to pull them up. Just the other day, this guy was walking in front of me. Seriously, his pants were below his underwear. Under his butt. It's ridiculous.

Danny Silverberg, second assistant director: When it came to the baggy-pants boys, those guys were selected [and] prefit, days if not weeks prior to that shooting day.

Mona May: It was so much fun to make fun of, it made me giggly even though it was five in the morning when we had to dress the extras.

Classic *Clueless*: Key Scenes

Meeting Cher . . . and Her Closet

So okay, you're probably thinking,
"Is this, like, a Noxzema commercial, or what?"
—CHER

Production info: The pieces included in the movie's opening montage were shot at various points throughout production, and at various locations, including several streets in Beverly Hills; the hallways of Grant High School, located at 13000 Oxnard Street in Van Nuys; the backyard of the house in Encino that doubled for the Horowitz home; and Burbank's Crocodile Cafe, the restaurant where Cher, Tai, and Dionne discuss Cher's "hymenally challenged" status. The scene in Cher's closet was shot on January 20, 1995, in the pool house on the Encino property/Horowitz residence, a private home on Louise Avenue in Encino, California.

What happens in this scene, CliffsNotes version: A montage that resembles a Noxzema commercial segues into our introduction to Cher Horowitz, who is captured in her "way normal" environment: a wildly oversize closet in which she picks out her school clothes using a computer program that—for real, no joke—seemed incredibly high-tech in 1995.

Amy Heckerling, writer-director: I wanted to do something that seemed typical and then say that we're aware, and we know this isn't real. To make it look like: Oh, here's all these teen movies and they opened with wacky montages and girls having fun and sexy stuff, and then say: "Yeah, *right*. It looks like my life's a commercial but: no, really."

MTV and commercials for young people were converging. People wanted energy more than to see a person's expressions.

Kim Shattuck, lead singer, the Muffs: I had no idea [our cover of "Kids in America" was going to open the movie]. In fact, later when we saw it . . . I remember cracking up, going, "Oh my God, that's me. *Uhhhh.*" I don't like to hear myself sing really, even though I sing. So when I heard it I was like, oh God . . . I wasn't embarrassed. It just made me go: *Oh God, there it is.*

The original "Kids in America," recorded by Kim Wilde and released in the US in 1982, almost became the opening song in Heckerling's Fast Times at Ridgemont High. *Instead Heckerling went with "We Got the Beat" by the Go-Go's and saved "Kids," the updated version, for her second high school–focused feature.*

Amy Heckerling: To me it's like: here it is. Here's these young people. It's fun. You're going to come into this universe and it's bouncy and happy and it's "Kids in America." It is a good song, actually, for what both of them were, in different ways.

Another song that could have become the kickoff piece of music for Clueless*? No Doubt's "Just a Girl," which is still featured early in the movie, but not as prominently as it might have been.*

Amy Heckerling: ["Kids in America"] was cut in and the Muffs were all excited. Then along came "Just a Girl," and Karyn [Rachtman, the music supervisor] said, "This is going to be huge, you've got to use it." I was like, "But I can't. I've already done all this stuff and [the band] already knows that they're in it." So it felt like, *Ooh. Where am I going to put it?* So I put it in the driving [scene], but I should have put it in a bigger place. But it came so late in the game. . . . Normally I would have wanted to feature it a lot more.

Originally, the *Clueless* crew was hoping to shoot the restaurant sequences at California Pizza Kitchen. But once the CPK people saw the final script, and saw how much breadstick-penis talk goes on between Cher, Dionne, and Tai, they said no. Says producer Adam Schroeder: "I think the whole idea of talking about boy parts in CPK, that made them uncomfortable."

Adam Schroeder, coproducer: It was always a mandate [to shoot portions of the montage] when we had the girls together, or we had locations that we were going to be shooting for the specific scenes. But Bill Pope was really just a fantastic, industrious cinematographer, who worked so fast and would see opportunities and bring them to us. When we would try things, most often they would work and become these great little snippets and pieces.

Amy Heckerling: Depending on how the scene is going, [that's] how much time I have for doing a montage piece. So I think the guy with the cherries when they're sitting at the bar—that was probably shot during the "Cher's a virgin" restaurant [scene].

Elisa Donovan, Amber: We would be prepping for other scenes and then Amy would see who was ready, and we would just shoot something on the fly. They were fun because it was all improvisation.

Steven Jordan, production designer: Cher's closet, which we built actually in a pool house, at the property we were shooting at, is probably larger than most of the bedrooms that kids in America grow up in.

Amy Wells, set dresser: For the closet set, I remember going to Warner Bros. and getting some antique chairs and re-covering them in really bright silk.

Steven Jordan: What I was going for in that particular room was lots of curves. The furniture was all cabriole legs. I think there were some gold chairs in there. I recall painting her room in pink and white stripes, which was basically—the inspiration there was the box from Victoria's Secret. Building that closet was sort of, you know, thinking, *What would any high school girl love to wake up to every morning?* But the closet, to me, was something that you just let your imagination run. It was all about fantasy. And the fact that she probably had miles and miles of clothing. That's why we put that dry-cleaning conveyor in the closet.

Amy Heckerling: The closet was based on somebody's home [that] actually had that installed, and it blew me away when I saw it. It was this big record producer who didn't want his clothes to be [tucked away] so that he wouldn't see them. He wanted to be able to see and know what he had.

Adam Schroeder: Then we were able to kind of bring that to life, which was really fun. Again, so absurd, but I think it was something people just dug. Big-time.

Jordan also remembered encountering something similar in real life that helped inspire the moving racks in Cher's closet.

Steven Jordan: I went to this collector's, this gentleman who, at the time was George Steinbrenner's partner, part owner of the Yankees. I went to his home because I needed some baseball stuff. He had a collection that was sold off at Sotheby's ten years [prior], and I went into his office and he pulled a painting off the wall. Behind this painting was just such a conveyor, with jerseys and uniforms going back to the turn of the century in baseball. It was crazy, and that was sort of the idea I had for Cher's closet.

That was much before I did *Clueless*, but I never forgot it. It was the silliest thing in the world but it made so much sense. . . . [The rack system] came from a dry-cleaning source, someone that supplies dry cleaning. We rented it.

Mona May, costume designer: We photographed all the clothes that were downloaded into the computer program, supposedly. We had to deal with the closet: we had to fill the closet with all her costume changes. So I was a big part of building that whole idea and the closet and making sure what we see on-screen is actually what she wore in the movie.

Amy Wells: You want to make sure that [the clothes] are consistent with the character. So that was something where we had to kind of interface [with Mona's department] on that, so that, especially the ones that were featured, that were hanging on the outside of the door and all that, would feel like they were real.

Mona May: [The idea for the computer program came from] Amy. Absolutely. Oh my goodness. That's the genius of Amy.

Amy Heckerling: I always thought, *I don't have a lot of clothes. But why do I even have to try them on when I want to go somewhere, to see what looks good with what?* All I have is black and dark blue so it doesn't really matter, but when I was a kid, I'd play with cutout dolls because they were cheaper than real dolls. I thought, *Why not make a cutout doll of yourself and then you could see?* You would have a cutout doll. When you go shopping, you know what clothes you have and you could see how it would go with everything. That would be a good thing to have. Then I thought, *Well, you could have it on the computer*. So we had a computer guy that made that program up [in post-production].

One of the other noticeable but less futuristic details in Cher's house is the massive painting of her mother that looms over the home's entryway. The portrait was painted by Victor Rinaldo, an old high school friend of Amy Heckerling's who created what Heckerling calls a piece of "classical disco" art using a picture of Alicia Silverstone as his guide. These days, the painting can be found in another family home; Heckerling has it stored in her garage.

Steven Jordan: It was a standard computer, but at the time doing that kind of stuff was in its infancy. So finding a graphic designer who can animate those hangers and create that skeleton-shell of Cher that then would start putting on clothes was a very difficult and labor-intensive process. I think today someone could do it and finish the whole thing by lunchtime. You know, the computers were very early; it was twenty years ago. It was quite a difficult thing and there was an awful lot of back-and-forth.

I still have somewhere in my office to this day—I came across it a couple of months ago—a screen grab, a photograph, of those hangers.

A lot of that, as I recall, was done in post-production. We probably put a green screen up on the monitor, and it went in later.

Adam Schroeder: There really wasn't anything there [when the scene was shot]. It was just the concept that was explained to [Alicia] and then we were going to have to pull it off in post. But it was just a very brilliant idea—if we could see what we looked like in clothes and then choosing our outfit for the day, what a cool thing that would be.

Mona May: It was pretty genius on Amy's part, to be able to see into the future.

The Great Debate

In conclusion, may I please remind you that it does not say RSVP on the Statue of Liberty!

—CHER

Production info: The first sequence in Mr. Hall's class—a.k.a. the "party with the Hait-ians" scene—was shot at Grant High School, 13000 Oxnard Street, in Van Nuys, California, on the first day of production: Monday, November 21, 1994.

What happens in this scene, CliffsNotes version: Cher engages with Amber in a debate over immigration. Amber flashes the "whatever" sign. Christian's eventual arrival is foreshadowed. Mr. Hall distributes grades, prompting a pseudo-suicide attempt from Travis and shock from Cher, who is stunned that she received a C when she's *clearly* doing above-average work in this class.

Amy Heckerling, writer-director: The first shot was [Alicia] doing the Haitians [speech], and Ken Stovitz had come by. She was just great. I thought she was adorable. And he looked at me like: *Wow!* Because that wasn't what we had been seeing and playing with [in rehearsals] up until then. It was like, when it was needed, she was fully loaded.

Bill Pope, director of photography: You just kind of hold your breath when you start a movie and you wonder if it's going to come alive. And almost immediately there was something special going on here. This girl is fantastic. Wally Shawn is fantastic. Everybody's character was fully formed.

I don't know what sort of preparation the actors went through with Amy. But day one, they showed up and there was no "We had to tweak the characters." They're just there, and they're just alive, and they're fully formed. The mood was right there. You don't have to tease it out. There's no panic, there's no re-rehearsals. It just started and you were in the movie. There was this great sense of wonder and relaxation and loss of anxiety. That's kind of what I remember. And the smell of the bathrooms.

Jeffrey T. Spellman, locations supervisor: When we shot that, it was like, we've got to take it to Grant [High School].

That school had it down where you actually could film there during school hours and you just knew that every fifty minutes or so, the bells were going to go off and there would be one thousand students walking through the hallways.

Danny Silverberg, second assistant director: In a situation like that, you've got a bell schedule, so you know you're going to be shut down for that five-minute period when there's a class transition. But you just go in knowing it and more often than not, you're in the middle of a fantastic take when that bell goes off. You wait five minutes and gear it up again and do it all over again. So it wasn't that big of a deal.

Elisa Donovan, Amber: There were classes going on. So if we had to go to the bathroom or something, one of the PAs would take us. So then you're going into the bathroom and you're dressed—like me especially, because I always looked crazy. So I would just be going into the bathroom with these other high school kids, who would laugh at me. Nobody knew who any of us were so it wasn't like people were asking for our autographs or something. You know, they were making fun of us. I was like: *Oh my God, this is just hilarious*.

Steven Jordan, production designer: One of the things I did was I changed all the windows in that classroom. They were basically the public school windows that we all grew up with, those big tall windows. And what I did is I converted them to arches, to tie in with the Occidental College architecture.

Amy Heckerling: There had just been a shooting there . . . there was violence in high schools in California. And here we come in and this one little corner, this one room, has got arched windows, it's painted a pretty color, everybody is dressed nice, and it's lit. And it's this little piece of fake happiness in this world where the kids, it seemed like they were walking in slow motion.

I know my movie is not what high school's like. People say, "Oh, how'd you research it?" Well, it's like, this is not real. Real is not fun. That's why we make movies. But sometimes [students] would walk by and look in and say, "Oh." It didn't occur to them that the building they were in could be made to look nicer.

Wallace Shawn, Mr. Hall: My first impressions were, how did [Amy] find all these charming people? People who were not tense about being, perhaps, in a big studio film. I mean, a lot of actors, quite naturally, would feel: *This is my big chance, I want to make a good impression. What if I do badly?* Well, that's not fun. So the whole atmosphere would have been brought down, in a way, by that type of desperation.

She had picked people for whom it was some kind of adventure to do this. I mean, Alicia, Stacey Dash—for some reason, they were more into having fun than being obsessed with their careers, their futures, etc. We were all just kind of living in the present, amusing ourselves from day to day on the set. That's, I think, probably the first impression I had on that first day: how is it possible that it's all going to be this much fun when there's a lot of money involved and a great big studio? Scott Rudin was probably even there that first day. I remember him as being in a wonderful mood and enjoying himself, every time I saw him on the set.

Alicia Silverstone, Cher: Amy created a great vibe on set from the beginning, so it was more exciting than anything else. I felt so supported.

Elisa Donovan: I was super nervous. . . . I had only been living in LA for a month, and I was living with a friend—a playwright, a dear friend of mine—who I knew from New York. I was basically renting a room in her house. I didn't really have an alarm clock, I just had this little battery-operated one that was digital. I was so nervous the night before that I couldn't really sleep. I finally fell asleep and I woke up . . . at five and my call time was five forty-five and we were shooting all the way in the Valley. The alarm just simply didn't go off. It was like a half-hour drive, and I hadn't showered or anything. I was just beside myself.

I dashed in the shower. I was completely terrified. I didn't even really know where I was going. I had to have the Thomas Guide in my lap. There was no GPS, you know? So when I got there, I'm racing out of my car and the first person I see is Scott Rudin. And I'm like, "Huuuuuuu—hi! Good morning!" He clearly had no idea what my call time was or anything. He was chipper and friendly and fine, and I was just like, *This could not be worse*. Then it was completely fine. I was only a few minutes late in the end. But I was completely scared.

Wallace Shawn: I had actually been a schoolteacher at one time and that was much more stressful than being in the movie. So I suppose I found it extremely entertaining and delightful to be a teacher where I already knew my lines. Any rebellion from the students was in the script. Of course, it's a gift to an actor to play an agreeable person, but one that's written in a way that's believable. What fun! You leave your anxieties at the door of your trailer and—for twelve hours or whatever that is in a day—those anxieties are not there.

Adam Schroeder, coproducer: You try to start the first day out with a very makeable day. It was very controlled. You're in the classroom. It's obviously important dialogue and all that kind of stuff. You're introducing some of the characters. But you know, I think Alicia mispronouncing Haitians as Hait-ians, which is fantastic, kind of set the tone.

Elisa Donovan: I remember Alicia, when she said Haitians, it was a mistake. It wasn't supposed to be that way. That was how she thought it was supposed to be pronounced. I was like, *Oh my God, is somebody going to—I can't believe*—I was sort of, I didn't know what to do. And Amy was like: "This is *amazing*."

Amy Heckerling: She mispronounced it, and the script woman and everybody started to run toward her to correct her and I had to block them all. I was like: "Stay away from the actress." She needed to have that assurance that she was saying it right. There's a cockiness to Cher when she's just going down the wrong track, and you just have to make sure people don't mess with that. So we continued, and I didn't tell her until later [that she mispronounced the word]. . . . Thank God [Elisa] didn't go over to her, because she was right there. Thank you, Elisa!

David Kitay, composer: [The music in that scene is] very American. Of course for her and her life, the idea that everything is just good—her world is good. That's the perspective that we were always making sure we were supporting.

Amy Heckerling: I had a lot of fun with the extras, too. . . . I had a lot of stuff for people to be doing, and they really all got into it. A lot of people had plastic surgery things [on their noses], and these things itch. So people were doing stuff with their [pens trying to scratch].

Adam Schroeder: There were a lot of nose bandages and chin bandages and telephones in the room.

Amy Heckerling: I thought, *Okay, we've got the plastic surgery people and they're itching*. And then I figured there are deals going on. People are buying and selling shit. So I had that kind of going on, too. So they're haggling and they're selling things. Then there was a lot of grooming and that was totally real from Beverly Hills High School. They would come in with these Caboodles—it was like a plumber or a workman would come in and open it up and there'd be all the different tools in all the different sizes: drill bits and screws and things in drawers. But it was all makeup and grooming stuff.

So I thought, *Well, let's play with these kinds of grooming situations*. So everybody had something that they were doing. People were organizing their CDs, they were straightening their hair, they were selling a watch, they were scratching their bandages.

Bronson Alcott High School is named after both Bronson Pinchot, Heckerling's former boyfriend, and Bronson Alcott, the father of *Little Women* author Louisa May Alcott, after whom Pinchot was named. Says Heckerling: "I liked the idea that Bronson Alcott was somebody who had a famous daughter who accomplished something at a time when it was very hard for women, and that he was one of the freethinkers, [part of] the pre-hippie alternative lifestyle movement. And [he] also was into educating women."

They were all very gung-ho. Everybody was cool and having fun and busy.

Jeremy Sisto, Elton: I remember when we did the first take, I was in the background maybe. . . . I don't even know exactly what I did but I must have done some big, over-the-top thing, because Amy came up to me after the first take and just said, "What are you—what are you *doing*?" *[Laughs]* And I was like, "Sorry, sorry. Let's go again."

I would love to see that first take because it was probably pretty ridiculous.

Elisa Donovan: I had this boyfriend in high school who would say *whatever* in the most, just, mean, dismissive [way]. When he would say *whatever*, it was like things were over. He would be like, "*Whatever.*" And it was so irritating to me. It would make me so mad. So when I read the script, I was like: *Oh, this is her word. Of course it is. Of course this is her word. This is my revenge, that I get to use this word on everyone now.* . . . I feel like Amy told me to do [the *W* sign]. Or maybe it was in the script. I think it was in the script.

I had a very distinct, visceral reaction to that word, so maybe that's why it sticks so much with people with Amber having done that. It definitely resonated at the time with me, in a major way.

Dean Wilson, prop master: I went to the school system and talked to them and got copies of the real report cards. So [the ones Mr. Hall distributes] are all actually authentic for the Los Angeles school district. . . . When the actors are looking at something, it's kind of nice to have something [real].

Yeah, I mean [Travis really] had D's and F's. You know: suicide time.

Wallace Shawn: I think most of the actors would feel as I did: well, if this could be our permanent job and we could come in every day and do this fifty weeks a year, maybe with a two-week vacation, we'd sign up. Because this is Amy trying to amuse herself. She's trying to give herself a happy experience by writing something delightful and directing it in a way that brings out the delightful aspects of the actors. So this is a very pleasant world that she's creating.

The Presence and Prescience of the Cell Phones in *Clueless*

When we watch *Clueless* through the prism of the present day—a time when, according to a 2014 Pew Research Center study, 90 percent of adults own cell phones—it's funny when Cher, her father, and Josh simultaneously answer their mobiles in the middle of a meal, or when Cher and Dionne talk to each other on their cells while standing next to each other in a high school hallway. But when we watched *Clueless* in 1995—a time when data collected by the World Bank indicates that a mere thirteen out of every one hundred Americans subscribed to cell service—the obsession with those phones not only seemed absurd, it looked downright alien to the average moviegoer still getting by in life with (*gasp!*) a landline.

Heckerling's decision to weave cell phones so prominently into the fabric of her movie may have been made primarily for comedic reasons. But, like so much in *Clueless*, all those Motorolas and Nokias provided a sneak preview of America's future.

Steven Jordan, production designer: Honestly, I think at the time cell phones were still relatively new and the fact that there was this obsession with them was just foreshadowing things to come. Telephones all fall under the prop department, and Dean [Wilson] just got an incredible assortment of phones. And it just turned out to be rather fortuitous that that's how life is today.

Dean Wilson, prop master: All the cell phones that everybody used, we promoted them. You would just talk to the different companies, you know, about [using their] cell phones and all of that.

I think [we used] Motorola . . . just about all the brands. Samsung. We had just about everything. I think [Cher's] was a Nokia. But I think when they did the publicity photos, the people who were doing the publicity photos didn't really like the Nokia. I think she's got a flip phone in that. But that really wasn't her phone, that was the phone that they liked. And you don't argue with them. You just give them what they want, make them happy.

[The phones] weren't as flashy and all that stuff, but you know, as long as the company saw it in one of the principals' hands, I mean, they were pretty happy.

Herb Hall, the "real" Mr. Hall and the *Clueless* principal: There were a few jokes at Beverly that people would perpetuate, just because people would come in and say, "Is that really true?" You know, we would spread this rumor that there was Evian in the water fountains. That kind of thing. And [*in sarcastic tone*],

"Yes, everybody has a cell phone and yes, they don't really talk to each other, they walk down the hall and talk to each other on the phone." That kind of thing. That was pretty much a standard joke at the school.

Here's a fun fact: the last name *Horowitz* was given to Cher unintentionally, and not by Amy Heckerling. "I didn't really give her a last name as far as in the script. She was just Cher," Heckerling says. But during the scene when Mr. Hall is handing out tardy slips, he ad-libbed the name "Cher Horowitz"—and it stuck. This also explains why Cher's report card says Hamilton on it; that's a name Heckerling says she told the props department to use on the report card, as an homage to Brad and Stacy Hamilton from *Fast Times*, before Shawn's bit of Horowitz improv. The minor continuity error, one that hard-core fans certainly notice, stayed in the picture.

Amy Heckerling, writer-director: Actually [the idea for the hallway cell phone scene] came many years before when there first started to be cell phones. I was on *Look Who's Talking* and the producer was on the set, but he was always on [his phone]. And these were bricks, right? And he'd be walking around in the background; sometimes we'd have to move him over because he was just, like, walking and talking. He'd be talking on his cell phone, then the associate producer would be walking around, talking on his. I remember my ex-husband and I were joking: "They're talking to each other." And it cracked me up. There they were, they were both together. Obviously they were probably talking to other people. But maybe not. It just seemed like a funny thing, that you could be with somebody and still be talking on your phone to them.

Paul Rudd: I remember thinking it was really funny that the phone rings and we all three [Cher, Josh, and Mel] answer our cell phones. I don't think that joke had ever been done before and I remember going, "That's *brilliant*."

Stacey Dash, Dionne: I had a cell phone at the time. It wasn't foreign to me. But I loved the way she used the cell phones in the movie.

It's just the genius of Amy. She saw what was coming, and that's what she's good at. She has great foresight.

The Introduction of Tai

Ms. Stoeger, my plastic surgeon doesn't want me doing any activity where balls fly at my nose.

—AMBER

Well, there goes your social life.

—DIONNE

Production info: The gym class scene on the tennis court—in which Tai arrives on the Bronson Alcott High School scene for the first time—was shot, along with all the high school exteriors, on the campus of Occidental College, 1600 Campus Road in Los Angeles, on Tuesday, December 20, and Wednesday, December 21, 1994, days twenty and twenty-one of production.

What happens in these scenes, CliffsNotes version: Cher makes a convincing case that she can burn more calories chewing a stick of gum than she can by playing tennis. Tai makes her first appearance in *Clueless*, completely unaware that, a mere four scenes later, she will be completely transformed via the magic of a movie makeover montage set to Jill Sobule's "Supermodel."

Adam Schroeder, coproducer: That was one of those scenes where you felt the style of it because the workout clothes—or the tennis clothes, rather—were so not tennis.

Amy Heckerling, writer-director: The school colors were black and white so they wouldn't mess up the palette of the different seasons. . . . I needed the things that would be throughout the year—the gym clothes, the cheerleaders' [uniforms]—those things to be black and white.

Mona May, costume designer: I think we wanted to make that scene and the gym clothes feel like they're accessorized, like they are also part of the wardrobe. . . . I think that was really important to Amy: that even in the gym clothes, they were like full-on.

Amy Heckerling: I really liked those outfits. . . . When I went to school, we had to wear these gym uniforms. They were either green or blue. They snapped. You had to sew your name on the pocket. They had short sleeves but they went like that [*gestures to indicate awkward sleeves*] and then there were pantaloons. I don't think there's anything as ugly as what those looked like. It was just like a Girl Scout uniform turned into pantaloons with stiff, ugly material. It was ridiculous. So I wanted the girls to look all nice.

Elisa Donovan, Amber: That outfit: that was just bananas. Who wants to wear bike shorts in the first place? I was just like, *Well, let's go for it. Never again in my life will I have cause to wear these*. That was probably the only [costume] that I went, "Oh my goodness." Satin bike shorts. But again, the whole ensemble was just so absurd and fantastic that there was never a question. I loved it.

Stacey Dash, Dionne: The sneeze that you hear in the film is my actual sneeze. Amy heard me sneeze at one of the read-throughs and she was like, "Oh my God. Is that your real sneeze?" And I said, "Yeah." So she wrote it into the movie. It fit perfectly because I had the nose ring. So it was a really good joke.

Amy Heckerling: I don't know if that was props, or if Mona found [the cell phone and water-bottle holders]. Mona would find things and she'd get all excited about [them]. Special, designer things to hold your water bottle—she would just go crazy over these things.

Herb Hall, the "real" Mr. Hall and the *Clueless* principal: It was freezing cold because it was December. I was on the set at about seven in the morning. It was just ridiculously early, and they had these gigantic parkas for all of us because it was so cold.

When I went into the makeup trailer, I was in the makeup chair and Cher, Alicia, was in the next chair over. She said, "Yeah, I heard that there's supposed to be a teacher from Beverly Hills High working today." And I said, "Yeah, that's me." She looked at me and she goes, "No, no no. There's this guy, I think his name is Mr. Hall, and he's a real teacher. He's not an actor. He's going to be working on this show."

I said, "Yeah, I'm Herb Hall. That's me." She goes, "No, no. It's not you because I went to Beverly and I know and it's not you." And I kept going, *What is she talking about? I'm Herb Hall. There's nobody else*. She kept insisting on it, so I said, "What did this guy teach?" And she goes, "Science. He was my science teacher." And I went, "Oh my God." There was a biology teacher at Beverly at the same time whose name was Mr. Hale. He was also black. We were both about the same height, both about the same build. Pretty much, if you saw us from a distance, the only difference was that he had a very large 'fro. And I said,

"Oh, you mean Mr. Hale." And she goes, "Hale? His name is Hale?" I went, "Yeah, he's the biology teacher. I'm Mr. Hall." She goes, "Oh my God. No wonder the guy would never call on me in class. Because I always called him Mr. Hall!" That was my introduction to Alicia. It was really kind of funny. It was a very common mistake.

Mona May: It was interesting how [Brittany Murphy] really was that [character]. She was a very up-and-coming young actress. This was her first break. She was kind of the lost little bird, in a sense. She came on set with her mother, she was still underage, kind of big-eyed—as in her first scene of the film, you know.

Herb Hall: She was really sweet and down-to-earth. She didn't put on any airs whatsoever. She was just a normal teenager. It felt like I was having a conversation with one of my students in my class. There was nothing about "I am a star," or "I'm going to be a star," or, you know, "I'm full of myself." I just got this impression she would be the kid you'd want to hang out with if you were in school. Go get a burger or go to the dance or whatever . . . She was so sincere that way. It was really refreshing.

Mona May: In the beginning [Tai] comes and she really is kind of like from another planet or another state, somewhere where the world of fashion is not as fashionable. That's what kids were really wearing at the time. That was the grunge look that represented what was in the schools.

Dean Wilson, prop master: I think Glen and I actually built [Tai's] notebook. That was something that we actually designed and drew and we let Steve [Jordan] look at it. Steve gave us ideas, stuff like that.

Herb Hall: Before we shot my scene . . . I was outside of a fence with Tai. They told us what they were going to do. "We're going to set this-this-this, and then on 'Action' we want you to count to three," I think, "and then come through the gate." Well, we never heard "Action." She and I were just standing out there talking, because she was really a nice kid. Then we suddenly realized. We went, "Have they started rolling the cameras? We've been out here talking a long time." We couldn't hear through that—I don't know what that stuff is, the baffling they put on tennis courts.

Then we went in and it was always: wear the parka up until the last second, and then as soon as you hear "Action," yank the parka off and go in so that we wouldn't be frozen when we walked on-camera.

Stacey Dash: I just loved the fact that we all had excuses [for] why we didn't have to play tennis.

Herb Hall: It's not in the final movie, but there's that whole thing with the tennis balls being shot [out of the machine]. I don't know if he did it as a joke or what it was, but the guy who was off-camera who was shooting the tennis ball, at one point he shot it so that it zipped right by my nose. And I did this double take on it. Then Amy said, "I like that. Let's do that again!" So then we did a whole bunch of these with this guy shooting the tennis balls and them whizzing by my nose so I could react to them, but that wound up not being in it.

Stacey Dash: I loved saying ["There goes your social life."] It is my favorite line in the movie. There were points where I would say it and then we'd all start cracking up, and we wouldn't be able to do another take until we stopped laughing. There was a lot of that. A lot of us breaking into giggle fits and Amy telling us, "We're not starting until you stop laughing." The more we got told to stop laughing, the more we laughed and, you know, we would get into trouble sometimes.

Adam Schroeder: I want to say that maybe the "balls flying at my nose" [line] and then Dionne's "There goes your social life" might have been a Cher line at one time. But it became a Dionne line and I'm not sure why. I just have a memory of that.

Stacey Dash: I think probably [it did] because I had more attitude and there was more of a rivalry between Amber's character and my character. I didn't really like her in the script, in the movie. For me, she was just there, as furniture. She didn't really exist. That was Dionne's feeling about her. I think that's probably why they gave me the line.

Elisa Donovan: When I first read [that line], I didn't even understand. I didn't get the joke. The joke was *totally* lost on me for quite some time. And then when we did actually shoot it, then I was like, *Oh ho ho ho ho, I get it!*

Bill Pope: [I remember] how well that joke worked. To tease a joke and make it work and figure out the timing. Each joke is a miracle. When you watch a comic performance, it's like, wow. Yeah. That's it. That timing right there. You know you got it. It doesn't take [these actors] very long. They're all really fast.

If you watch closely during the scene between Cher and Josh in the kitchen, just before Tai sings the Mentos jingle, you may notice that Paul Rudd has an, um, unconventional approach to sandwich making. Says Rudd: "I hate condiments. I can't stand mayonnaise or ketchup. So when I had to go in and make a sandwich, looking back now, I think I put mayonnaise right on the turkey and not on the bread. That's the kind of thing that will bother me now for years."

Making a Cameo at the Val Party

Let's do a lap before we commit to a location.

—CHER

Production info: The sequence was shot at a private home in the Granada Hills neighborhood in Los Angeles. Shooting began on Tuesday, November 29, 1994 (day five on the production schedule), and lasted for four days.

What happens in this scene, CliffsNotes version: Cher tries to hook up Tai and Elton, a plan that initially seems to succeed thanks to the magic of flying clogs and Coolio. Suck and Blow is played. Murray's head gets shaved.

Donald Faison, Murray: They had a bunch of extras who were my age or around my age. We were playing music all night long. We're all dressed up really cute. When they break, we're all hanging out with each other, trying to pass time and stuff. So it totally felt like a party. Making that movie, in a lot of ways, felt like a party. We were a bunch of kids hanging out, and hanging out in big groups. That's all a party is: a party is a bunch of people hanging out in a big group and having fun.

Danny Silverberg, second assistant director: Working in that small environment with all those people is tricky. I think we had smoke in there, which means no air-conditioning. So it's hot and uncomfortable.

Breckin Meyer, Travis: Party scenes are always weird because you have the fake smoke being blown in, you have a ton of background people smoking fake cigarettes, which, oddly enough, smell weirder than real cigarettes. We're also smoking fake weed in the scene. . . . Bad weed smells awful, but bad herbal cigarettes also smell terrible. I remember that distinctly, having a headache from all the smoke/fake smoke.

Donald Faison: It took a long time to shoot that scene and I remember falling asleep [at one point], and being woken up by Tara Reid, who was not in the movie but just came by the set to hang out. Which was really odd. I went to high school with Tara Reid so when she woke me up, it was kinda like, "Yo, what are you doing here?"

Nicole Bilderback, Summer: Tara and I . . . we had like a mutual group of friends. [She] and I hung out quite a bit back in those days. Yeah, so I want to say I do remember her just stopping by to hang out, to say hi to everybody. When you have a whole cast, who's all, give or take a few years, all around the same age—and it's a small world here in LA so everybody kind of knows everyone. So when you're working on a set . . . people are inviting their friends to come visit.

Twink Caplan, associate producer and Miss Geist: My nephew was in *Clueless*. He was in the party scene. Yeah, it was hilarious. . . . He was in the party scene and he walks behind somebody when Brittany hands the joint to somebody else. He's got a hat on with flaps, and he looks adorable.

Jeffrey T. Spellman, locations supervisor: [The location] was written as a typical Valley house. But what is a typical Valley house? We needed this big backyard for the party scene and needed it to be [in] a good neighborhood because, as I recall, we were there for a few all-nighters to get the work done. We found it up there in Granada Hills.

Donald Faison: I remember us getting there, to do the scenes, and me being like, "This doesn't look like Beverly Hills," and them being like, "No, this is supposed to be in the Valley." You know, I didn't live in Los Angeles, I lived in New York, so I thought the Valley was part of Beverly Hills. That was a little confusing.

Steven Jordan, production designer: My recollection of the really big job we did was all that lighting at night. The Christmas decorations: I think that's really where we just went over the top. I think the nature of that party, the only place you can go is over the top. Bigger, louder, brighter. It's not a place to nuance. You have to work in very broad strokes.

Amy Heckerling, writer-director: I'm a sucker for glowing colors. I was very happy to be able to use a lot of twinkly Christmas lights. The palette for that part of the movie was reds and greens. I was trying to steer away from the cool colors.

Bill Pope: That's something I've done since, several times, as a way to sparkle up a party and give a general ambience at the party. You don't have to overlight it. You can light it like a party really is.

Amy Heckerling: It was also a place where we were using more rap music. The kids were being a little looser than they normally would be. They were usually uptight about what they do and don't do, and this is a situation where they're letting their hair down because they're out of their neighborhood. Emotionally, it was all about forcing Tai into a role she didn't want to be in, but she goes along with things fairly easily. So if you say, "Here's this boy that likes you, this boy that you should like," she'll go with that. And if another boy comes along, she'll go with that.

I was thinking about what Cher's agenda was, and emotionally where Tai would be. And how this would affect Travis and how they were misled by Elton's motivations. So those were the main points I had to deal with. And then finding a silly way to do them and have some details that would make it feel like a real, fun party in the Valley and not just, here's a bunch of young people in really baggy pants and they're all drinking. I was never into that much reality. I was always sort of like: what's more fun and prettier and more romantic than real reality?

Alicia Silverstone, Cher: I don't even think Cher had fun at that party. I'm sure that I was not in the party scene, like, in the party vibe. She was just like: It's all business. You go in, you go in there, you see what's going on, and if it's not working, you've got to go. It was like a business transaction or something.

Breckin Meyer: One thing I remember about that [scene] was me trying to rail-slide, which my character does when [Tai] enters the party. My character does this weird run-and-jump and rail-slides on the banister, and I think, eventually, they absolutely did not use mine. It was probably a stunt skate guy. I think it's a three-foot-high rail, a hand banister, and the producers were like, "If you get hurt, it's kind of the end of the movie for Travis?"

Donald Faison: Sean Holland, who's also in the movie—he plays Lawrence, who's the guy who's shaving my head. He came with a song. He was a rapper and stuff like that . . . [and] he played me one of his songs. I remember saying to Amy, "Amy, I think this should be the song in the show." And she was like, "Well, let me hear it." And Sean, he sat everybody down, all in one room, and we watched Sean perform the song. That wound up being the song they used in the movie ["This Time" by Phunke Assfalt]. Not "Rollin' with My Homies," the other song, when they come into the party. That was his song. It's pretty cool.

If people look really closely, though, Sean Holland played

two parts in that movie. He's the guy dancing with Amber with the tank top and the crazy hat, and then he's the guy cutting my hair. A lot of people don't recognize that.

Elisa Donovan, Amber: I just created this sort of spastic dance that she would do. I think that's when it started, when we first shot that scene. . . . Then I did some of it also, when we had the other party with the Mighty Mighty Bosstones.

Breckin Meyer: A lot of the stuff we kind of—not came up with on the fly, because the script is pretty solid, but just the way you do things. The way you get passed around, the way you jump into the crowd, the way we bring Brittany over to the table and dump ice on her head by accident, stuff like that.

Dean Wilson, prop master: Everybody's drinking there so we have to make the prop drinks. Actually, they're drinking caramel-colored water, unless it's a beer. And if it's a beer, they were probably all drinking nonalcoholic beer.

Alicia Silverstone: I love that scene when I see it. I love the Suck and Blow thing—am I saying that right? I love that, when Jeremy [Sisto] gets in there and tries to snag a kiss. I just love it. [*Laughs*]

Amy Heckerling: A friend of mine, she was in her twenties and she wanted to have a party but she didn't really have a place to have it. You know, not a big party, she wanted to have some of her friends come over. I said, "Oh, you can do it at my house." Essentially I was just hanging around, watching movies, doing whatever I'm doing, but there's a party going on at my house. That was one of the things I observed. They were playing that game. I said, "Huh, what's that? I'll use that."

Actually, you have to really work to make it not work. It's easy to do. What I liked was that I wanted to have a situation where somebody has to kiss somebody at a party and the old standbys just seemed too immature. And also a game that involved a credit card seems kind of different.

Alicia Silverstone: I definitely hadn't heard of it. I didn't know it at all. I've never heard of it again since then.

Breckin Meyer: If Travis was any good at trying to woo Tai, he would have realized he should have dropped the [credit card]. Because I was oddly good at it and had no intention of doing that, which I think—it's gentlemanly but also, at the end of the day, he wasn't great at it. He wasn't great at [Suck and Blow] because he was good at it. I think being bad at that game probably benefits you more than being proficient at it.

Nicole Bilderback: Of course when you're going to play Suck and Blow when you're in Beverly Hills, you're going to use a credit card. But I remember us trying to do it, like me trying to do it, and, you know, credit cards are thicker and heavier and I couldn't suck it long enough to hold still to pass it on to somebody else.

Adam Schroeder, coproducer: I think we had to do a fake cardboardy one because the sucking part was difficult. Ooh—that sounds bad.

Nicole Bilderback: I remember that was kind of a thing everyone kept trying. Even the producers were trying.

Everyone's like, "Suck harder! Suck harder!" I'm like, "I'm sucking hard! I'm sucking as hard as I can!" That became, like, an ongoing joke.

Alicia Silverstone: I love when Murray gets his hair shaved and Dionne's all freaking out. That's cute.

Stacey Dash, Dionne: I loved the freaking out. I loved every time I got to freak out. I thought it was really cute and really funny that Dionne always had these temper tantrums, which is so far from who I am.

Amy Heckerling: I liked the idea that Murray would shave his head because his friends were [doing it] and they thought it was cool, but his girlfriend didn't think it was cool, and [they'd] have a conflict about that. Which would also give [Cher and Tai] the "How are we going to get home?" situation. The "How are we going to get home?" was a big part of what the party needed to accomplish for me, story-wise. . . . We made sort of a wide lens on Donald when you see the first close-up on him. So he's kind of round and his smile is really big, a little distorted.

Bill Pope: You start on Donald Faison's face and you don't show that he's bald. Then the joke is that he's bald, or becoming bald. That's the reveal. There was a topper to that, there had to be a topper to that, but I can't remember what it was. That's a mechanical joke scene.

Donald Faison: It was finally time for me to shave my head but they didn't want me to shave my whole head, they just wanted to shave the top of it so that when I have on hats throughout the other scenes, I still have hair on the side. And I remember them shaving my head and me looking like George Jefferson by the end of the night.

Breckin Meyer: On-screen Donald had all these cool hats and lids and all these great Kangol, Sam Jackson–type hats. And in reality, every time you knocked his hat off, he was George Jefferson at twenty years old. So it was fantastic for me and Rudd to just know that any time we wanted to, we could see what Donald would look like as George Jefferson. That was a bonus.

It's such a specific, distinct haircut. And Donald rocked it well. But also, just to be a twenty-year-old guy with normal hormones and normal vanity and have your hair look like a fifty-year-old laundry owner's—it's not a great look. I should say, George Jefferson owned a dry-cleaning business. It wasn't a laundry.

Stacey Dash: Yeah, he did. He looked like George Jefferson. That's hilarious. And I was like, "You've got to shave your whole head. You cannot go around like that. That is a no-go."

Donald Faison: Look, I'm a light-skinned black guy who kinda resembles Sherman Hemsley. So if you shave my head to look like that, guess what? I'm going to look like that.

Alicia Silverstone: Oh, I don't remember that. [*Laughs*] Oh, I see, because of the sideburn kind of thing, right? I can see that now that you said that. But I don't remember having that thought at the time.

Amy Heckerling: We had his head partially shaved for early scenes and he would be wearing a cap. I forget scheduling, how we worked it out, but we had it look as though he still had hair.

He was kind of not very happy with having to look like [George] Jefferson for a few weeks. His head was bald in the middle, so for take two, three, four, we were actually shaving. Then we were just repeating ourselves.

Nina Paskowitz, lead hairstylist: You want to be able to do a couple of takes, so you've got to put the shaving cream on in a certain way so that if you're actually shaving it, you can then take two and it can still look regular. So you only do parts of it, so there's always an area that still has hair. So you shave that off and go: *Oh, you can actually see the hair being removed.* I seem to remember us doing it pretty easily and not having to do a lot of takes of it in that bathroom.

Bill Pope: I remember the difficulty of just being in that bathroom. The bathroom was a nightmare. All bathrooms are nightmares, especially on an actual location where you're not on a set and you can't pull a wall and have room to work. You have to just wedge in the door and figure out blocking.

Amy Heckerling: I wanted Breckin Meyer to be in a position where he's trying to impress [Tai] in whatever ways he can think of. And so, you know, trying the stage-diving act.

Breckin Meyer: It was a time when I was following Pearl Jam around, and all [Seth Green and I] would do was crowd-surf and stuff. So that was just fun. It's actually less fun to do it in a movie because instead of jumping on actual people, you're jumping on stuntmen. So you have all these burly stuntmen who are dressed as eighteen-year-old partygoers and they catch you in a very supportive way as opposed to a normal crowd-surfing environment, where you're just landing on heads and elbows. Here, it's like you have a very strong, callused hand on your thigh the entire night. Not that there's anything wrong with that. I have nothing against a strong, callused hand on my thigh.

Jeremy Sisto, Elton: I remember there was this kind of dance that was popular when I was in high school, or a couple years before that . . . it's this weird funny dance, and I remember doing that and kind of feeling good about it—like, it was funny. I remember feeling insecure about having to dance on-camera and then getting through that and then feeling all right about it.

Mary Ann Kellogg, choreographer: I remember rehearsing with Alicia and Brittany that they had to do this kind of Bertolucci reference. You know, when the two girls dance in [*The Conformist*]—I think they're in that big hall. She has to go down on her knee and Brittany has to go around her.

Amy Heckerling: *The Conformist* . . . I just love that movie. There was that scene where the two women are dancing together. I just thought that was really beautifully done. It was hard to do it in the Val party. It needed its own space and light. But I felt like Cher dancing, you would look to Cher. But Cher wanted to be showing off [Tai], so it was more of a presentational thing. That was the reason behind that. Now I feel like watching *The Conformist* again. That's a gorgeous movie.[17]

I wanted to put Tai in the position of needing to be rescued and make it as though Elton had helped when, in reality, he had nothing to do with anything. So the idea of getting hit in the head with a clog—because people are doing sort of a move together and a clog comes flying across the room and hits her in the head. Well, we did the take a few times with a clog flying off and we also had a foam-rubber clog that we made.

It happened so fast that you didn't really see it. When you throw something, it's just a couple of frames in a darkened party room.

So we had to animate it slower and have a fake clog, I think it was drawn in. . . . We had to create a special effect essentially

17 *The Conformist* is a 1970 film directed by revered Italian filmmaker Bernardo Bertolucci (*Last Tango in Paris, The Last Emperor*). In the *Entertainment Weekly* cover profile of Silverstone published in March of 1995, she mentioned that she had just run into Bertolucci moments before the interview, which took place at the Four Seasons in Beverly Hills.

on regular film that was not shot for special effects, of a slower, darker, more noticeable clog going from the girl's foot and hitting Brittany.

Mary Ann Kellogg: Before we had kind of goofed around with [the idea of kids] dancing on the pool table. Standing up on the pool table, dancing on the pool table. But the room was really low so the actual set—I don't think they could actually stand up on the pool table and dance without touching the ceiling.

The shoe would have gone into the ceiling instead of straight. Then it becomes oh well, okay, so you have to sit on the pool table. That ["Rollin' with My Homies"] movement comes organically out of what those kids would have done.

Amy Heckerling: I liked [Coolio] for that part of the movie because I wanted something that involved hand movements, or movements that everybody would be doing together that could mess up Tai. The song that I was originally thinking about when I was writing it was "Slide, slide, slippity slide." [*Heckerling is referring to Coolio's 1994 hit "Fantastic Voyage."*]

We had to sort of finesse things to make it look like they were deliberately doing this and not just trying to make a shoe fly off.

Mary Ann Kellogg: One of the things Amy said was this scene, this movement, had to play while the girls were also sitting down at that café.

Donald Faison: [That song] worked so well because Brittany Murphy sang the crap out of it with just that one line, when she said, "Rollin' with the homies."

I honestly believe that's why everybody remembers the song, because one, she's so cute when she sings it. Two: you didn't expect that voice to come out of that girl when she sang. So when she does that line, it's like, "Holy cow, she can sing?" And then they start dancing. That's why everybody remembers that song. And also the hand gesture, you know, the waves? That makes no sense. It's a wave. But it just works with that song.

Mary Ann Kellogg: That's the one thing about doing it on the day is that I'm meeting people for the first time. They're meeting me for the first time. You don't have a lot of time to explore what makes them look good, how their character would move.

So we're all kinda playing around. Amy's there, I'm there, the actors are there. This is the way I remember it, anyway. Then something just kind of happens and you hit on something. And you go, "That's it. That'll work. That'll make sense."

Jeremy Sisto: I feel like [the hand movement] was brought to me, like, *Here's what you're doing*. . . . I feel like I can't take credit for that. I feel like if I had something to do with that, then I would have bragged about it before. And I have never bragged about it.

Breckin Meyer: I just think it's sweet when Travis gets booted to the side for Jeremy [after Tai gets hurt]. My heart breaks a little bit for him when he gets kind of shoved aside.

Amy Heckerling: At one point, [Cher's] outside and she's feeling very good with her accomplishment and I wanted to see that the party was getting later into the evening, and somebody would be throwing up in the swimming pool, and a couple would be making out in the pool. It's a part of the night where people have already found each other if they're hooking up or whatever, or they've done too much and they're sick.

Bill Pope: I remember how waterlogged some of the people were that sat around that pool. I remember looking at the extras and going, "God, they look like prunes."

Danny Silverberg: I think we spent some time looking for the guy who was throwing up in the pool. We brought over a bunch of people for Amy to look at and approve of: this will be the vomit guy.

Amy Heckerling: The ADs and I were going through saying if any of the extras wanted to play a couple in the swimming pool making out, they would get extra money for that because they would be wet.

A couple of people volunteered, a cute guy and a cute girl. And I thought, *Well, they'll make a nice couple*. So we asked them if they wanted it, and they looked at each other and thought, *Yeah, okay*.

Years later, I was walking down Melrose and I hear some people going, "Amy! Amy!" And I turn around, and it was them. They met that night. They're engaged. She shows me the ring that's been in his family.

I don't know how that marriage worked out, but it was really sweet.

Adam Schroeder: Who knew there was a *Clueless* marriage?

The Mugging of Cher Horowitz

Oh no, you don't understand. This is an Alaïa.

—CHER

An a-what-a?

—MUGGER

Production info: The central portion of this sequence—which involves an argument between Cher and Elton, followed by Cher being held up at gunpoint—was shot on the evenings of Wednesday, December 14, and Thursday, December 15, 1994, days sixteen and seventeen of production, in the parking lot of Circus Liquor, 5600 Vineland Avenue, in North Hollywood. The portion of the sequence in which we see Josh and Heather's date interrupted by Cher's phone call was shot in a dorm room at Occidental College on Thursday, January 5, 1995, day thirty of the shoot.[18]

What happens in this scene, CliffsNotes version: After brutally rebuffing Elton, Cher gets ditched in a liquor store parking lot. She's then held up at gunpoint while wearing a dress by a totally important designer, then forced to call Josh and ask him to pick her up; she does so by using some weird contraption called a pay phone.

Amy Heckerling, writer-director: I remember what the inspiration was for [that scene]. I was having dinner with some agents. I think [Ken] Stovitz was there. And they were telling me about this other agent they knew, who used to be a big slob and then got married and this woman did a makeover on him and got him all these nice suits. He had an Armani suit. He gets held up and the [robber] tells him to get on the ground. He's like: I can't, this is Armani. Because he's so afraid of his wife—that if he messed up the suit, she would be mad at him. The idea that you're more worried about, in this case, it was his wife, than being shot—it reminded me of that old Jack Benny joke: "Your money or your life?" Then there's the longest pause ever on radio . . . and he goes, "I'm thinking." I liked the idea that you could be threatened with something so drastic, and something so stupid would mean more to you. So that was where that [scene] came from.

---

18 Circus Liquor also was featured as a backdrop in Snoop Doggy Dogg's 1994 video for "Murder Was the Case." Today it remains a fully operational liquor store, one that's impossible to miss thanks to the thirty-two-foot-tall neon clown out front.

Mona May, costume designer: I think this is the most sophisticated and dressed-up that we see [Cher] in the film. . . . I think it again lent itself to the scene. It really was important when [the mugger] makes her go down [on the ground], that this is a very important designer. An international designer: somebody from Paris. Not just anything you get at the mall. . . . At the time, he was one of the top people working out of Paris.

It really was silk: sexy, but in a very Cher high school way, even though Alaïa—probably at the time, the dress was $2,500 or $3,000, which translates to $5,000 or more now.

Amy Heckerling: Mona made [the jacket]. So the dress was the Alaïa and the jacket was Mona.

Nina Paskowitz, lead hairstylist: I just love the palm fronds, all the feathers on her. We just wanted something fun and playful and up, but I don't like hairdos that look done, so it's very deconstructed at the same time.

Mona May: I think also the feather outfit, the feather jacket—her standing alone in this forbidden Valley parking lot of a liquor store makes her so out of place. She maybe belongs on the runway. But she's on the pavement.

Jeffrey T. Spellman, locations supervisor: As a kid, my younger sister, Kat, always had nightmares about clowns, right? So many people do. When she would come to town, I'd always make sure she came to the Circus Liquor and she was like, "Oh, it's so creepy." To me it was like, *Wow, that's the quintessential Valley liquor store*. I guess it's been in a lot of stuff since then. I've seen it in other things. Thank God they haven't changed it too much.

Richard Graves, first assistant director: That clown has a light bulb in an unfortunate place. It's very strange.

Jeremy Sisto, Elton: I sing part of the Cranberries song in the beginning of [that sequence]. I remember adding that. That was the only thing I added in the movie. It was just like I'm serenading her for a second.

I'm not sure exactly why they chose the Cranberries but I'm sure it had something to do with the fact that it was popular. Maybe it was a little like, only private school kids would listen to it. You know?

Alicia Silverstone, Cher: I loved shooting that scene with Jeremy, where I get out of the car in a huff.

Adam Schroeder, coproducer: James Russo was supposed to play the robber who mugged Cher at the clown liquor store. There was going to be a little bit of an homage to *Fast Times* because he was the robber at the 7-Eleven at the end of it. He's going to rob Judge Reinhold and Sean Penn does something Spicoli-ish [to stop it]. It was going to be a little bit of an homage. At the very, very last minute—he was cast and he wasn't able to do it.

Marcia Ross, casting director: He was shooting something else, and he wasn't finished and they wanted him on the set by a certain time. Because he couldn't make it by a certain time, they decided, you know, we're going to recast it.

Barry Berg, coproducer and unit production manager: I called his agent and I said, "Look, we want him at a certain time." And she said, "Well, he feels that's too early." I said, "Well, it's not really about what he's feeling. The director is asking that he come down so she can rehearse with him and she's comfortable with what he's going to do in the performance and so on. So we'd like him there on time." And she just refused.

So I picked up the phone and called Scott and said, "Hey, there's a little problem here." And he said to me, "Well, what would you recommend we do?" And I said, "I recommend we replace him." He said, "Well, we've only got a couple hours." And I said, "Scott, between you, me, and Amy, we know a lot of actors that would be happy to come down here and do this role." He said: "Replace him."

I had to call the agent, and I'll never forget the conversation. She picked up the phone and said, without my saying anything, she said, "We *just* talked about this. He's not going to show up at two o'clock." And I said, "Well, let me just stop you. He doesn't have to show up at all. He's fired." There was silence on the phone. She said, "What do you mean?" I said, "He's fired. We're going to replace him." And now the backing and filling started: "Well, wait a minute. I'm sure he wants to do this." And I said, "No, no. It's over. It's over." So it was over, and we got another actor to come down and he did a wonderful job with the part. And that was the end of it.

James Russo did not respond to requests seeking comment for this book.

Jace Alexander, Mugger: I've been in this business for over forty years and my story is not only unique to that film, but it's also unique to any actor's experience.

Marcia Ross: This all happens during my lunch hour. I was sitting at my desk and I had a list of people, but I had to run it by Scott and Amy to make sure they were okay with them.

And one by one, I would [get], "Okay, yes to this person." Then I'd call and leave a message and, well, if they didn't call me back in fifteen minutes, I had to go on to the next one. Of all things, we had a couple of people we loved, and I reached out to them but they didn't get back to me within the hour. I had, like, literally an hour to do this.

Adam Schroeder: It was the most horrible thing that can happen on a production: that one of your actors doesn't show up.

Jace Alexander: I was in my second year at the American Film Institute and I was editing my thesis project. I had written a script for a movie with a good friend named Bradley White. We had just completed the script and we had arranged a meeting with Scott Rudin, who was nice enough to meet us in his office and talk to us about the script. We had a very good meeting, and the next day, I was driving in the Valley doing some sort of business related to my thesis film, editorial or something like that. And my pager went off. This is back when people had pagers. It was a number I didn't recognize, so I stopped and—I think I had a cell phone back then, one of those big Motorola things that look like a toy now. And I called the number and the person on the other end went, "Scott Rudin's office."

My heart literally jumped out of my chest, because at that moment, I thought that meant that he was interested in this script, in this movie. I was so excited, I can't tell ya. I said, "This is Jace Alexander." And she goes, "Hold, please, for Scott Rudin." I was like: *Oh my God. Oh my God. Oh my God.* And Scott gets on the other line and he goes, "Jace?" And I'm like: "Yeah?" And he goes, "Um, kind of a strange question, but what are you doing tonight?" And my heart sank. It was an odd thing to say and it clearly had nothing to do with the script and his tone was—I couldn't read it.

I said, "Ummm, well, actually"—and I was telling the truth—"I'm directing a play at the Mark Taper Forum second stage, and it's a one-woman show and it's the second night of only three nights and I kind of feel like I should be there." And he goes, "Oh, really? Huh." And I said, "Well, what's up?" And he goes, "Well, my friend Amy Heckerling is doing this little movie and we lost an actor and I thought of you." And like, my mind was reeling. I could not grasp what he was saying because this kind of thing just isn't really ever said to anybody. I said, "I'm so sorry—what? What are you saying?" And he goes, "Well, she's shooting a movie and we lost this actor and I wanted to see—but if you're busy . . . ," and I said, "Well, no, hold on one second." So I said, "Well, where is it shooting?" He said, "In the Valley." And I was in the Valley. I said, "Well, when would she need me?" And he said, "Well, like, now." "Like *now*-now?" He goes, "Yeah. Yeah, the scene's shooting in a couple hours." And I said, "Well, where are they shooting?" And he said the address was just like Victory Boulevard and something-something, where that liquor store in the movie is.

I looked up where I was. I had no idea where I had pulled over. I was literally less than half a mile from the location. Like, just happenstance. I said, "Um, okay. I think, yes."

Marcia Ross: I think Scott was in a meeting with Jace Alexander, who was writing something for him. He said, you know, Jace is a good actor. And that's how Jace ended up [in the movie].

Jace Alexander: [Scott] said there's a scene where the guy robs the lead. That was kind of my wheelhouse. Basically, for whatever reason in my career—I went through this recently in my head, and I've had a weapon in my hand in about 85 percent of the things that I've done.

Now, you have to understand, I had had an agent my whole life. At that point, I was segueing from acting to directing and I didn't really have an agent in Los Angeles but I had one, sort of. And I called this lady . . . at Abrams Artists. I said, "It's Jace. I just got offered a role in a little movie. I really know nothing about it. But I think they really need to cast it. Can you get me some money?" She was like, "Well, let me see." She calls me back in like five minutes and she goes, "Yeah, I think they're going to pay you some decent money."

I think it was in the neighborhood of $10,000, which, back then, for one scene was a very, very nice thing. It paid for my second year of film school.[19]

This is the other lesson about casting—I think I was the last person [Scott] had seen in his head. We had literally met the afternoon before, so he knew that I had been an actor and he had probably seen me mug somebody somewhere. Like maybe in the Broadway show *I'm Not Rappaport*, where I played a mugger. He just put two and two together, and he knew that I was in LA.

Amy Heckerling: That's funny. I didn't even know.

Jace Alexander: So I drove the half mile [to Circus Liquor]. I pull up to the parking lot and I say to a PA, "Hi, my name is Jace. I'm here for—" and he goes, "Oh yeah, sure." He takes me out of the car, he brings me into a room, and this woman goes, "Hi." And she looks me up and down. She goes, "Oh, I'm doing the costumes. Yeah, that T-shirt that you're wearing is great. The jeans seem to work. Here, try this leather jacket on." And I'm like, "I've just got to be honest with you guys: I have no idea—" She goes, "Oh, no one's even told you?" At that point, somebody rushes over the sides of the scene to me.

Then they hustle me into this trailer and I sit down and right next to me is Alicia Silverstone. And the AD goes, "Hi, Jace. This is Alicia. You'll be doing the scene with her." And she goes, "Oh, hi!" And I was like, "Hi." I told her that I just

19 For those keeping score: that's the same amount Ross was paid to cast the entire movie, although Ross says she later received an additional $5,000 as a bonus.

found out about this, and I said, "You want to run lines?" She goes, "Yeah, that would be great."

So we start running lines and I said to the AD, "When do you think they're going to be ready?" They go, "Probably in just a few minutes." So they get me out of the hair and makeup trailer, they bring me onto the set. I meet Amy Heckerling for the first time. We're standing there. We rehearse it. They light it for maybe about forty-five minutes because they had already done some prelighting. And all of a sudden they start rolling the camera. Basically, what you see is one of the first takes. I ad-libbed a couple of little lines, mostly at the very end. But other than that, it was what it was.

Amy Heckerling: Before he runs away, he says, "Thank you." That was him. I thought that was really cute.

Bill Pope, director of photography: I'd never met him before and he just showed up and did that part. I'm going, is that guy a real gangster or is he a comedian or what? His timing is perfect. Then [Amy] told me who he was and I went, "Oh, that makes sense."

Amy Heckerling: He's Jane Alexander's son.[20]

Adam Schroeder: Jace was just fantastic. He really did us a great prop and a favor.

---

20 Jane Alexander is an acclaimed actress who has been nominated for multiple Oscars, Emmys, and Tony Awards (she's won two Emmys and one Tony). In 1993, a few months before *Clueless* began production, President Bill Clinton appointed her to serve as director of the National Endowment for the Arts, a position she held until 1997.

Jace Alexander: The whole thing was maybe two or three takes each? It was very quick. It was over before I even knew that it had started. You know, Heckerling knew exactly what she wanted. She knew exactly what she was doing. They had all been shooting for a little bit. Alicia was in full-on Cher mode and was nailing every take. Yeah, it was right on the money.

The irony is that I was a working actor since I was basically eight years old, and a very steadily working actor as an adult in New York doing Broadway and TV and movies, but mostly movies and theater. To this day, it is the most recognized work that I've ever done. People stop me all the time and go, "I was watching TV last night: you're in *Clueless*!" I can't tell you how many people of every single age group stop me and talk to me about *Clueless*, because it's always on somewhere in the world and it's become an iconic classic.

It's crazy, right? Completely crazy. And it was my last acting role. I quit acting when I went to AFI. That was just a complete lark. I wasn't auditioning, I wasn't looking for work as an actor. It was my swan song and it was out of left field.

Calvin Klein, Christian, Cher, and the Big Bosstones First Date

She's a full-on Monet.

—CHER

Production info: The scenes in which Cher introduces the Calvin Klein dress that "looks like underwear" and heads off on her first date with Christian were shot during a few dates of production, including Friday, January 13 (shoot day thirty-six); Monday, January 23 (shoot day forty-two); and Tuesday, January 24 (shoot day forty-three). The interiors and exteriors were filmed at the Encino home that doubles for Cher's house. The epic first Christian-and-Cher date/Mighty Mighty Bosstones party scene was shot over two days (Thursday, February 2, and Friday, February 3, 1995, days fifty and fifty-one of the shoot) at the MOCA Contemporary (152 North Central Avenue), a part of LA's Museum of Contemporary Art that is now known as the Geffen Contemporary at MOCA.

What happens in these scenes, CliffsNotes version: Christian picks up Cher, who's dressed in a barely-there Calvin Klein dress. Mel reminds Christian, using colorful language, that if he gets murdered, he won't be missed, while Josh festers in a pool of jealousy. Cher and Christian head off to the party, where the Bosstones perform; Christian displays an interest in guys, to which Cher remains oblivious; Josh dances awkwardly; and Amber confirms her full-on Monet status.

Mona May, costume designer: Calvin Klein was an established designer, of course. But the underwear theme was big at the time. Not only the dress itself being the spaghetti-strap, very simple slip, but just, it connoted underwear. It connoted something that was forbidden, that was too revealing, in a sense, even though it really wasn't. I mean, it's a simple dress.

Amy Heckerling, writer-director: I don't know if that actually was a Calvin Klein. But I liked the idea of: "Says who?" "Calvin Klein." It just looked good on her.

It wasn't overtly sexual. It wasn't low-cut. And it wasn't the father that said that [it was inappropriate at first]. Josh notices she looks hot and wants to make sure she doesn't go out like that.

Mona May: What was fun, too, was to play with the cover-up, which was another little riff on it. Because the cover-up was sheer.

Amy Heckerling: I liked the idea of, sure, I'll cover it. [Alicia] was very cute when she did that.

Mona May: I think the cover-up was Vivienne Tam, which was a pretty big designer. But you know, we had to try many different things to figure out what's going to work in that scene and what's going to give us that laugh or the right feeling. It was interesting; it took a lot of different trials. We did more revealing stuff and it just didn't work. It was too slutty.

I think it was important that it was cream, too. Again: an innocent color, cream, because it wasn't red or black. But it had the feeling of an undergarment.

Dan Hedaya, Mel: Mel respected [Cher]. But he set the parameters. When she came down dressed in that skimpy outfit, it was unacceptable.

Justin Walker, Christian: I remember that [scene] was so much about the way that Christian moves. Like a breeze. Like a swirling breeze on a beach.

Dan Hedaya: One of the things he says, to the kid, the punk who came to date her, it's a line that scores of fathers have told me, *I wish I said that at some occasion, when somebody was coming to date my daughter.* And you know which line I'm referring to: "I've got a .45 and a shovel. I doubt anybody would miss you." It's a genius line. A *genius* line.

Amy Heckerling: My brother came up with the line—well, it's not that he came up with it, it's just like he said it once. He was saying that about a guy I was seeing. So I thought, *That's funny.* I put it in the movie.

Justin Walker: I mean, a guy tells you he's going to bury you with a shovel, and you roll out of that, no problem? That says a lot about where the confidence and the swagger and the movement and the priorities of the character are.

Paul Rudd, Josh: I do remember seeing the movie for the first time, and when I say, "I'm going to [the party to] make sure that she's okay," and [Hedaya] goes, "Yeah, you do that." And then I walk out, and he just looked up. In that look, it was like: *Oh, he knows everything that might [happen]*. I didn't realize he had done that. . . . I remember going, *Whoa, that was really amazing. What a really great choice to do that.*

Nina Paskowitz, lead hairstylist: Once she decided that she was going to wear that really simple, little, cute white dress, it's like: we don't want anything really with color [in her hair] but we want a tiny little bit of bling. I don't even think the word *bling* was invented yet—just something that would pop a little bit and keep her hair really simple.

I think we shot the car [scene] first, I'm not sure. But we threw [that clip] in her hair as she was getting in the car and went, "What about this? Oh yeah." I'm showing her in the mirror—"Oh my God, that's so awesome." So cut to: now she's dancing in that scene [at the party] and everything. I said, "You know, wouldn't it be really fun if her hair was more playful?" You're moving around, you want it to move. It's like when you wear an elastic and you put it around your wrist. People didn't do stuff like that, so I said, "What if we just stick [the barrette] on your dress, clip it to your dress?"

Okay, so cut to: three years later on, I had that baggy with the [same] clip, with the scene number and everything marked on my peg-bulletin board. I would bring it along with me on shows just to have, just in case of whatever—you never know. So now

I'm on *She's the Man*, and I'm doing Amanda Bynes's [hair] and I'm doing her brother, making them look like the same person. I said [to Amanda], "You know, I put this clip in Alicia's hair in *Clueless*." She's like: "Oh my God, that's my favorite movie." She started screaming. I said, "Would you like to wear it in the scene?" And she almost had a heart attack she was so excited and honored. So it's come around a couple of times. Now I just have it put away in a drawer to make sure no one loses it.

Dicky Barrett, front man for the Mighty Mighty Bosstones: We certainly liked *Fast Times at Ridgemont High* and the stuff Amy Heckerling had done. At the time, we were experiencing tax problems and we needed some money. That opportunity came along, and I don't think, being a punk-rock ska band, that we would have jumped at it if things were different financially for us at the time.

It turned out that we really liked the movie, as much as guys from Boston can appreciate a movie about rich Hollywood kids.

Adam Schroeder, coproducer: We were trying to figure out a band that would be kind of cool and different and very party. I think we had them for just the one night, so we had to shoot them out quickly. We had to shoot them out first, I think.

Steven Jordan, production designer: We just sort of treated [the scene] like a rave. There was a lot going on in there architecturally, I believe: big girders and beams inside. I sort of fed off of that. We put a stage in there, is my recollection. Again, that was just a big rave and a mosh pit.

Mary Ann Kellogg, choreographer: I remember this thing where Brittany, she's kind of a wallflower, right? We picked out people [to stand next to her] that we thought would be funny.

We created a lot of little bits, more than what made it in the film, just so [Amy] would have enough to work off of. But I remember the Mighty Mighty Bosstones that day. There was a lot of energy in that room. A lot of dancing.

Bill Pope, director of photography: I'm sort of giving Amy entrances and exits to scenes, iconography. Again: I'm trying to make a movie-movie. I'm not trying to break new ground. I'm trying to remind people of other movies and older movies and classic movies. That [opening] shot is out of a forties musical, basically. Start out of nowhere and pull back and see everything at a party.

Richard Graves, first assistant director: It is a very elaborate shot because the camera's pulling back straight over the heads of a bunch of extras who are all trying to act like they're partying, and they have to sort of dance their way right, just outside of the frame, so it doesn't look like your camera's going through the Red Sea. It's a tricky shot to execute as far as staging, but it's kind of an industry standard now. You've probably seen a shot like that any number of times, but it's hard to execute. And at the time it was a little harder to execute because of this piece of equipment that was cumbersome and prone to break down.

Charlie Messenger, head of extras casting: I remember visiting several times on that [set] because I think certain difficulties arose between the kids. The party scene was shot near the end of the film, and I think there were some [extras] who didn't get along with each other. Or who thought they should have gotten the upgrade [to be part of the cast], or who were jealous, or who had issues with some of the principals. So there was a certain amount of maintenance that I had to do at that point.

It wasn't unusual, no. But it happens more in that age range. If a kid has been there for the full shoot, you develop friends and you develop enemies, unless you were a pretty super kid.

Adam Schroeder: We used a lot of extras multiple times to keep it real and create that world. You don't think you're recognizing people; it's kind of that great subliminal thing that's part of the crowd in this film.

Amy Heckerling: I'm always worried when you get a lot of people [in a scene]. It takes longer to move everybody around. But it went surprisingly easy. And the Bosstones were fun.

Dicky Barrett: If you remember the fashion, she had everybody dressed in tanks and baby blues and those kinds of pastel colors. Everyone was dressed very Easter-y as far as we could see. There wasn't a lot of room for Scottish tartans and the stuff we liked to wear.

Jeremy Sisto, Elton: I just remember thinking the Mighty Mighty Bosstones were pretty funny and entertaining. When they do those scenes, they have to lip sync to themselves and stuff. So I felt like it was one of the first times I saw that. Well, it wasn't the *first* time I saw that. But I just remember being impressed by their level of commitment to the lip-syncing of it all.

Dicky Barrett: I think we performed live a few times, and then we performed to a track for the majority of the day. Both things were going on. My biggest disappointment was seeing all these kids dancing to us who had little sense of how to dance to us. That didn't matter, they seemed to be enjoying it enough. But during the first take, I did a vicious stage dive onto a good chunk of them. And it looked good and [Heckerling] loved it. She goes, "Oh, that's great, that's great." So then every take after it, I had to do a stage dive again. She'd go, "Do the stage dive again." Which I did, but as the day went on—and you know, I got drunker because the Bosstones were drinking vodka. . . .

Richard Graves: The Bosstones had never worked on a movie or anything. They had no idea what was involved or really what was expected of them outside of playing. They started drinking sometime in the afternoon. They were kind of out of it by the end of the day.

Amy Heckerling: [Were they drunk?] Could be. But they were fun. They were game.

Dicky Barrett: [The scene] was filmed in downtown Los Angeles, right across the street from the O. J. Simpson trial, which was going on at the time. We didn't really know what we were doing. Doing a movie for money to get out of tax problems: it didn't feel very punk to us. The O. J. Simpson trial sort of added to the depressing air that was in downtown LA. We were far from our beloved Boston. So we got a gallon bottle of vodka that we had to hide from a lot of people. I don't think anybody really cared that the guys in the band were mixing drinks all day.

Richard Graves: We worked around it. They didn't have anything very precise to do. Luckily we were doing their stuff first because we were starting with that [part of the] scene. So the fact that they were, like, drunk off their feet didn't matter quite so much because they didn't have any scenes with [Alicia]. They just had to pretend to be doing their songs. I'm sure that, depending on when the shot was done, they're a little less synchronized than earlier in the day.

Dicky Barrett: As the day went on, my stage dive got sloppier and certainly less enthusiastic. So if you watch the scene, you see me almost wilt onto the heads of these kids who were not prepared for what I was doing. It's been mentioned to me that it's one of the worst filmed stage dives in history. It's not exactly Eddie Vedder climbing the walls at a club in Seattle. I just kinda—waaaa—fall, you know. Somewhere between the second and three hundredth stage dive of the afternoon, I had a head full of Cape Codders.

Justin Walker: I'll tell you this. I fancy myself a hell of a dancer. A *hell* of a dancer. And Christian definitely fancied himself a hell of a dancer . . . [The Bosstones] are cool dudes, from Boston, like me. But for me to get my freak on, that would not be it.

The vibe on set [for me] was that I was going to turn out the dance. Like this is me, doing what I do best. I'm a damn good dancer and I could have done ten times what was called on me for that moment. But that whole thing was about, like, funking down. The dancing is on right now, with whomever came into my path. Her. A dude. Another girl. That's what was going on there.

Elisa Donovan, Amber: I didn't take [the Monet line] personally at all. No. I took it more like that it was sort of a commentary [on Amber].

Danny Silverberg, second assistant director: Dean [Wilson] is actually the guy at the Mighty Mighty Bosstones party who's talking to Josh. The "one adult in the party" is Dean, our prop master.

Richard Graves: The prop master did not look anything like the guy you'd expect to see on a movie like that, because he was this late-middle-aged, overweight guy. His name was Dean: a very good guy [and a] good prop master.

I remember we singled him out. We said, "Amy, we just thought it would be funny if Dean was that guy." Because he did look like a guy who would never be at that party.

Dean Wilson, prop master: Amy had come up and asked me if I would just stand there and do it. And that was the first time I'd ever been in a movie so I said, "Okay." [Do I remember what we were] actually talking about? No. Not a clue. Not a clue what we were talking about.

Paul Rudd: I remember thinking that it was funny that I would just be there talking to a grown-up. I don't remember what we were talking about.

Dean Wilson: That's the only [movie] I've ever been in that I was supposed to be in. I've been in some reflective shots. I've been in accidental shots, but not ones where I really was supposed to be there.

Paul Rudd: I do remember . . . being kind of freaked out that day, because the night before—I was at Jerry's Deli with a friend of mine. We were having dinner and there were these policemen sitting next to us, and I told her, "It must be really hard to be a cop in LA. It's got to be the hardest place to be a policeman." She said, "New York must be hard." I said, "Yeah, but it seems like everything's contained. If anyone did anything, you can't get away quickly." So we were having this conversation.

Anyway: [I was] going out to my car after we finished dinner, and a guy jumped out and put a gun to my head and demanded that I give him all my money. And I didn't really have

Amy Heckerling made her directorial debut with 1982's *Fast Times at Ridgemont High*. *Clueless*, which was initially developed as a TV show, then became a motion picture, gave her an opportunity to return to the high school movie genre.

Both Heckerling and Carrie Frazier, who was the casting director for *Clueless* while the project developed at Fox, had no doubt that Alicia Silverstone was their perfect Cher.

After *Clueless* was dropped by Fox and picked up by Paramount, the movie's new casting director, Marcia Ross, played a pivotal role in making sure that Paul Rudd was among those being considered for the role of Josh.

Stacey Dash, who nabbed the role of the "regal" Dionne, remembers that she and Donald Faison, soon to become her on-screen boyfriend Murray, had immediate and natural chemistry together.

The young stars who comprised the core *Clueless* ensemble, clockwise from back left: Justin Walker (Christian), Jeremy Sisto (Elton), Donald Faison (Murray), Brittany Murphy (Tai), Breckin Meyer (Travis), Alicia Silverstone (Cher), Stacey Dash (Dionne), Elisa Donovan (Amber), and Paul Rudd (Josh).

With the iconic plaid ensembles worn by Dash and Silverstone, costume designer Mona May took the classic schoolgirl look and put a contemporary, high-fashion spin on it.

As Amber, Donovan wore the most consistently outrageous costumes in *Clueless*. "Nobody wears that clothing in the real world," Donovan says of her character's fashion choices. "It's strictly for the runway. But in her mind, that's how you roll."

"I don't want to be a traitor to my generation and all, but I don't get how guys dress today": All the young dudes and their droopy drawers.

Makeup supervisor Alan Friedman observes Silverstone as she shoots part of the scene in which Cher prepares for the "brutally hot" Christian to come over to watch "*Sporadicus*." *(Photo courtesy of Alan Friedman)*

Friedman does not rely on mirrors. That's why he took Polaroids of the various looks on the principal actors and extras throughout the *Clueless* shoot. Here are a few of the many faces of Silverstone, Dash, Murphy, Donovan, Twink Caplan (before

and after Ms. Geist's makeover), Rudd (with and without chin pubes), Faison (the George Jefferson look and sporting hair), Meyer, Sisto, Walker, and an unidentified extra wearing one of the film's ubiquitous nose bandages. *(Photos by Alan Friedman)*

Heckerling and Silverstone sort through the extensive apparel in Cher's closet. The walk-in—make that live-in—closet was created in the pool house at the private home in Encino that doubled as the Horowitz residence.

Heckerling chats with her actors during a break in Mr. Hall's class. The scenes at Grant High School were the first ones shot during production.

Silverstone as Cher reminds us all that "it does *not* say RSVP on the Statue of Liberty."

Silverstone accidentally mispronounced "Haitians" while filming the debate scene, a flub that Heckerling made sure to keep in the film. "There's a cockiness to Cher when she's just going down the wrong track, and you just have to make sure people don't mess with that," says the director.

Cell phones weren't nearly as prevalent in 1995, which made the idea that Cher and Dionne would be talking on them, to each other, completely absurd. In 2015, it still seems absurd because—duh!—Cher and Dionne would *totally* be texting instead. (By the way, that guy wearing khakis in the background, as this scene is rehearsed? That's DP Bill Pope.)

Twink Caplan and Wallace Shawn, both personal friends of Heckerling's, enjoyed bringing the Ms. Geist and Mr. Hall relationship to life. "Every time I see him," says Caplan, "it's like he's still my husband."

Dash's favorite line in *Clueless* is Dionne's zinger during the tennis court scene, "Well, there goes your social life."

Murphy was the only principal actor in *Clueless* who was under the age of eighteen. Members of the cast and the crew remember that she had a wide-eyed, bubbly quality that was not unlike that of her character, Tai.

A bashful Meyer hangs with a happy Silverstone, Sharon Murphy (mother to Brittany), and Brittany Murphy during a break from shooting the Val party scene. *(Photo by Nicole Bilderback)*

Heckerling confers with Sisto, Silverstone, and Meyer while shooting the Val party scene.

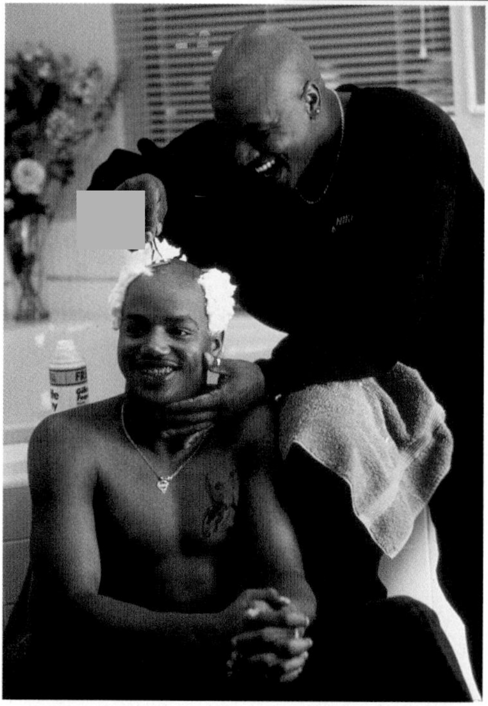

Murray (Faison) keeps it real while his buddy Lawrence (Sean Holland) gets down to head-shaving business.

Because Heckerling wanted *Clueless*'s color palette—including its costumes—to reflect the four seasons, Cher (Silverstone) and Tai (Murphy) dress in Christmas red during the holiday party in the Valley.

Silverstone shows off her Alaïa party dress, topped with a feather-collared jacket designed by May.

Jace Alexander was cast as the mugger befuddled by Cher's Alaïa mere hours before the scene was shot. Says Alexander: "I've been in this business for over forty years and my story is not only unique to that film, but it's also unique to any actor's experience."

The scene in which Cher, Dionne, and Tai discuss Cher's virginity was originally scripted to take place in a California Pizza Kitchen. According to producer Adam Schroeder, representatives for the chain passed on the chance to get a *Clueless* shout-out because "I think the whole idea of talking about boy parts . . . made them uncomfortable."

Dan Hedaya, who plays Mel Horowitz, says he appreciated the relationship between Cher and her dad when he first read the screenplay: "I liked how it was written and how the character was written. The tough love."

Walker and Silverstone, wearing the hair clip that stylist Nina Paskowitz would later let Amanda Bynes borrow for a scene in *She's the Man*.

Moments from the party with the Mighty Mighty Bosstones, including Elton (Sisto) with "total Monet" Amber (Donovan); the quite possibly inebriated Bosstones onstage; and Christian (Walker) and Cher (Silverstone), busting a move.

Ron Orbach, who played the driver's ed instructor, was amazed by Silverstone's ability to power nap between takes, then hit her lines like a total pro.

Breckin Meyer, Elisa Donovan, and Donald Faison show one another some love on-set.

Images from the *Clueless* wedding album: Heckerling, Silverstone, Caplan, Julie Brown, and others gather around the monitor; Silverstone and Rudd sharing a moment of "Tenderness"; Heckerling and the cast in a moment of wedding day joy.

The marketing campaign around *Clueless* made Silverstone and Cher's oh-so-Beverly-Hills lifestyle a central focus.

Clueless goes to the beach: Silverstone arrives at the premiere on July 7, 1995. *(Photo © Ron Galella/ Contributor via Getty Images)*

The cast of *Clueless* the TV show, left to right: Shawn, Donovan, Rachel Blanchard (the new Cher), David Lascher (back center; the new Josh), Faison, Dash, and Caplan. *(Photo © ABC Photo Archives/ ABC via Getty Images)*

Rudd appeared in one episode of the *Clueless* TV series, playing a character named Sonny who was interested in Cher, as well as *Sassy* magazine. *(Photo © ABC Photo Archives/ABC via Getty Images)*

In attendance at a special LA screening of *Clueless* in 2014: costume designer May; Heckerling; Dash; Stephanie Allain, a film producer who moderated a Q&A in conjunction with the screening; Silverstone; and Donovan. Even though twenty years have passed since its release, reverence for the movie only continues to grow. *(Photo © Araya Diaz/Stringer via Getty Images)*

any money on me. He goes, "You don't think this is a real gun?" He was all tweaked out on something, and he shot his gun next to my head. And I just remember looking out of the corner of my eye, and [my friend] had gone back inside—she saw what was happening—to get those policemen. She did, but it was too late. Then they went to try and chase him, but they couldn't find him.

It was a weird premonition. It was a strange kind of conversation. But I didn't have any money and so I said, "Look, man, I've just got my backpack. You can have it." He's like rifling around by my car and he just grabs my backpack. The only thing that was in it was, I had like a Discman and my script. My *Clueless* script that had all of my notes and everything in it. Those were the only two things he got. Then I remember having to go to work the next day, and it all was a bit of a delayed reaction. I remember thinking: *Whoa. That was really crazy. A guy shot a gun next to my head. And now here I am, like, ten hours later, dancing.*

Mary Ann Kellogg: Paul is . . . a specific actor who has really thought out what he wants to do. So I didn't have a lot of interaction with him, because he's a very good dancer, he's very specific about his character.

[The part where Josh is dancing]: That's all him. Those were his choices and even in other things—I think I've done other things with him and Amy—he's one of the actors that really likes to take it on himself, if it doesn't involve another person and wouldn't require him to dance with someone else.

Paul Rudd: There was no working out anything. It was just like: dance. Dance badly. That's easy to do. I didn't put a lot of thought into it.

Dicky Barrett: I run into some of the people in the movie every once in a while. Paul Rudd, I see him and I feel a connection with him when I see the guy. He's super nice to me. I'm sure in your research, you're probably having a tough time finding anybody that says anything unkind about that guy. And if you do, give me their names because I'll have it out with 'em.

Elisa Donovan: I'm pretty sure that that was my last day of shooting and so I have a very distinct memory of that . . . saying bye to everybody and taking some pictures.

I was amazed that it was over already. It was certainly the longest project I had ever worked on: a couple of months. I had never worked on anything for that long at that point. So it felt very—yeah, it was certainly sad. Then you have that feeling of: *Oh gosh, now I have to go back to trying to find a job!* [*Laughs*]

Mary Ann Kellogg: You know what? I must be in [that scene in] *Clueless*. Because I still get residuals from it.

Dicky Barrett: My lifelong friend and Bosstone roadie, Mark Higgins, is seen in that scene breaking down our equipment later. He was really just breaking down our equipment but they continued to film. It looked like the party was over, people were passed out, and he was just doing his job. He's always been excited about that.

You want to hear a funny story? I told you I was drinking vodka. And at some point it was important for us to get a picture with Alicia Silverstone, or at least, you know, the people making the movie, for promotion, would like the band and Alicia Silverstone [in a photo]. She wasn't at all interested in that.

But my friend, who roadied for the band, he's from Boston. Alicia Silverstone was the girl in the Aerosmith videos. And Aerosmith was very important to us because they're from Boston. Higgins said to me, "You know, if you can"—and he gave me his camera, he always had a camera with him—"ask Alicia Silverstone if she'll take a picture with me." We're doing a photo shoot and everything. As I was walking away, then I remembered. I go, "Oh, oh, Alee-sha." I was very close to her and she was looking the other way. But after saying her name, like, three times, I realized she was ignoring me. She heard me and it was like, what is going on here?

"Alee-sha, Alee-sha, Alee-sha." Then I heard her say to her publicist or whoever she was with: "Could you please tell the drunk guy my name is 'Alicia'?" I was pronouncing it wrong. . . . I clearly heard her say "Alee-cee-a," and then I go, "Oh, I'm sorry, Alee-cee-a, could you please take a picture with my friend High-gins?" [His name is] Higgins but I called him High-gins, to make fun of the pronunciation. And she goes, "What?" Sure enough, I got the picture: Higgins and Alicia, standing there together. And I knew at that time—the way she talked to me and treated me, I go: she's going to be a very big star.

Photo courtesy of Dicky Barrett

"You're Driving on the Freeway!"

I swear to God, woman. You can't drive for *shit*.

—MURRAY

Production info: Dionne's frightening foray onto the freeway was shot on December 6, 1994 (day ten of production), on the Long Beach Freeway, or the 710, a location frequently used in Hollywood sequences where free rein of a multilane highway is needed.

What happens in these sequences, CliffsNotes version: After an assist from Murray, Cher realizes that Christian is gay. Then Dionne accidentally steers her red BMW onto the freeway, which leads to a great deal of panic-driven screaming.

Amy Heckerling, writer-director: That [freeway scene] is very personal to me because I don't drive on the freeway. But every now and then you find yourself in a lane you can't get out of that turns into the freeway, and then I really just scream until I'm off the freeway. I'm just so scared. When I first got my driver's license, I was hit by a drunk driver [in LA]. So I'm very panicked about being hit hard.

The idea that everybody's going really fast, and I know how much people don't pay attention. It just scares me. Cars—you trust that you have this control over them, but you can't completely. So it just all scares me a lot. You know, I realize that that's kind of stupid and

Always wondered who's actually Gail, the mother of Josh, who can be heard when she calls the Horowitz home looking for her son? That would be Amy Heckerling, who also acted as the telephone voice of Rudd's mother in the second film they worked on together, *I Could Never Be Your Woman*. "If ever he needs a mother on the phone," says Heckerling, "I can do it."

people could laugh at that. To go, "The freeway: Ah!!!" [The scene] is making fun of my problem.

Jeffrey T. Spellman, locations supervisor: That [location is] down in Long Beach. That's Shoreline Drive, which is a popular stretch of road that you can shut down. It leads to the 710 freeway. It's one of those few that you can do [on] weekdays in Los Angeles. . . . It's used in *Iron Man*. On *Criminal Minds*, we've used it. It's in almost everything.

Bill Pope, director of photography: They always shut you down in Long Beach because that's the end of the run. They can shut off the very end of the freeway, and people just have to get off an exit earlier and they'll give you the very end of the freeway.

Danny Silverberg, second assistant director: I don't know if you've ever seen the rig that we use, but you use an insert car, which is basically a movie version of a tow truck that's towing the picture car, the one that's being photographed with the actors in it. They don't have to do any real driving, certainly in the freeway scene.

Although there are, in that scene, some free-driving shots where the actors are actually driving and the camera car is in front of them shooting them, which makes it look amazing. But along with that insert car, you have a train of other support vehicles that are going along with you on the road. You've got follow vans, where you have supporting makeup, hair, wardrobe people and additional camera people: grips, things like that. Also smaller trucks: stake beds that are holding additional equipment, whether it's film magazines, lenses, things like that.

Amy Heckerling: In between, when you're riding to the [location] or back from it, you feel like you're on a parade float.

Danny Silverberg: You can tell from the wide shots that there's not a lot of traffic on the freeway around them. But most of the sequence is played in tight [shots], which I think really, really works well.

Adam Schroeder, coproducer: Stacey could drive so it wasn't dangerous in any way. A lot of actors put on their résumés "can drive stick," or "drive," or "ride horses," and all this kind of stuff and then you get to the filming and they can't do any of those things and you're in trouble.

Stacey Dash, Dionne: I love to drive and I love cars so I had no problem doing it. But the rest of the parts were controlled. We were on the back of a jib, so we didn't have to worry about anything. You know, the parts where I'm closing my eyes, I'm not actually driving. But it is funny because you do think I am driving, and there I go again, having a huge temper tantrum because I'm stuck on the freeway and Murray's not giving me the right directions. He's not teaching me right. *[Laughs]* It's his fault.

Danny Silverberg: When it's Stacey Dash really driving the car with two other actors in with her and we have real traffic around them—you know, our traffic—I think that lends an authenticity to it. I think [the actors] probably were a little more amped up for those shots.

Stacey Dash: We had big rigs coming by us. A motorcycle gang drove by us. It was cool. It was really cool.

Alicia Silverstone, Cher: Filming in the car when we were screaming on the highway—it was such a blast.

Donald Faison, Murray: Me turning around and screaming into the camera wasn't in the script. I did that on my own. It made it and I was like, that's really awesome.

Bill Pope: It's all about [Dionne] going too slow: the Hells Angels go by and flip the bird and all that stuff. People are honking. That silly screaming at the camera shot: "*Ahhhh!*" It was really funny.

Donald Faison: When we were shooting the scene I didn't have a clue—I didn't see the danger in driving on the freeway, you know what I mean? Coming from New York, where I felt like we're all aggressive drivers here. Going into LA and being like, "The freeway? It's empty? What are you talking about? There's nothing to be worried about."

Then you talk to people and now, after living in LA for a long time, I would never take a first-time driver onto the freeway. That would be the most dangerous thing in the world.

When Cher Met the Messiah of the DMV

I had an overwhelming sense of ickiness.

—CHER

Production info: Cher's less-than-successful driving test was shot on Monday, December 12, 1994 (day fourteen of production), on streets adjacent to the VA Medical Center at 11301 Wilshire Boulevard in Los Angeles.

What happens in this sequence, CliffsNotes version: Cher's lack of driving skills is officially confirmed, despite the fact that she's wearing her second-most-capable outfit. During her much-anticipated driving test, she sideswipes some parked cars, then gets taken down several pegs by an instructor who shall forever be known to all as the Messiah of the DMV.

Ron Orbach, Messiah of the DMV: I knew who Amy Heckerling was because I knew *Fast Times at Ridgemont High*. So I knew she was somebody who was really smart and good with comedy. When I met her I liked her enormously and she was really . . . just kind of a kooky, funny, not someone who seemed to take herself very seriously. That made me very, very comfortable. I think that's probably why I got the job.

Amy Heckerling, writer-director: He was wonderful. He was a friend of Scott Rudin's—Scott Rudin found him. Scott Rudin was a casting guy before, so he knows a lot of people.

Ron Orbach: I arrive on the set and go to the makeup and hair trailer. It's probably six thirty a.m. I walk in and—the visual would be helpful for this, but you'll have to imagine it. You know how in the makeup chairs, sometimes girls will sit forward with their heads almost between their legs and their long hair kind of flipped over? The hair people will brush it that way. That's kind of how I discovered [Alicia Silverstone].

Then she sort of comes up to do the reverse—you know, like, she comes up and leans her head back and now her hair is being brushed the other way. But she's completely slack-jawed and her eyes are closed. She looks like she's in a stupor. Then they finish her hair and now they're doing her makeup and her head is now straight but it's still slack-jawed and eyes closed and they're putting the makeup on. At some point—and I'm observing all this—at some point she turns to look at me and as quickly as I can, I say, "Hi, I'm Ron Orbach. I'm gonna be working with you today." She opened her eyes, really for the first time that I could see: "Hi. Hi, how are you doing?" And she closes her eyes back down. And we don't speak again.

Then we get to the location in Beverly Hills, and we're in the Jeep.

Mona May, costume designer: This outfit was very important because that was going to be her adulthood. She's going to get the driver's license, she's going to be free. She needed that white special shirt. Then she didn't get it, so she put something else together. But then also, what happens on the other side of that scene: she doesn't pass the test and she becomes the loser. So there's something pathetic about her, too, in that outfit.

It was too much, you know. She was trying too hard.

Ron Orbach: Alicia's sitting in the driver's seat. Again, eyes closed, looking like she's sleeping or something, I couldn't tell. But when action is called, her eyes open, she goes, and it's basically spot-on: hits every line, every moment, perfectly. "Cut!" And she goes back to sleep. And this keeps happening, over and over, take after take. "Action!" Bang! She's up and going like a complete pro, perfectly, really hitting everything. "Cut!" She goes right out, unless Amy comes over to talk to her, to give her a note or something.

Twink Caplan, associate producer and Miss Geist: I remember between takes she was so tired, she fell asleep in this car. I'd try to feed her liquids to keep her up, you know?

Ron Orbach: After a while, we're on a break, maybe at the craft services table or something. And I just couldn't help myself, so I said: "Hey, Alicia: What's up with that? What's going on? Are you okay? I thought maybe you had narcolepsy." I'm like, *What the hell is going on?* She says, "No, no. It's just that I'm in practically every single frame of this movie and I've got to get my rest wherever I can just to conserve my energy." Well, I mean, I was just knocked out. Because what an amazingly savvy thing for an [eighteen]-year-old actress to be doing. To be that self-aware and that self-possessed, to me, was quite stunning.

Alicia Silverstone, Cher: I'm glad he thought I was being smart! I was just supertired and trying to sleep whenever I could.

Paul Rudd also recalls shooting one of his car scenes with Silverstone and noticing that she was power-napping between takes. "I turned around and I was like, Oh my God, she's asleep!" he recalled. "Then five minutes later, she was awake and doing the scene. I do remember she was just working like crazy."

Ron Orbach: Then they take me out in the Jeep to do, basically, the stunt shot. Which is—there's a stunt driver, not her, driving the Jeep and sideswiping the vehicles that are parked on the right, you know? Except they never told me that's what they were going to do. In a way, I probably could have sued them because no one ever said, "Yeah, don't worry. You just sit tight. You're buckled in." Remember: it's an open-air, somewhat open-air—I don't remember if there was a roof on [the Jeep]. There wasn't, was there? And we're basically having an accident with me in the car. You know? So I don't recall precisely my face as that's going on. But I assure you they probably captured something very real, no acting required. I was completely freaked out that we were taking mirrors off of the cars parked there. You know, the stunt driver was doing exactly what had been choreographed, but they kind of neglected to tell me, which I always found amusing.

Adam Schroeder, coproducer: I didn't know that. Sorry, Ron! Oops—hazard pay!

I did not know that, but I have to imagine he was safe at all times and never in danger. It was a professional stunt person and whatever we hit was not a real car. It was something rigged to bounce. But apologies to him.

It was good for his performance. It's method acting.

From the notes on the Clueless *production report dated Monday, December 12, the day this scene was shot: "CHER'S JEEP HIT . . . PICKUP TRUCK DURING STUNT WITH DAMAGE TO BOTH CARS. ESTIMATE OF DAMAGE TO FOLLOW."*

Schroeder did not recall a pickup truck getting hit, and Danny Silverberg, the second AD, could only barely recall it.

Ron Orbach: We finished [the scene] and Amy was very happy, and Alicia couldn't have been lovelier, and I kind of forgot about it. [Later] they invited me to a screening. I thought, *This is going to be some stupid-ass teenage bullshit that I could give a rat's ass about* . . . but I walked in and sat down, and the opening credits are these kind of kooky, multicolored graphics that are sort of fun. Immediately, I was sort of like: *Oh, this looks like this could be fun*. . . . Then when I saw it and I heard the reaction from the crowd—and it obviously wasn't just teenagers. The people were largely people who had worked on the movie: actors, crew people, etc. I was just really bowled over by it.

It was only years later when I would be on the road with a show and someone would recognize me—somebody, you know, several generations my junior, the kids that had grown up with that movie and for whom it is such a seminal yardstick in their young adulthood—somebody would recognize me: "Oh my *God*. It's the Messiah of the DMV! Oh my God!" Literally, literally, people would be on their knees begging for my autograph. "Would you just say the line? Just say it, please? Just say it." It happens, any show that I do, if there are people, kids, in their twenties or thirties—I say *kids* because I'm now in my sixties—

they may not know me, they may not recognize me. I usually wear a beard nowadays. But when they read my bio and they see that I did *Clueless*, they're like: "Oh my God." It becomes this reverential, awesome thing to them. Which I find endlessly delightful, because it connects me to people of that generation in a way I wouldn't be otherwise.

I'm very proud of the fact that I was in it.

The Virgin Who Can't Drive Has an Epiphany

That was way harsh, Tai.

—CHER

Production info: Cher's epiphany—when she realizes she's the one who loves Josh while standing in front of the Electric Fountain, a Beverly Hills landmark located at the intersection of Santa Monica and Wilshire Boulevards—was shot on Friday, December 9, 1994, day thirteen of production. Most of the Beverly Hills meandering that precedes her epiphany, including the moment when she passes by the so-called Witch's House at the intersection of Carmelita Avenue and Walden Drive, was shot on the same day; additional second-unit footage of Cher's "walkabout" was shot on February 7, 1995, the day that *Clueless* officially wrapped production. The "virgin who can't drive" confrontation that segues into Cher's epiphany was shot on Tuesday, January 10, 1995, at the Encino home that doubled as the Horowitz residence.

What happens in this scene, CliffsNotes version: After Cher learns that Tai is smitten with Josh, she almost starts ralphing, then goes on her version of a walkabout on the streets of Beverly Hills (and into some shops, because she's only *human*). Once she arrives at the fountain, she finally realizes what every other girl (and some guys) realized while watching this movie: that she's totally, butt-crazy in love with Josh.

Adam Schroeder, coproducer: Brittany really went for it, and it was a different side of her than we had all seen. And that's always a lot of fun. There had been rehearsals and that kind of stuff. But she kind of really hit it, and I think it just became this great, iconic "You're a virgin who can't drive." At that time, what's the worst thing you could tell a teenage girl, right? How low can you go?

During the DVD features on the Clueless *Blu-ray release, Brittany Murphy noted, "Actually, when I filmed it, I was a virgin who couldn't drive."*

Mona May, costume designer: I think that the plaid [outfit Murphy wears] does work in a way where: she's got the power, she's got the plaid, she's on, and the other one is not. So I think yes, in that moment, she kind of became Cher in a sense.

David Kitay, score composer and producer of Jewel's "All by Myself" cover song: I was working around that ["virgin who can't drive"] scene and it was just kind of not coming. It was tricky. Then I just slowed [the main theme music] way down. I mean, waaaaaay down, right? . . . So it ended up just being a hyper-hyper slow, still version of that theme, just really holding with the idea of trying to get inside Cher and her experience of what is going on in her that she doesn't even necessarily understand. And it just worked. And, of course, [that leads] into the song that I got to produce, by Jewel. I was kind of proud of my guitars over the fountain. That was fun. I liked that bit.

Karyn Rachtman, music supervisor: "All by Myself": I'm 99 percent positive that was Amy's idea.

Amy Heckerling wanted to use the original version of "All by Myself," as recorded by Eric Carmen, a song that has since been covered numerous times by various artists. But, as Kitay explains, the rights couldn't be secured.

David Kitay: We couldn't get "All by Myself," the original. So then, Jewel was a hot number at that moment. So it became a thought: "Hey, why don't we do it with Jewel?" I think Karyn might have even started that ball rolling.

Amy Heckerling, writer-director: I don't want to say bad things, but I felt like that version kinda sucked the life out of things. It was just *too*—too slow and draggy. I like the original.

David Kitay: That's why most of that scene plays without any vocals, if you'll notice. There's the very first two lines, I think, and then she dumps the vocal and maybe brings it back in for "All by myself," [the chorus], I think. And then my guitars take over and we're done.

Richard Graves, first assistant director: There's a house that [Amy] always called the Witch's House; it's this sort of strange-looking, fairy-tale-looking house in Beverly Hills. I think we had to have a shot of [Cher] walking by that just because, for Amy, it was iconic. I'd never seen it before.

Bill Pope, director of photography: I don't remember many locations, but the one that I really remember is the fountain.

Amy Heckerling: In *Gigi* when [Gaston] decides, "Wait a minute," and he's walking and he's silhouetted and then he turns around and [there's] the color and the fountain: of course, that's France and this was Wilshire Boulevard. But I wanted that. That moment stays with you when you see *Gigi*. It's exhilarating. You can't really do those things in the modern world in Los Angeles, but you can have fun with them.

Bill Pope: So now I gotta go rent *Gigi* and find out what the hell that fountain was. It's not like it's just stuck in my memory banks, that fountain. But in hers, it's an icon. Everybody has their own film iconography. I just copied it, straight out. Same colors and everything. We lit it up and Alicia's doing her *Gigi* thing where she realizes that she loves Paul.

We filmed [at the fountain] for a few hours. There were just numerous car accidents right next to us. People would drive by, they'd see her or they'd see the lights and [*makes loud crashing noise*]! That's one of the busiest intersections in Los Angeles and cars kept crashing into each other. We were like, "We've got to hurry and get out of here before we either get arrested or we hurt somebody."

Amy Heckerling: There are times where you drive by there and they have the lights on a timer with different colors coming up, and other times where it's not, it's just white. So I wanted the color business, but I wanted it to come on at a certain point. And the water wasn't high. So we had to do a thing to make it go up much higher. You have to pump more water in. I mean, I'm not the one that did it. But I wanted it higher, to make more of an impact. We may have put gels in and extra stuff. That's actually one of the pretty things in LA to drive by.

Adam Schroeder: We were shooting it at magic hour so that the light was going to be perfect. So we didn't have a lot of time to get it done. It was all the things—stopping traffic and getting the crane to go right and getting the lights in the fountain to go off, right at the perfect time when she's right at her mark and all. It was a crackerjack moment to get that right.

Kissing Paul Rudd

In the immediate aftermath of seeing *Clueless*, millions of women, and probably just as many gay men, wanted to be Paul Rudd's/Josh's significant other.

In *Clueless*, two ladies got to do just that, at least in the pretend-movie sense: Susan Mohun, who played Heather, Josh's pseudointellectual, kinda-sorta college girlfriend, and Alicia Silverstone, who, as Cher, won Josh's heart the minute she proved she could totally school Heather in the classic game Who Actually Said It: Polonius or Hamlet? In their roles as Josh's love interests, Mohun and Silverstone landed the opportunity of a lifetime: the chance to kiss Paul Rudd on-screen. But are some of those on-screen lip-locks as dreamy as they seem?

Susan Mohun, Heather: Paul Rudd could not be nicer. . . . I felt very at ease with him, even though we had a random kissing scene, which was never my favorite.

Paul Rudd, Josh: I remember she was really cool. She was funny.

Susan Mohun: There's a kissing scene on the bed [in Josh's dorm] that mostly got cut. . . . That's always sort of awkward. The camera guys were like, "You have to start kissing and keep kissing and then we'll tell you when to stop." Because they have to cut it, you know—they want to cut in when you're already kissing and they want to cut out when you're still kissing. And again, it's totally awkward, because you don't know this person. And they said, "When we say cut, you can stop." Jokingly, I think the cameraman said, "You know, I said cut ten minutes ago. I don't know why you guys are still making out." Which was, of course, horrifying to me. Not true, too, by the way.

Bill Pope, director of photography: The kissing story sounds right. The whole cast was always fun, and we wanted them to stay loose and unself-conscious.

Paul Rudd: I had never done anything like that, a kissing scene. But it was pretty chaste.

Susan Mohun: They were joking around with it, which made it obviously funny and easier and not a huge deal. We were not naked. It was not a sex scene, so it wasn't that big of a deal.

Amy Heckerling, writer-director: I really wanted to make sure Paul looked really good [during the kiss with Cher on the staircase]. So it was a combination of angle and lens and where his head would be so that it was foreshortened a little bit, but not extending a nose. I think I drove Bill Pope a little crazy.

Bill Pope: You can't take your eyes off either one of them, and the awkwardness and everything in that scene. The loveliness of the setting. Again, I think the staircase might have been Amy's idea.

Amy Heckerling: [I adjusted] until I felt like, *Oh, he's looking good.* I wanted that. I mean, it's a movie for girls. It's not just, oh, make the girls look pretty and then the guys are character-actor lit. No: the guys have to look good. And this is his moment. And then he's amazing, he's great.

Paul Rudd: We were making edits and rewriting things on the day. I feel like that one, as compared to other scenes, it wasn't like: okay, the scene is written and we go in and just do it. It seemed like that one was kind of being created a little bit on the day.

I do remember having a very clear understanding that teenage boys all around the world would be so jealous of me right now, because I'm kissing the girl from the Aerosmith videos. And being fairly psyched about it myself, might I add.

Amy Heckerling: Afterward, it was one of those times where the crew was going, "That was a good scene." I'm going: "You haven't talked to me in . . . wow! Good!"

Paul Rudd: I remember my [then-]manager afterward, when it came out and everything, saying, "Oh, you didn't kiss her right." I remember him saying that. He goes, "You should have grabbed her."

I think for years, I was like, *Oh, man. I kissed her wrong in that scene.*

Alicia Silverstone, Cher: It was really easy with Paul—especially the wedding kiss.

The Wedding

As if! I'm only sixteen.
And this is California, not Kentucky.
—CHER

Production info: The wedding of Mr. Hall and Miss Geist—not of Cher and Josh, because: as if!—was shot in the backyard of the Encino home that doubled as Cher's house. The wedding dates, i.e., the two days during which the sequence was shot: Thursday, January 19, and Friday, January 20, 1995, days forty and forty-one of production.

What happens, CliffsNotes version: Miss Geist and Mr. Hall get married. Cher catches the bouquet thrown by Miss

Geist, thereby winning a bet regarding which girlfriend could snag the flowers. To the tune of General Public's "Tenderness," Cher and Josh share a major, openmouthed kiss, bringing our movie to a happy, romantic ending.

Steven Jordan, production designer: We must have set up that wedding five or six times. We would set it up in the backyard the day before. The weather would come in, we'd take it all in and dry it all out. The rain on the movie that year, in January, was just phenomenal. And finally the sun came out. We were able to shoot it.

Amy Wells, set dresser: I don't remember the rain. I mean, I remember setting up and putting everything out. We had a lot of flowers. It's a pretty big scene, a lot of decoration. . . . We brought in the chairs, the flowers. We had to do a riser, all that kind of stuff. It was just like doing a regular wedding, except it's not.

Bill Pope, director of photography: By then, everybody was their characters.

I remember looking up and seeing the boys around the table and they were talking amongst themselves, boys about girls. And they were making husband jokes: Henny Youngman–ish husband jokes. And I was like, they already have this rapport with one another and they are a unit.

Donald Faison, Murray: We were all really tight already, by that time. That was toward the end of the movie. That was one of the last days of shooting. It was great to have us all together. When you look at it, it's like, wow, there's the three besties with the three besties, you know what I mean? It was great.

Elisa Donovan, Amber: Jeremy and I were supposed to be sitting together at the table. And I think I had a couple of lines, too, and they had to get cut because Jeremy wasn't there for some reason. [*Laughs*] Maybe I shouldn't be saying that. I don't know what happened but he wasn't there. So I was super bummed because . . . they just sort of cut it out, whatever I was supposed to do. Which wasn't a lot but, you know. I still wanted it to happen.

Jeremy Sisto, Elton: I do vaguely remember running to set or something weird about that day, so that must have been it.

Amy Heckerling, writer-director: I remember Donald was having some trouble saying some of the words in the dialogue. So I go, "Okay, okay, we got it." Because I felt like sometimes it was easier for him when the camera wasn't on him. Then I start to film what they all think is Breckin's close-up. But actually, I start the shot on Breckin and we ease the camera over onto Donald, so we catch his line when he thought he was off-camera. But then Breckin went, "Hey, wait a minute!" Because he saw that the camera wasn't on him.

Donald Faison: Breckin and I, we pretty much shared a trailer when we were filming the movie and we only had two scenes together. That's when I'm arguing with Dionne, and then, I want to say in Mr. Hall's class or Miss Geist's class. We didn't have a lot to do [together]. That was the one time we actually interacted throughout the whole movie. We were like, that's cool. At least we know we end up buddies.

Breckin Meyer, Travis: [Playing Suck and Blow] is the only time I think [I'd] come close to kissing Brittany, because we never actually kissed and we've played boyfriend-and-girlfriend probably four or five times. Even in *Clueless*, at the end of the movie, I'm supposed to give her a kiss at the wedding scene. Because Brittany has always been so close to me and like a sister, you'll see in the movie that I just kiss her on the top of the head, like she's my half sister or something.

Adam Schroeder, coproducer: The entire cast and everybody was dressed to the nines. . . . That was really fun because [Paul Rudd] wasn't with the full cast ever, except for that. So that was really cool.

Paul Rudd, Josh: I was excited because finally I was getting to shoot with other people when, it's like: we did the readings together, we were around together, we would shoot different scenes on the same day. Like I said, I became friends with Breckin and Donald, so I was psyched to finally get to shoot a scene with everybody.

Donald Faison: When [Paul] says, "I'm totally buggin' myself," that was improv. When you see us laughing at the end, we're literally laughing for real because nobody expected him to say that. And how he said it.

Paul Rudd: I think sometimes I would say, "I'm bugging." Not buggin', bugging—"I'm bugging myself." And then we kept trying to do different versions of it. Then we all couldn't stop laughing for a little too long.

We got real punchy and couldn't stop, to the point where the crew and Amy, they were getting a little annoyed. We were shooting outside. We were racing against the light: *Come on, guys. Keep it together.*

Breckin Meyer: We lost it. That was it, that was the end of the day for us. We could not do it.[21]

21 From the "Language Arts" feature on the Blu-ray release of *Clueless*.

Stacey Dash, Dionne: That's how much fun we were having. You never knew: It could be just one word that hit somebody funny, you know, or hit somebody's funny bone and the next thing you knew, it was just contagious.

Mona May, costume designer: My favorite! I love the wedding! Because I got to design everything . . . For the guys, what's really cool is to have that eighties, edgy, hip look. So it's kind of like skater punk for Travis. I think Paul Rudd had a 1950s, shawl-collar jacket, and the sharkskin blue for [Christian's tuxedo]. It just really was funky cool. I wanted [the guys] to have some more character.

Paul Rudd: I remember liking the suit that I wore, with the black tie, and that I was psyched that Amy wanted to put me in a thin black tie. I was like, "Yes! Right on!"

Nina Paskowitz, lead hairstylist: Sadly, what I remember was that I got sick the day before. I ended up suddenly having to leave the set and having to go almost to the emergency room. It was a weird thing. I went to my doctor that next morning and he's like, oh, you've got what's called slapped-cheek disease. I'm like, what's that? He's like, well, in kids it's like a cold. In adults, it's more like getting almost the chicken pox. It's, like, horrible. Because I was around so many kids, I probably got it from one of the background kids or someone's brother or sister or somebody.

So DJ, who was my second or third [hairdresser], ended up doing Alicia's hair for that scene. It all worked in the end. It was beautiful. I was really, really disappointed not to be there. It's the only scene I missed and of course, it's that huge scene.

Twink Caplan, associate producer and Miss Geist: It was fun for me because I forced Amy to be my best lady, my best woman in it, even though Cher was there.

Amy Heckerling: I'm the bridesmaid with her when they walk down the aisle.

Twink Caplan: If I was going to get married, even if it was fake, Amy would have been my maid of honor. She edited most of herself out and she was shy, you know, to be on that side of the camera. But she did it for me and I loved it.

Alicia Silverstone, Cher: My mom and Amy were both in the scene, so that was fun.

Paul Rudd: Carl Gottlieb was in it briefly and was a friend of Amy's. I think he was the priest who marries them at the end. The thing I knew about him, because I was such a Steve Martin fanatic, was what a great comedy writer Carl Gottlieb was, and that he was Iron Balls McGinty from *The Jerk*. That was totally mind-blowing to me.[22]

Wallace Shawn, Mr. Hall: I also found that part of the plot so moving and adorable, the way they set us up, Miss Geist and myself. The decency of these characters and the way they do nice things, not really out of principle but more out of instinct. In this world that Amy has created, some of the rules of the world are set up so people learn to be more compassionate and

22 Gottlieb did indeed play Iron Balls McGinty in *The Jerk*, a film he also co-wrote. Gottlieb also was a writer for *The Smothers Brothers Comedy Hour*, and co-writer of the first three *Jaws* films. Another notable wedding cameo: the woman sitting next to Rudd during the wedding is Bronson Pinchot's mother.

nice to each other and understanding of each other, without consciously adopting new principles. This is the meaning of the film.

Twink Caplan: I was really humbled to even work with Wally. I really adore him. He is just a lovely man in every way: gentlemanly, and just kind and so smart. Every time I see him, it's like he's still my husband.

We actually did one thing where I walked down the aisle with Paul and kissed him because that was going to be in a dream sequence Cher had. But then it got edited and we didn't use it. [It was] something like, Cher has this dream that I guess Paul marries me, you know, because she's going to the wedding anyway. She has this nightmare that it's really him [marrying Miss Geist]. I guess subconsciously she's—you know what I mean?—figuring out all this stuff. . . . That day I got kissed by both guys: Paul and Wally.

Mona May: I got to design the wedding dress for Twink, for Miss Geist.

Twink Caplan: I loved the dress. . . . I remember Mona got me a slant board [to lean against instead of sitting] because my dress was absolutely fitted to me. It was like a size 2 and it was designed for me and fitted for me and everywhere I went—[if] I went to eat something, Mona would be behind me. "Don't eat that! I'm not going to make the dress over!" Because if you gained an ounce it wouldn't fit. It was the most stunning dress. A high collar—it was just gorgeous.

Mona May: We wanted to make Miss Geist beautiful, to kind of come out of her shell. Here she is: it's almost like unveiling her to the world. To me, it was very Paris, with her little fascinator that I made for her on the top of her head, with the flower. Kind of the very architectural dress, which was interesting and hard to make because it was kind of the Morticia shape. But she had a high collar in the back and also the back open. I don't know if we ever even see the back open in the film. It was quite an interesting design and I think beautifully executed by my seamstresses. And I think it just turned out gorgeous on her.

Barry Berg, coproducer and unit production manager: I guess it's something that as a guy, I probably didn't really understand and that was that they really wanted a terrific-looking, special, expensive wedding dress [for Miss Geist]. And I kept saying: "Well, guys, it's just a film. Nobody—they won't know how much we spent" . . . [but] we did spend quite a bit of money on the wedding dress. And Twink looked beautiful in it.

Mona May: And then the bridesmaids: I got to make all the bridesmaids' pink little outfits—shift dresses with little jackets. Also I got to dress Amy. It was so much fun.

Stacey Dash: I remember really trying to get the bouquet. That's what I remember.

Amy Heckerling: I used to play this game with my daughter. It always ended with people getting married when we played Barbies. She always wanted a wedding at the end, right? So we'd be playing Barbies, then all the dolls would start fighting in a big mob at the end over who caught the bouquet. It would turn into a wrestling match. Then they would all jump off the table. You know, we were just screwing around.

So I wanted the girls [in *Clueless*] to be really fighting, really aggressively fighting. And they were all being very tame. So I put back on my bridesmaid outfit so I could get in the middle of them and just start pushing them around. They weren't doing anything. They were just being polite. So I got everybody to push around. Then they all fall on the floor, and [Cher] gets up triumphantly. The falling just happens because everybody is shoving and pushing.

Alicia Silverstone: I remember having the instinct that Cher would be superaggressive and crazy going after the bouquet.

Elisa Donovan: The bouquet throwing—I mean, it was all really fun. I remember it being difficult to move in that dress. It wasn't a tight dress, but the material—I think the waist was really tight or something. When I was falling I was like: *Oh, I'm really falling down. I'm not going to be able to get back up!*

Danny Silverberg: [When Cher and Josh kiss] in fact, we all had to wrap our head around: Are they brother and sister? They're not brother and sister, are they? No. They're kissing right in front of us. No, they're not.

Paul Rudd: [The kiss] was—you get a little nervous. But also, I was psyched.

Growing up you hear these actors, and granted, they're talking about sex scenes and not just kisses, but they're like, "Oh, it's all technical. Nothing's there. Nobody's excited. It's all just kind of embarrassing." I remember thinking, "Is that really true?" And then I remember thinking, "This is pretty awesome."

I sound like a total perv.

Adam Schroeder: Karyn [Rachtman] had found an Oasis song called "Whatever," which was a big part of the movie—*whatever*—and it was very Oasis-y and it was a very cool song and sounded great. The deal was that they were the end title song, but the song [would start] before the movie's over. So it's not just on the credits, it's on the end of the movie. That was very important to them. . . . But it wasn't as happy and fun as you wanted with Josh and Cher, the wedding, and then Josh and Cher kissing. We ended up using "Tenderness," the [General Public] song.

Oasis wasn't happy about that, because we wanted to go from "Tenderness" right into the Oasis song on the credits. And it was end credits, so it was actually good. End credits are usually not bad, but they're a scroll of crew. But this was actually [the names of the] actors and the director and the production heads and it was this kind of shiny thing we had designed. But they weren't happy with that. So we ended up not being able to use that Oasis song "Whatever," which was a bummer. Because that seemed so perfect.

Mona May: [The wedding] was all about the ending and the happy ending. Where everybody found themselves: they all had the boyfriends, they all were together, really getting along. I think I wanted to make the wedding just super exciting. And kind of life-affirming.

Cutting *Clueless*: The Editing Process and the Scenes That Got Deleted

"Easy, easy, easy."

That's how Debra Chiate describes her experience editing *Clueless*, an endeavor that, according to Chiate, took roughly eight months and began while production was still under way. Chiate, who previously worked with Amy Heckerling on a short film when Heckerling was studying at the American Film Institute, as well as both of the *Look Who's Talking* movies, says she was cutting scenes and "keeping up pretty much to camera" as filming chugged along. She then worked alongside Heckerling to shape the movie as a whole once production wrapped.

It all went so well, she says, because she and Heckerling share a common sensibility.

"We think similarly," Chiate says in a New York accent nearly as thick as her collaborator's. "We're both musically driven. We have the same taste in a lot of things."

Chiate and Heckerling also agreed that for a breezy comedy like *Clueless* to work, it needed to be properly paced. That meant condensing some scenes and losing others. No hugely significant plot points, conversations, or events were removed, but some "scenelets," as Heckerling calls them, did wind up on the cutting room floor.

Amy Heckerling, writer-director: For this movie, I had all the material that I wanted. I didn't have a lot of extra stuff. It was all very, "Here it is, now let's put it together." The only variable was the timing and spacing for voice work, which we wouldn't have until the very end.

Debra Chiate, editor: I knew how much [Amy] shot. I knew what she wanted. The challenges were structuring it. The challenges were keeping all the characters alive.

Amy Heckerling: We never really had a sense of how it was going to work until [Alicia Silverstone's voice-over] came in because it was such a nutty thing. Her voice: we were recording, even during mixing. Right up until the very end.

[Before Silverstone's voice-over], it was always with my voice, so it never felt like you were transported into it. It always felt like a work in progress. . . . That version was very wacky. I wish I had a copy of that. Because you'd see this beautiful young blond girl and you hear this low-class, older female speaking in Val speak.

Debra Chiate: There was a point where we watched about a reel of cut footage once it was assembled in some kind of order. I think Twink was there, and Amy, and we watched it. And I think we just thought: *Okay. We're onto something here*. I didn't know. But it just had a feeling that it stayed on this very fine line of not being over-the-top and not being, I don't know what the word is—it just stayed on that fence, you know, the tone of it.

What happened when Amy came in was she shortened a lot of the scenes but didn't lose the essence of anything. So it felt like things went more shortened, yet better and tighter, and moved on. Every scene made [sure] the next scene was there for a reason. . . . I know there were a few scenes we took out. Nothing off the top of my head where I thought, *That's too bad we have to lose that.*

The most significant of the "lost" scenes took place in the girls' bathroom at Bronson Alcott High and featured a conversation between Cher, Amber, and Dionne in which Sassy *magazine was referenced. A snippet of it was included in the movie's trailer.*

Amy Heckerling: There was one little scene where the girls are in the bathroom and Cher says, "What do you think of Christian?" And they're all looking in the mirror and putting on makeup.

Debra Chiate: I think Scott Rudin really liked that scene. I don't know if that's the one where Amber says, "Shuffle the cards and deal."

Amy Heckerling: Amber says something snotty and she's got a big hairdo. And Alicia goes, "I missed this month's *Sassy*. Is big hair back?"

Debra Chiate: There's a scene where they're outside, yeah: "Where should we go get yogurt? Which yogurt store is better?" That didn't stay very long.

Amy Heckerling: When Josh is teaching her how to drive they go by Dionne's house and [Cher] says, "Oh, let me off here instead of"—I didn't continue it, but he lets her off there and she's with Dionne and Murray. They're going to go get frozen yogurt and they're arguing about whether they should go to Humphrey's. There's one place where they blend in the toppings and another place where the toppings go on top. And they're having an argument about which is better . . . and Murray thinks toppings are wack, that he wanted them blended. It was a little ending to that other scene to keep [Dionne and Murray] alive, doing their silly stuff.

Another scene slated for inclusion very early in the film featured Cher picking oranges and joking with a gardener who works at the house.

Amy Heckerling: Oh, that was just her getting up during the day when you see her with the maid and they're making orange juice. I had a little bit more of a conversation between those two and she went out for one second and was tossing an orange back and forth with the gardener. I just wanted to show that she has fun in her house with the people that work there.

Debra Chiate: I think Amy wanted to emphasize the fact that you're in Southern California, and what are things that are Southern California that are great? That you can just go outside and pick an orange off a tree.

A telephone conversation between Cher and Elton—described in the shorthand of the shooting schedule as "Cher talks to Elton on the phone" and "Elton is brought into Cher's scheme"—was also ditched because it wasn't crucial to the plot.

Debra Chiate: There was a scene where she's making a healthy smoothie talking to Elton on the phone.

Amy Heckerling: She was trying to recruit all her friends to help with putting the teachers together. So that was a conversation where she would be telling somebody what to do . . . it wasn't necessary because just seeing her do what she does with Dionne seemed to be enough.

Also nixed: a brief scene of Cher standing in line at the DMV prior to going out on the road with the Messiah of said DMV.

Amy Heckerling: It [was] probably to establish it was the DMV and driving. But I think I probably, ultimately, figured out that you would get that from the test.

Perhaps the most difficult moment for Heckerling to cut was a portion of the skate park scene that originally featured a young school newspaper reporter. The actor who played that budding journalist? Mollie Israel, Heckerling's daughter.

Amy Heckerling: The movie cuts out when [Tai and Travis] wave to each other and Cher knows that things are going to be good. She knows Tai won't be thinking about Josh anymore. I had a scene where there's a kid from a junior high, a newspaper reporter, who's from her school paper interviewing him. [Travis] was very sweet with the little kid, and then the girls come over and we see that, you know, Brittany is very touched by that. They talk and Cher leaves and she knows that those two are going to be together. I felt like the moment—the information was conveyed by the looks between [Tai and Travis].

My daughter was not at all happy with me. She was adorable and Breckin was adorable with her. Sometimes you have to take out stuff that you like, or stuff with your relatives, because the information is conveyed in a more visual way and it's enough.

Heckerling may have (briefly) upset her daughter. But, according to Chiate, the filmmaker's parents were pretty happy with the initial cut of the movie.

Debra Chiate: Sitting down and screening it [for the first time], I'm sure it was for Amy. She probably had her parents there or something, a few people. In my head, I think her mother or father said, "Now, that's a good movie." It just got the seal of approval, you know, pretty quick.

Amy Heckerling: Yeah, that's unusual. Usually they're the ones with the most notes. My mother especially.

Part Three

THE IMPACT OF *CLUELESS*

The Screening and Selling of *Clueless*

Once *Clueless* was edited and in mostly completed form, it was time to show it to key people at Paramount, then start test-screening it with actual audiences. Once higher-ups at Paramount could see they had something special (and potentially lucrative) on their hands, the marketing team, in conjunction with Adam Schroeder and others on Team *Clueless*, had to devise a strategy that would convince potential ticket buyers *Clueless* was something special, too. Fortunately, they had a couple of advantageous allies on their side: star Alicia Silverstone, who was already known to the coveted *Clueless* demographic as America's Video Vixen Sweetheart, and MTV, which played a big part in promoting *Clueless* on a platform widely watched by future Cher Horowitz disciples.

Adam Schroeder, coproducer: We finish the film and then the director has ten weeks of cutting, and the producers get in there during that time, and you work with them, and then you show it to the studio. I remember we showed it to Sherry [Lansing] and the other executives in the Paramount screening room. And you're a nervous wreck because you think it's great, but God only knows you're living in a bubble. After which you walk over to Sherry's office, and I've done this many times since then, but you walk over to her office and she gives you her thoughts. And she literally said—we could hear her laughing in her seat and all, and that was always a good sign—she said, "This is fantastic. I don't have anything I think you should change. I think you should lock it"—finish it, you know, color timing and any of the other kinds of things you do. And then she gave us more money for the soundtrack. It's never happened to me before where it was just so positive and she was so incredibly supportive, and then gave a bit more money for finishing costs.

Twink Caplan, associate producer and Miss Geist: Sherry's got the most engaging laugh. It's this very beautiful, powerful laugh that makes everything okay. It's like sprinkles. Amy and I were elbowing each other every time she would laugh. And we knew. It was . . . oh my God. Extremely exciting. I had my grandfather's pocket watch around my neck just for luck. And I never bring it out, because it's like one hundred years old. But it was incredible.

Sherry Lansing, former chair and CEO of Paramount Pictures: She's right, Twink—I laughed my head off through the whole thing. I probably had no notes. I said, "I love it, I love it." So I thought everyone else would, too.

Amy Heckerling, writer-director: There was one note, after seeing it, from Sherry. Alicia is looking all daydreamy and she says, "Looking for love in high school is like looking for meaning in a Chevy Chase movie." And Sherry Lansing was like, "Oh, no, he's a nice guy. I see him socially at some charity things and stuff. So can we change that from Chevy to somebody else?" So I put in Pauly Shore and it didn't seem to hurt anything. I mean, maybe it hurt Pauly Shore's feelings, which I'm sorry for. . . . That was the only note I got.

Arthur Cohen, chief of worldwide marketing, Paramount Pictures: Some movies, you have to open. Some movies, maybe you'll open. And some movies you'd love to open. And this was one that we really loved to open.

Michelle Manning, executive vice president of production at Paramount Pictures: I think everybody thought it was going to do well. It's not like it exceeded our expectations. Everybody had very high expectations for it. We had good screenings. Kids loved it.

Amy Heckerling: In Hollywood, they talk about these quadrants—there's younger males, younger females, older males, older females—and how you want four quadrants [to respond positively]. The scores were sort of uneven in that it really spiked with the younger females. So I was kind of afraid, because this other movie I had done that had done well, *Look Who's Talking*, that had much higher scores [across all four quadrants].

I thought *Clueless* was good, if not better. Everybody's got their own personal favorites, but it was shocking that the numbers weren't nearly as high and they just really spiked in that one quadrant. And I was like, *Oh no, what should I do?* After the screening, Sherry showed me the numbers and I said, "I'm sorry, I'm sorry." And she said, "What's the problem? We've found our audience, now we're going to sell it." So they were cool. They were fine, they knew what they had to do. They knew what would work.

Adam Schroeder: I feel like it was a different time where maybe young girls, I don't know, thirteen to thirty-five, wasn't a quadrant that was gone after in such a way. But it was a quadrant that wasn't being served, either. Maybe Sherry realized that was going to be a great thing for this film. But those test screenings are always terrifying. Because you always leave in doubt even if you get great scores.

Sherry Lansing: That demographic was so strong, and maybe this was one of the first films that really tapped into that demographic of young girls. It remains so strong today with *The Hunger Games*, with *Twilight*, whatever it is. Young girls coming out is enormous, and then that spreads.

Elisa Donovan, Amber: There was a test screening that Alicia, Donald, Justin, and myself, and Paul Rudd, went to, and we all sat in the back row. And as soon as the movie was over, I just looked at Alicia and I was like, "You are going to be a huge star."

Debra Chiate, editor: I remember having meetings after the screenings and all the executives were excited. Like, how can we start the lingo going on talk shows?

Arthur Cohen: At the beginning of any of this stuff, you release a few photographs, a few things to long-lead press, and you start building a budget. But you really can't do much until you see enough of the film to know whether it's good or not.

If you start building a budget that's large, it's hard to come back off of it with the talent. And if you build a budget that's too small, you're not servicing the movie right. It was a B+ budget. This was a phenomenon that was manufactured.

The important thing in movies like that, and *Forrest Gump*, and *Titanic*, and other movies we've done, is once you've set a tone and a goal, you have to stay true to it. If you breach it—and this was pre-Internet even—the audience knows it right away.

Setting a tone for marketing Clueless *meant selling the movie as something fun, glossy, and youth-oriented. That approach permeated everything, from the movie's one-sheet (the Hollywood term for the movie poster); to in-theater displays, or standees; to TV commercials; to the cutesy* Clueless *swag distributed to members of the media.*

Michelle Manning: I remember it being about the girls and that one-sheet. Everything was sort of stylized and pushed. It was to make something, not hyperreal, but more fun and not edgy. So it was about showing the wealth and the spirit of the movie.

Adam Schroeder: We were doing the poster shoot for the one-sheet and we went back to the house where we shot [Cher's] house. The photographer David LaChapelle was shooting the one-sheet, because often we got people—Herb Ritts would shoot one-sheets. You want beautiful photography. So David LaChapelle shot the one-sheet art, and then we also had this really fantastic in-theater standee. The one-sheet was the three girls on the steps of Cher's house with the phones . . . in their best outfits that they wore. I think they were outfits from the movie. Then the standee was the three girls, and they were putting on makeup, and it was a big heart thing that had a mirror treatment on it. So it was like they were looking into the mirror. It was expensive. It wasn't just a cardboard cutout. They spent money to make this special, unique thing, which was pretty cool.

Except I remember I was at the AMC Universal and it was in the front lobby and I was all excited: *Ooh, my first movie and look at this great standee!* And I'm looking at it and some people are coming over to look at it. And I'm like: *Ooh, let me hear what they're going to say.* And I remember these teenage girls said, "Ooh, what's this? A movie about teen prostitutes?" It was kind of crushing. . . . I went home very sad.

Arthur Cohen: We didn't take it too seriously. If we saw a [TV] spot, if somebody tried a spot that we liked, we would put it on the air without testing it. Because we knew—there were four or five of us who knew what it was. And once we knew what it was, it was easy to do things.

Amy Heckerling: The executives told us: "We've got a team that's so excited about this stuff." The marketing people were making little dictionaries and they were giving out fluffy pens . . . [it was] the stuff that you gave to the writers and press people, to make people excited about it: Here's this special little world you're going into. In case you don't understand, here's a little vocabulary guide. It was very cute. They were jazzed. They were coming up with ideas for things they hadn't ever done before.

As far as selling merchandise to the masses goes, Schroeder says that attempts at prerelease cross-promotion with other products didn't really go anywhere.

Adam Schroeder: We tried. I know we tried. But it just wasn't a known quantity. And I remember we showed the movie to MTV very early on to do our thing with them, and I think there were attempts to show it to other, possibly, marketing alliances. It just wasn't that desirable. Because it wasn't known and it didn't have a cast that was famous and all.

Ultimately, generating interest in the movie came down to a couple of key things: selling the allure of Silverstone and making maximum use of Paramount's connections with sister company MTV. Prior to the release of Clueless, *Silverstone's face was splashed across magazines like* Entertainment Weekly *and* Seventeen. *And in the days immediately before the movie opened, she was on MTV on a practically hourly basis.*

Adam Schroeder: Alicia had currency and we really put her out there, and then we put the other cast members out there as well. Then once the movie came out, Alicia really took off in a huge way.

Arthur Cohen: [Alicia's] agent was difficult, okay? And not constructive. And that's all I'll say.

Alicia was fine. Alicia was actually pretty great.

What she did, she really hit it big. She was smart enough to know that a movie is more than just ninety days shooting. You've got to do the rest of it.

Adam Schroeder: MTV Films was just starting at that time, they were just starting their label. Viacom [Paramount's parent company] owned MTV and MTV Films was going to do movies. And we came to them, maybe before we even made it. We said to them, "Would you be interested in partnering with us and making this your first MTV film?" And they passed on it.

They didn't feel this was what an MTV film was going to be or should be. We said okay, fine, it could have been a good alliance . . . but then, the movie turned out really well. We went [back to MTV] and we showed them the movie and they loved it. We ended up doing this huge marketing alliance with MTV, where we produced these special interstitials. We came back and shot five little one-minute pieces, with Alicia and some of the other cast, totally original, that they spread throughout their programming for the couple weeks prior.

Sherry Lansing: One of the things that we were incredibly blessed with when Sumner Redstone bought the company was that MTV became a sister to us. And a sister we could often use to market to that young demographic.

Adam Schroeder: We did these special shoots and one of the shoots we actually did was a confessional, like in *The Real World*, where Cher is in a room, and she does a confessional about something that happened to her. So we really tried to tie into the MTV programming with our characters. You know, with the same production team and all. It was a big deal.

Arthur Cohen: I think during the last week [before the movie came out]—this is from memory, but we were on air every twenty minutes. So that's a lot.

Ken Stovitz, Amy Heckerling's agent: The great irony was that I begged [MTV Films] to get involved with the movie and then they didn't, but they just sold it like *shit* on their network. I mean, they sold it like crazy on their network.

Adam Schroeder: To have that kind of exposure on MTV—and you know, movie studios will buy time to play the trailers and TV spots on MTV and other networks. But this was its own dedicated campaign, which was really, really cool.

Arthur Cohen: The reason it was hard for, we'll call—I'm looking for the right term—the outsiders [to predict the movie's success] is that for teen movies, you spent the bulk of your [marketing] money in the last four days. So, you know, you really drive it home. Most of them make up their mind [about what to see at the movies] in the last forty-five minutes. I'm telling you the truth. It may have changed, because time has passed. But that's the way it was.

[*Clueless* was] the most fun [project I worked on at Paramount]. *Titanic* was the most satisfying, *Forrest Gump* was extremely satisfying. *Braveheart* was amazing and a miracle. This was the most fun. Everybody liked each other, everybody was having a good time, everybody would call one another and say, "I just got this great idea!"

For a marketing department, the greatest thrill for everybody that I've observed over the years is when a movie comes out of no place and, because of your effort, it becomes something. This is one of those movies.

The Story Behind the *Clueless* Soundtrack

The *Clueless* soundtrack—a thoroughly nineties mix that dips primarily into that widely defined pool called alternative rock, but also dabbles in rap, pop, a touch of complaint rock, and a dash of retro covers—was released on July 4, 1995. A year later, it had sold enough copies to be certified gold; by February 4, 1998, it was certified platinum.

The soundtrack was released on Capitol Records, which, not surprisingly, orchestrated the inclusion of several of their artists on the CD. Most of those bands and solo performers had only the most basic sense of what *Clueless* was about when they agreed to allow their voices and music to be associated with it. But as a result of that association, some (though not all) either pocketed a decent chunk of change or still collect a nice little regular royalty check. And all of the *Clueless* soundtrack contributors eventually learned that being linked to Amy Heckerling's teen classic would earn them a level of street cred that would last for two decades and counting.

Adam Schroeder, coproducer: At the time, soundtracks were a big marketing tool and they could be very important to a campaign. And record companies would give advances to films for the soundtracks. We actually had a $1 million advance from Capitol, which was really huge and exciting and amazing, because that stuff doesn't happen anymore at all.

Karyn Rachtman, music supervisor: Capitol Records was already involved. They had already gotten the soundtrack rights . . . and it was funny for me because, right as I was being asked to do this movie, I was also being asked to become [a] vice president of Capitol Records. It worked out great for me because not only was I the music supervisor on the film, I was also the record company. I had a lot of control—not enough. I had some control.

Adam Schroeder: What happens when you're working with a record label, they want you to use their artists. Which was great. Capitol is historic and they have incredible artists.

Karyn Rachtman: Amy had great taste in music and I think she could relate to me on that level. She liked my taste in music from some previous films.

Amy Heckerling, writer-director: Just as language expresses who [the characters] are, I mean, the college boy is going to be listening to the new Radiohead kind of music. And music from Seattle. Cher's going to like happy, poppier stuff, and also all the rap stuff. Which was kind of different then. It was also like, "Slide, slide, slippity slide"—there was happy, fun rap.

Karyn Rachtman: The song at the end title . . . ["Tenderness"]. Based on [Amy] wanting the song . . . I kind of knew what direction to go with other songs, what she was looking for.

Amy Heckerling: I wasn't saying, "Oh my God, this has to sound completely 1994. It can't be songs from 1990." I just wanted stuff that had the right feel for the movie, that made me feel so happy, and felt contemporary and cool. But I didn't want to be snobby about it: "Oh, that's two years ago."

Was this just stuff that I liked? Yeah . . . "All the Young Dudes." The people that I liked then—the Bosstones. I liked Radiohead. I liked the Beastie Boys and Gwen Stefani.

Karyn Rachtman: [With] "Shake Some Action," with "Alright" by Supergrass, I think with clearly "All by Myself," "Just a Girl"—they all fit the story. They fit. They were very much a part of the time.

Adam Schroeder: Capitol wouldn't let us put ["Just a Girl" by No Doubt] on the soundtrack because the soundtrack was filled and they weren't Capitol artists at all. . . . I'm so proud that it's in the movie, but it would have been really cool to have been on the soundtrack.

Karyn Rachtman: I was blown away; I thought that was such a great song. I wanted to put it on the record and make it our first single and the president of the record label said no. I was so pissed.

But he didn't think it was a single. That's like the big joke or whatever. And they wanted it to be a single from our film. No Doubt and their management and everything, they were into it. They hadn't done anything yet. What a great opportunity for them. And the record company said no.

It's still in the movie, it's just not on the soundtrack . . . but it should have been on that record. It would have made that record even better.

Adam Schroeder: The soundtrack did really well. We went platinum. But I don't think any singles charted. Luscious Jackson was our first single and Jill Sobule was our second. I think Coolio did go out as a single but he had, that summer, "Gangsta's Paradise" from *Dangerous Minds*, that Michelle Pfeiffer movie. So that was his single that summer, and we were kind of like, his other single.

That's where I go back to my *If only we had No Doubt* . . . but I think the sum of the parts is all great, and I think it encapsulates the movie really beautifully.

Track Listing

"Kids in America" by the Muffs

Appearance in the movie: It's the track that opens the film and provides the soundtrack to the Noxzema-style commercial montage.

Kim Shattuck, lead singer and guitarist, the Muffs: We had our cell phone, like a big, gigantic shoe phone kind of cell phone, in the car, that we were only allowed to use if the president of Reprise [Records] called us. Because it was so expensive and it was coming out of our budget. So we were like, don't use it unless it's somebody important. He called on the big shoe phone, and we're like, "Oh my God. What's going on?" He wanted to know if we wanted to do a song for *Clueless*.

So we had a choice of three songs. One was "Kids in America," the other was "Go All the Way" by the Raspberries, and the other was a song that some songwriter wrote. Just some random songwriter. They gave us a cassette to listen to in the car.

We heard "Kids in America." I'm like, yeah, I like that song. It's melodic. I didn't realize that the lyrics were so dumb, but I liked the melody. But I really liked "Go All the Way" by the Raspberries. It's a really good song, but Babes in Toyland did it right before that and we didn't want to also do it because we just thought that would be creepy. And then we didn't want to do the song that the songwriter guy wrote, because it was probably the dumbest song we'd ever heard.

They gave us $10,000 to record it, which, for one song, you would think we'd be able to come way under budget. But we didn't. . . . I've never gotten any money for it. The first original $10,000 they gave us to record, apparently it was an all-in deal. . . . You know, I have no regrets. It was cool to have it be in the movie.

"Shake Some Action" by Cracker

Appearance in the movie: This song pops up twice when Cher is in proactive mode: first during the montage where she starts working to raise her grades, then again when she starts pitching in with the Pismo Beach relief effort.

Karyn Rachtman: I'm 98 percent positive that I found that song. I did not know it was a cover.

David Lowery, singer and guitarist, Cracker: The song that we have on there is actually a really obscure cover of [a song by] the Flamin' Groovies. . . . I guess we'd been playing that live and, I don't know if it was the music supervisor or whoever put together the soundtrack, had seen us do that.

Adam Schroeder: We did that remake with that band. That totally felt right. But again, they didn't put it out as a single.

David Lowery: We've had some pretty big hits. That wasn't really a radio hit for us but that's definitely in the top ten of tracks that get streamed and spun and stuff like that for us. It's had really a long-term impact on our career, basically.

Actually, the cool thing about that is the guys who wrote that, you know, the Flamin' Groovies, they were pretty obscure . . . I think one of them told me that was the most money they made off of anything their entire career. And it came like almost twenty-five or thirty years after they wrote that song.

We were paid a quarter million dollars for that song, on that soundtrack, to record it and put it on there. . . . But that was the height of our popularity. That was about the going rate. And that was also when the music business had a lot more money than it does now.

"The Ghost in You" by Counting Crows

Appearance in the movie: It's on Josh's car stereo after he picks up Cher, post-mugging, and drops off Heather.

Adam Schroeder: We had to have [Adam Duritz], the lead singer, come to sign off on it. We really wanted to use the song, it was just cool. You know, the Psychedelic Furs but being re-done by Counting Crows, a very big band at the time.

Karyn Rachtman: Amy likes those eighties songs.

Adam Schroeder: We had him come to the lot to see it and he loved the movie and signed off right then and there. But you always run the risk of, they're not going to let you use it and then you have to find something else.

David Lowery: That guy's a movie freak. When [Adam Duritz] lived in Hollywood, he had an entire theater basically in his basement. Movie chairs and everything. We used to always go there and have movie night.[23]

"Here (Squirmel Mix)" by Luscious Jackson

Appearance in the movie: It's playing after the Bosstones party has wound down and Christian is making plans to hit a "happening after-hours."

Karyn Rachtman: We loved that song. That song was [by] a Capitol act. They were signed to the Beastie Boys' label, [Grand Royal]. I don't remember how it came about, but that was the first single from our soundtrack.

---

23 Lowery has worked with Counting Crows, coproducing their 1999 album *This Desert Life.*

Jill Cunniff, bassist and vocalist, Luscious Jackson: I think we were an important part of the label at that time, and they were prioritizing the band. We had to approve it. We met with the team music supervisor and we got the gist and it sounded really great. You know, we were very picky about our stuff and that one was a good fit. So we were psyched.

Kate Schellenbach, drummer, Luscious Jackson: We always wanted to support other women who were doing their own thing. It's still, especially in the film industry—there's like a handful of successful directors that are directing movies for major studios. I think whenever we could, we would try to connect ourselves to other creative women who were leading the way. Definitely Amy Heckerling is one of those people.

Gabby Glaser, guitarist and vocalist, Luscious Jackson: The song was originally a rock 'n' roll song. . . . One day in the studio, I actually don't think I was there that day, our coproducer Tony Mangurian switched it to a disco beat.

Jill Cunniff: They call it a different name [on the soundtrack]: the "Squirmel Mix." Remember what a Squirmel is? It was that toy that was on TV: it looks like a little furry snake and it has a string on the end of it. The guy would be like, "This is the greatest toy ever!" It had two little beady eyes. He would wind it around the paper. Then you get it home and you can't do anything. It's this crappy little thing on a clear piece of plastic. And on the commercial it was like, incredible. That's what that reference is.

Kate Schellenbach: This actually worked out perfectly because I think the movie itself is female-positive. It's pretty mild; there's not really bullying. It's encouraging. As New York girls who grew up in the city, we couldn't really relate to the whole

California rich-girl, high school scene, but I think . . . we liked the fact that it's all about individuality and, just, positivity, and that kind of thing. And incest, of course.

"All the Young Dudes" by World Party

Appearance in the movie: It's what the baggy-pantsed dude-bros walk to in slow motion while Cher bemoans the way boys dress these days.

Karyn Rachtman: I think I was trying to update the record. It's funny because I don't usually do that. When I've worked with Quentin [Tarantino] in the past, I would never suggest that. But I felt like with this, it's what people were doing. You're recycling fashion in a new way. You're recycling music in a new way. That cover was pretty damn close to the original. But I love World Party. It worked out fine.

Karl Wallinger, World Party: I didn't really even know that much about the film because it was such a specific thing. I loved the song. It's incredibly slow, which is amazing, and there's nine seconds of it in the film. So I was quite astonished, really.

"Fake Plastic Trees" by Radiohead

Appearance in the movie: It's what Josh is listening to when he raids the Horowitz fridge; Cher hears it and asks, "What is it about college and crybaby music?"

Karyn Rachtman: Amy wanted the whole Radiohead thing. I was scared—you know, [because of] the line in the movie—and because I had just started at Capitol and Radiohead was a Capitol band.

Radiohead actually were very good sports. They said, put "Fake Plastic Trees." It whines enough and it's not on their record, so they'd prefer that. [The acoustic version that's on the soundtrack] wasn't on their record, it was a B-side. It's a great song, actually . . . It's one of those songs that I've come to appreciate a lot more as I get older.

"Change" by the Lightning Seeds

Appearance in the movie: It provides the soundtrack to the montage in which Miss Geist and Mr. Hall find love.

Karyn Rachtman: That was on one of their records. . . . It's a great song, I remember that. I don't know if I found it or Amy found it. I loved it, though.

"Need You Around" by the Smoking Popes

Appearance in the movie: It plays over the closing credits instead of the Oasis song once marked for that position.

Josh Caterer, vocalist and guitarist, Smoking Popes: After we signed with Capitol Records, one of the things that also happened was that I got a publishing deal with PolyGram, and they just started looking for movie soundtracks for our songs to be in. I think *Clueless* was the first one that they found for us, although they ended up placing songs in about four movie soundtracks, I think. There was *Tommy Boy*, there was a movie called *Angus*, which was a good movie, and then there was *Boys*, starring Winona Ryder. . . . The only thing that we agreed to in advance was that the filmmakers could use our song. Where they placed it was entirely up to them.

So even now, I'll have friends who tell me, "Hey, you know, we were watching this movie *Clueless* last night and sort of fell asleep toward the end, but the credits were rolling and we heard this song come on and we were like, hey, that sounds familiar. Who is that? And it turned out to be you!" Which is sort of like, our song ends up being the hidden track.

The *Clueless* soundtrack is the thing that has survived that era of our career [and] continues to generate more publishing income than anything else we ever did. . . . It is something that has generated fans for the band over decades now.

"Mullet Head" by the Beastie Boys

Appearance in the movie: It provides the soundtrack to Travis's skateboarding competition.

Karyn Rachtman: Amy really wanted the Beastie Boys. We managed to get it because they liked the movie and we had Luscious Jackson and, blah blah, they let us have it. The Beastie Boys never license their songs to movies. They just don't. We got very lucky with that.

"Where'd You Go" by the Mighty Mighty Bosstones

Appearance in the movie: It's one of two songs performed by the ska-punk band during the movie's second big party scene.

Karyn Rachtman: I remember I thought they were really nice guys. I thought they were perfect. I think [Amy] thought they were perfect. . . . I still talk to one of them every once in a while. I mean, they were the perfect party band to play that scene.

Amy Heckerling, writer-director: I don't know if they're like anybody else, but it was like the Specials kind of feel. And fun for college stuff.

Dicky Barrett, front man for the Mighty Mighty Bosstones: I think [Karyn] picked [which song to use on the soundtrack] and we didn't mind. We loved all of our songs. It wasn't like we were choosing from the Green Day catalog—"Which hit do you guys want?" It was like, "Which obscure college-radio track are you interested in us playing? And we'll do that for you."

"Rollin' with My Homies" by Coolio

Appearance in the movie: Surely you know that this song is featured prominently during the Val party, and again when it makes Tai cry over Elton during the restaurant scene.

Coolio: I was just asked if I had a song that could possibly fit in the movie, and it just so happened that I did. The actual song, "Rollin' with My Homies"—those were the original lyrics for "Fantastic Voyage." That's what I was going to put out for "Fantastic Voyage" in the beginning. A friend of mine—actually it was a guy who worked for Tommy Boy. His name was Ian. He heard the "Fantastic Voyage" song and told me that if you change your lyrics a little bit and make it more universal, he said, I think this song could do good. So I took the lyrics from "Rollin' with My Homies," which were the original lyrics, I took those off, and I rewrote the whole song. And the rest is history.

My first album sold two million copies plus. I kinda became a household name from that. It's kind of a weird thing. "Rollin' with My Homies": I mean, it sold a few copies but it didn't do great or anything.

Karyn Rachtman: It was kind of funny, right, because it was a rip-off of his own song. It was bizarre.

Coolio: The reason I chose to do something with the lyrics as well was because I was getting ready to go on tour. I'm one of those people, I like to break shit down and overanalyze shit. . . . [But] I just went with it. I didn't want to have to ponder over writing an all-brand-new song, you know, if I had the moves like that. It was because I needed to make it happen fast and I wanted to go ahead and record it, so as I was looking through my line book, I came across those lyrics.

I just wanted to make something that was kind of hood, that was kinda street . . . because the movie was kind of squeaky clean. It's weird, though, I wouldn't imagine them spending the kind of money they spent on that soundtrack.

"Alright" by Supergrass

Appearance in movie: It's the buoyant Britpop track that plays while Cher takes photos of her friends.

Karyn Rachtman: They were ecstatic to be a part of it. They were so cool. I just thought that song—to me, that really felt like the movie.

"My Forgotten Favorite" by Velocity Girl

Appearance in the movie: Ironically, the one song with *forgotten* in its title is also the hardest song to hear in the movie. It plays very faintly during the restaurant scene, before "Rollin' with My Homies" kicks in.

Brian Nelson, guitarist, Velocity Girl: I remember going to see the movie and being told beforehand when to listen for our song, because it was so sort of quiet and obscure. It sounds pretty puny compared to some of those other songs on the soundtrack.

Occasionally, in my civilian life, I talk to people who find out I was in a band, and when they find out I was on the *Clueless* soundtrack they all know that movie. And then I have to go into the story about how they have to listen really hard.

I still get maybe a couple hundred dollars in royalties off of the *Clueless* soundtrack every year, which is kind of surprising to me. And surprisingly nice.

"Supermodel" by Jill Sobule

Appearance in the movie: The happy (and ironic) musical accompaniment to the Tai makeover montage.

David Kitay, *Clueless* score composer and cowriter of "Supermodel": "Supermodel" was just one of those really fun, fast experiences. David Baerwald, Brian MacLeod, and I were kicking around a couple of ideas and then . . . we went and bought some teen magazines.

Karyn Rachtman: David Baerwald was in a band in the eighties called David + David. They had a big hit called "Welcome to the Boomtown." I've worked with him a lot: he wrote the Ethan Hawke song for *Reality Bites* and he wrote a song for *Romeo + Juliet*, which ended up in *Moulin Rouge*, "Come What May," that Nicole Kidman and Ewan McGregor sang. He's a great songwriter.

David Kitay: On one of the magazine front covers it said, "Do you want to be a supermodel?" Then we literally played those chords—we just kind of called them out and played them in one pass in the span of three and a half minutes. It was done. It just kind of existed.

Every lyric in that was based on a teen mag line. . . . We just went out, got stoned, and bought every teen mag they had and ran with it.

Jill Sobule: They asked if I wanted to do the song and I was at first a little bit reluctant, because I don't sing other people's songs and I was trying to have people know me as a singer-songwriter. But then I thought, *Am I stupid?* And it's a really good song. What should I be prideful about? Although I did add the middle section . . .

Karyn Rachtman: She added one line: "I'm not gonna eat today and I'm not gonna eat tomorrow. Because I'm a supermodel." Which bugged me for some reason. I mean, it was funny. It was clever. But it bugged me, first of all, because eating disorders first came on the scene [in the nineties] and also because that was never an issue in *Clueless*.

Jill Sobule: I was also a person that had eating disorders when I was in my twenties so I felt like I just had to add my little thing. I think one of the many reasons why I probably had [an eating disorder] was from looking at magazines and supermodels. And that affected me. So I think I just tried to subvert it a little bit and still keep it fun.

I agreed to [record the song] but I think I might have had, not a bad attitude, but I wasn't excited. And then when I saw it, I was so proud. [I went] from being, you know, some sort of snobby person to being like, "I'm in *Clueless*, everybody!"

The Very Beachy Premiere of *Clueless*

The premiere of *Clueless* was held on July 7, 1995, on a beach in Malibu where stars walked a red carpet laid out over the sand and MTV recorded some of the prescreening proceedings, which would air starting July 14, as part of an hour-long *Clueless* MTV Beach Party special.

Members of the cast and crew of *Clueless* were there, of course. Luscious Jackson and Coolio performed. During the MTV *Clueless* movie special, hosts Daisy Fuentes and Jenny McCarthy conducted goofy interviews with some of the stars in attendance, which, unless the clips have been taken offline, can still be viewed on YouTube. During one segment, McCarthy subjects Henry Thomas—who auditioned for the movie but did not get cast—to a *Clueless* quiz that asks him, along with

Yasmine Bleeth, to identify the meanings of slang terms from a movie that, presumably, they had not yet seen. (Honestly: doesn't Elliott from *E.T.* deserve more respect?)

In keeping with Hollywood premiere tradition, a number of other celebrities who are not in the movie showed up to check it out, too. Bleeth was joined by her *Baywatch* costars Jaason Simmons and Nicole Eggert. Stephen Dorff, David Arquette, Marcia Cross (then of *Melrose Place*), Kimberly Williams, and actress/*Sports Illustrated* swimsuit model Angie Everhart were there, too.

Yes, it was a night that no one would ever forget. Or at least one that a few people associated with *Clueless* still remember, a *little* bit.

Adam Schroeder, coproducer: I had this idea to have the premiere at the MTV Beach House. But the MTV Beach House in Malibu was too small, so we ended up having it on Zuma Beach, where they got a giant Jumbotron and put it on a cliff and put couches and food stands and a stage and a whole premiere on the beach. We had Luscious Jackson and Coolio perform their songs from the show. They did a premiere special on the network. It was fantastic.

Paul Rudd, Josh: I remember going, *Whoa, this is a big deal.* I had never been to a movie premiere, I don't think. This was also its own, strange kind of thing: on the beach and MTV was there. I remember Jenny McCarthy was there and Bill Bellamy was there.

Alicia Silverstone, Cher: I was hosting a show with Daisy Fuentes for MTV. I went back to my trailer at some point and was supposed to be on camera for the MTV thing, and the security guard, rightly so, didn't want to let me back in without credentials. I'm not sure I ever had any. Or I lost them, not sure. Luckily after a while, someone came out to get me!

Amy Heckerling, writer-director: My agent came and he brought his dog because it was on the beach. They had couches on the beach, which I think is a very cool-looking thing . . . but I'm not really a beach person. I'm very pasty. Which is the complimentary way of saying it.

Marcia Ross, casting director: I was wearing a jean jacket, one of my favorite vintage pieces, that fell off at the beach, never to be found again.

Alicia Silverstone: I brought my dog, Sampson, as my date for the red carpet.

Barry Berg, coproducer and unit production manager: I took my daughter to the premiere. She was just knocked out by the movie. Even at ten. So I knew I was in trouble immediately.

Kate Schellenbach, drummer, Luscious Jackson: We got picked up at our hotel in a stretch limousine and then they drove us to Malibu. But they decided to avoid traffic by going over the mountains and it was super windy and we all got really carsick.

Jill Cunniff, bassist and vocalist, Luscious Jackson: It was one of our early gigs. It definitely felt like, *Ah, now we're stepping into this other realm of exposure*. MTV liked us, but we were never the MTV darlings. It was nice to get that boost.

Gabby Glaser, guitarist and vocalist, Luscious Jackson: It was very California, very Malibu, very the beach, awesome, outdoor party. Actors were there. And Coolio was there, and he was funny. Flirtatious.

Coolio: I remember going to the premiere—they had it on the beach—and basically getting white-boy wasted.

Gabby Glaser: He said something to me that made absolutely no sense. But that was okay, you know. White-boy wasted: that's funny.

Kate Schellenbach: I think we played maybe one or two songs and it was broadcast on MTV and then we watched the movie on the beach.

Justin Walker, Christian: From a professional standpoint, your job after you get a movie like that, where you get a break like that, is to get another one before it comes out. That's job number one. That didn't happen. I tried. I really tried. I was up for everything. But that didn't happen. So the *Clueless* premiere itself was bittersweet for me.

Amy Heckerling: I was going out with Bronson Pinchot. So they put a little red carpet on the beach and there were people there to take pictures. And all the photographers are going, "Bronson, over here! Bronson, over here! Bronson, over here!" And they're asking me to get out of the way, because they want to take pictures of him. And then somebody told them that I was the one who made the movie. Then they were going, "Oh, Amy: over here! Oh, Amy: over here! Bronson, can you move out of the way?" And this is basically stupid, showbiz stuff, but Bronson's quite a sensitive person. I had to deal with the effect that that had on his psyche for a while.

Elisa Donovan, Amber: I was late because I was shooting *90210* and I was on set that day shooting in Van Nuys. . . . My agents had to orchestrate me getting out as early as possible that day to make it. Suddenly everybody's like, "Wait, there is a stretch limousine outside for Elisa. Who is this chick?" "Where has she come from and why is she so important?" [*Laughing*][24]

They got me out of there as early as possible but it was still too late. So I wound up taking this enormous limousine through the canyons. I remember calling my mom, "I'm on my way, I'm in this huge car and I'm all by myself and I'm late." I had friends meeting me at the premiere. I got there and the movie was already half over.

Jeremy Sisto, Elton: I honestly don't think I've seen the whole movie. But I was out of the country shooting another movie at the time, so I missed the whole premiere.

Paul Rudd: I remember thinking that, as they were showing it on the beach: this is a fun party, but no one's really watching the movie.

Amy Heckerling: That [setting] kind of doesn't work for a movie because you're waiting for it to get dark and it doesn't get dark until extremely late, but people are there much earlier. They start the film and there's still dying light so you can't see it very well. And the ocean is quite loud. So you can't hear it.

But as an event-y thing, it was fun.

---

24 Donovan played a recurring role as Ginger LaMonica, the visiting best friend of Tiffani-Amber Thiessen's character, Valerie Malone, during the sixth season of *Beverly Hills, 90210*.

Summer Sleeper: The Critical and Box Office Success of *Clueless*

The movie was done. The soundtrack was out. The MTV promotions and various Alicia Silverstone magazine covers had been disseminated for public consumption. It was finally time to find out if moviegoers would embrace *Clueless*.

"If advance buzz is right, this could be one of the summer's sleepers," predicted a *Dallas Morning News* story published on July 15, 1995. Four days later, on Wednesday the nineteenth, the film opened in 1,470 theaters across America and quickly proved that the advance buzz was right: Paramount Pictures had a sleeper hit on its hands.

That Wednesday, *Clueless* brought in nearly $3 million, making it the number one movie in the country, ahead of *Apollo 13*. On Friday through Sunday, the movie played on more than 1,600 screens but business dipped a little, ultimately giving it a second-place finish at the weekend box office, behind the Tom Hanks NASA drama, even while playing on fewer screens than any other movie in the top ten. Within its first five days of release alone, *Clueless* made $15.8 million, more than enough to recoup its modest production budget and then some. It earned largely positive reviews from critics in major media outlets, including the *New York Times*, the *Los Angeles Times*, *New York* magazine, *USA Today*, the *Washington Post*, and the *Wall Street Journal*. The months following its US release would also

> "Effervescent, unflappable, supremely pleased with herself, Cher (delightfully played by the much-publicized Alicia Silverstone) is the comic centerpiece of *Clueless*, a wickedly funny teenage farce from writer-director Amy Heckerling that, like its heroine, turns out to have more to it than anyone could anticipate."
>
> —KENNETH TURAN, *LOS ANGELES TIMES*, JULY 19, 1995

> "The movie emerges as a breath of fresh air in a summer where most of the comedy has been formulaic. Tech credits are also superb, down to the outlandish costumes, carefully chosen song score, and opulent Beverly Hills estates—gaudy enough to make even the Clampetts and the brats on *90210* eat their collective hearts out."
>
> —BRIAN LOWRY, *VARIETY*, JULY 17, 1995

bring more good news, as the film began to do better-than-expected business overseas and earn some awards for Amy Heckerling.

All the success was a thrill for the writer-director and everyone who worked on *Clueless*. But after the struggles at Fox and the discouragement she faced when she tried to pitch her affectionately satirical coming-of-ager to other studios, for Heckerling, the sudden love for her Beverly Hills baby was also vindication. She had been right all along: people would love Cher and her world exactly the way she originally envisioned them. And now, it was time to celebrate.

Adam Schroeder, coproducer: We went on that Friday night. Amy and I filled up a limo and we went from theater to theater just to see, is anybody in the theater?

David Kitay, composer: Amy and everybody else [were] in one car, and Breckin Meyer and I were in another car. That's always kind of a fun, magical thing to be able to do. When you're sitting in the back of a theater and people are liking it and laughing and having a good time.

Amy Heckerling, writer-director: I usually do that unless I'm totally depressed about what's going on.

David Kitay: It was great. People loved it. They laughed at all the right places, they felt in all the right places.

Dicky Barrett, front man for the Mighty Mighty Bosstones: We were on the Lollapalooza tour. We drove the bus to a theater, a multiplex at a mall. We all got out and went in and saw it. We were very nervous—it wasn't the days of the Internet where you could just Google it or check what people were saying about it. So we sat in there and watched the movie, thinking we're either going to go crawling out and run for our bus or do what we ended up doing, which was stand up at the end and go: "That was us. We're the band. That was us!"

Steven Jordan, production designer: Oh my God, I was so pleasantly surprised. [The movie] was great. And it was funny. I was working with Darren Star at the time and he came into my office—"I saw your movie this weekend. Oh, so great." Which was nice.

Donald Faison, Murray: I always wanted to do *Sixteen Candles* or *The Breakfast Club*. I wanted to be in a movie like that. And while making it, I thought, *Aw, this isn't that*. Then I saw it and was like: *Holy cow. This is exactly what I wanted to do*.

Stacey Dash, Dionne: We could tell that it was going to be a huge hit. We knew. Or at least I did.

"[Silverstone's] Cher doesn't know the name of anything and she has an unfortunate experience explaining Haitian immigration policy to her class, but she reminds me of Judy Holliday's blonde ditzes from forty years ago: The more she babbles, the shrewder she seems. The surprise of her character in *Clueless*—which is based, amazingly, on Jane Austen's *Emma*—is that she's more interested in looking great and being nice to other people than she is in her own happiness. Is there a catch somewhere? How can virtue be encased in an ethos of consumerist narcissism? But Heckerling loves Cher and her friends: Their posing conceals a small gift of poetry."

—DAVID DENBY, *NEW YORK MAGAZINE*, AUGUST 7, 1995

Elisa Donovan, Amber: The weekend that it opened, people started recognizing me immediately, which was so bizarre. I was in the Beverly Center, taking the escalator up. I was with a friend and all these girls started crowding around at the top. They were pointing and jumping up and down. It was a huge crowd. I said, "Oh, there must be somebody famous coming up the escalator because these kids are going bananas." And then we get to the top and I realize, *Oh my God, it's me*! They all swarmed around me, and it's so funny because people often speak to you in the third person when they recognize you. "Oh, look at her. Look—she looks so nervous!" Or, "Oh, she looks so good in person!" They're kind of pointing at you like you're not real. It's so bizarre, and that was the first time I had ever had that experience. And I said, "I can't believe this is really happening."

"Alicia Silverstone makes a delectable teen queen in *Clueless*, a candy-colored, brightly satirical showcase for her decidedly visual talents. Thus far famous mostly for being famous (mostly in Aerosmith videos), Ms. Silverstone finally gives a film performance that clicks. As a pampered Beverly Hills clotheshorse, she's mostly a one-joke princess, but the joke happens to work."
—JANET MASLIN, THE *NEW YORK TIMES*, JULY 19, 1995

Donald Faison: That was my go-to when I wanted to be with a girl. I'd say, "Come over and let's watch *Clueless*." Absolutely. *Clueless* was the ultimate wingman. They loved the movie. They didn't give a shit about me being in the movie, they just loved the movie, period. I didn't start getting girlfriends until *Clueless* came out. It worked well for me. It's true. It's because I kept it real. That's exactly right. Because I was keepin' it real.

Paul Rudd, Josh: I had never been in a press junket or anything and we had to do a press junket. I remember I did my press junket with Stacey and Justin, so we were all in the room. Inevitably, every single critic that came in to talk to us, nine times out of ten, they started this thing with, "You know, I'll be honest with you"—even before the camera would go on. They'd say, "I went into this thing thinking I was going to hate this movie. I had a *blast*." Every critic was coming in and talking about how they expected this thing to be dumb, they didn't want to see it, and they loved it. They thought it was really smart, really funny, really sweet. Again, not having any kind of experience with any of that before, I kind of took it all with a grain of salt.

"*Clueless* is a smart and funny movie, and the characters are in on the joke. Cher (Alicia Silverstone), who lives in a mansion and looks like Cybill Shepherd, is capable of lines like, "Why learn to park when every place you go has a valet?" But she puts a little satirical spin on them. She is one of the most totally self-absorbed characters in a movie since the heroes of *Wayne's World*, and yet she isn't a victim, and we get the idea she will grow up tough and clever, like her dad (Dan Hedaya)."

—ROGER EBERT, *CHICAGO SUN-TIMES*, JULY 19, 1995

Bill Pope, director of photography: My wife and I went to a dude ranch with our daughter. There was no phone service, no nothing. We were out riding horses in Colorado or Wyoming or something. Somebody came in from the office with a fax that my agent had sent me of the *New York Times* review. I'd never gotten a good review or recognition for anything. And there was my name, mentioned in the *New York Times*. It felt good. The critics loved it. And I thought, *Wow. It's not just me that loved it. The world's starting to recognize this movie*.

Amy Heckerling: It's not that I read all of [the reviews]. But I read enough to know that it was the first time in my life something was completely accepted all over the place. And that freaked me out and blew my mind. It's like when you've been starved to death and somebody says, "Here's some food." And you go, "Okay, I better not have too much because this will kill me."

Paul Rudd: Scott Rudin called me the morning it came out, and it had gotten good reviews. He said, "Congratulations. Don't get used to this." It was kind of a successful movie, and then *Halloween* 6 came out, and afterward Scott said, "Ah, yes. The actor's nightmare."

Adam Schroeder: We were the little movie that could, so the studio was wonderful that following week. They kept the marketing up because it was this potential sleeper. They were very dedicated to it succeeding because they knew it could succeed.

"Heckerling doesn't quite pull off Cher's character transformation. The materialism in *Clueless* is almost as scary as the hopelessness in *Kids*. Whatever. Silverstone is the babe of the moment. And she's learned how to back up her sexy pout with shrewd comic timing. You think maybe a star in the making doesn't count for something? As if."

—PETER TRAVERS, *ROLLING STONE*, JULY 19, 1995

Amy Heckerling: People would say great things about *Fast Times*. But at the time that it opened, they didn't even want to put it in many theaters. It was just that it did well in California, so they opened it in the rest of the country. There was no advertising. There were hardly any reviews. It wasn't given a release like it was a real movie. And then with *Look Who's Talking*, they put it on the shelf for six months. . . . It was scoring in the nineties, but they were acting like, "This movie—we can't sell it."

And *Johnny Dangerously* didn't do well at all. So I thought, *I suck, but I really want to do this stuff.* I got to do this one, [*Clueless*], that was really the closest to me. Not "me" as in who I am, but what I like to do and see. The idea that it was getting good reviews—and not [as] an afterthought, like, "Oh, this came out a couple of weeks ago, maybe we should review it"—and the marketing people were doing their job, it was too rich for me.

Twink Caplan, associate producer and Miss Geist: The critical acclaim that *Clueless* got actually meant more to me than anything because Amy really got her due.

Carrie Frazier, *Clueless* casting director while the project was at Fox: [Elizabeth Gabler at Fox] wanted it so badly and was terribly upset when it went to Paramount. Then when it became a hit, the story I heard is that she came in with the grosses, put them on the table, and said, "You idiots! What were you thinking? Look what this movie did! I told you it was going to be good!"

Gabler would not comment for this book, despite multiple attempts to set up an interview via her office and the communications department at Fox.

Adam Schroeder: Usually what happens is you get the matinee numbers from the East Coast first. And they were really, really promising. Sherry [Lansing] was just the most incredible person because she made the calls [to tell us] herself.

After that first weekend, Clueless *would go on to earn $56.6 million.*

Sherry Lansing, former chair and CEO of Paramount Pictures: In today's dollars, it's probably a lot more. Those numbers, [all] that time ago, were really great.

Amy Heckerling: Ken [Stovitz] was always calling, really excited. He was so much a part of it. He was the one that wouldn't let it die. So it was real validation. But afterward, actually, I took my parents and my kid and my then-boyfriend, Bronson, and we all went to Europe on a vacation because they'd never done anything like that before and I wanted to take my family somewhere. When you make a movie, you spend a lot of time on it. And I had a little girl. I wanted to do something for my family and for my baby.

During the fall of 1995, Clueless *began to open elsewhere around the world: in the UK, Australia, Mexico, Germany, Hong Kong, and a number of other countries. While American comedies generally do not play as well overseas as they do at home,* Clueless *did respectable international business. By mid-January of 1995,* Variety *reported that* Clueless *had earned $20.7 million overseas, in addition to the $56.6 million it had already made in North America. (According to IMDbPro data,* Clueless *has made $77.3 million worldwide, but figures for its cumulative international box office, as well as home video and DVD sales, were not available, according to a Paramount representative.)*

"No one lately has said a good movie must also be a good film. This one is best taken as a thing of bits and pieces, attitude and gestures. It's like a restaurant where you go for the food and go back for the atmosphere. Or for the waitress. Silverstone is a giddy delight, a beguiling performer, and an icon for her generation."

—RICHARD CORLISS, *TIME*, JULY 31, 1995

Ken Stovitz: Every international buyer I've spoken to loves *Clueless*. I don't know why. I don't know how.

Amy Heckerling: Australia and Germany have been good to me over the years, for some reason. I don't know why. Because my name is Heckerling? My family's from Germany? Australia: I don't know. Seems like a fun-loving country.

*In December of 1995, it was released on home video and became one of the most popular rentals in the country. In January of 1996, when a massive blizzard dumped nearly two feet of snow in many locations on the East Coast—and in some places, even more than that—*Clueless *even provided a sense of calm during the storm. A* New York Times *story reported that the Video Room, a video store in Manhattan with a clientele "whose predilections usually run to sophisticated fare," could barely keep the high school comedy on its shelves during that winter weather event. (Within two years,* Clueless *would generate more than $26 million in rental revenue alone, according to figures reported by* Variety.*)*

The winter of 1996 also brought more good Clueless *news. In January, shortly after the New Year began, the National Society of Film Critics named* Clueless *the best screenplay of 1995. On February 8,*

"Crammed with pop-culture references to everything from cellular phones to skateboarding to Starbucks (she scores one of her biggest laughs just by showing a Mentos TV commercial), Heckerling's script has even more and better teenspeak lines than *Heathers*. 'I don't want to be a traitor to my generation, but I don't get how boys dress these days,' Silverstone complains, as the slo-mo camera trails a quartet of droopy-pantsed, backward-capped, tie-dye-T-shirted, goatee-chinned boys. All the girls in the preview crowd cheered."

—JOE BROWN, *WASHINGTON POST* "WEEKEND" SECTION, JULY 21, 1995

"The film bobs along like a designer balloon, pumped with wry observations on Marky Mark and Mentos ads."
—SUSAN WLOSZCZYNA, *USA TODAY*, JULY 19, 1995

1996, the Writers Guild of America nominated Heckerling's work in the best original screenplay category, alongside Woody Allen for Mighty Aphrodite, *Aaron Sorkin for* The American President, *Randall Wallace for* Braveheart, *and P. J. Hogan for* Muriel's Wedding. *Wallace ultimately won for* Braveheart, *a Paramount release that would go on to be named Best Picture at the Academy Awards. But the WGA nomination suggested that perhaps* Clueless *had at least a shot at an Oscar nomination for its screenplay.*

Amy Heckerling: With the Writers Guild, I was nominated for best original screenplay. It is an original screenplay, if you consider *West Side Story* an original screenplay. If you're going to say, there was *Romeo and Juliet*—well, [*West Side Story*] was a whole other world. Everything is based on some great classic or material. Unfortunately, I told people about *Emma*, so when it was submitted as an original, the Academy decided the category should be adapted. So that's crazy, because then I'm competing with *Sense and Sensibility* that year. Usually things that are nominated by the Writers Guild, since it's the same people voting, 99.9 percent of the time it's exactly the same as the Academy Award nominations.[25]

Wallace Shawn, Mr. Hall: I think she should have won the Oscar for that screenplay, but I don't think adapted from an-

25 The winners of the Academy Awards in the screenplay categories that year were Christopher McQuarrie's *The Usual Suspects* in the original category (where it competed against Paramount's *Braveheart*) and Emma Thompson's script for *Sense and Sensibility* in the adapted category, where there was apparently room for only one take on a Jane Austen novel.

other medium was a fair category. Everything we write is inspired by great works of the past. Her script was inspired by Jane Austen's book but it wasn't what people ordinarily mean by adapted from another medium.

Arthur Cohen, former worldwide marketing chief, Paramount Pictures: Some of that goes down based on what else was going on at the studio. I don't want to tell tales out of school here but some of the way those things resolve themselves is sometimes a little nonlinear.

Amy Heckerling: Of course I was disappointed. But what can you do?

Clueless the TV Series and the Merchandising of Cher Horowitz

Shortly after the release of *Clueless*, Amy Heckerling and Paramount Pictures decided what their next collaboration should involve: more *Clueless*.

Clueless the TV show was developed with three women—Heckerling, Twink Caplan, and Pamela Pettler, who also would initially serve as show runner—as executive producers, with Scott Rudin, Adam Schroeder, and Julie Brown (Ms. Stoeger) among the producers. It landed a spot on ABC's fall 1996 schedule, in a time slot smack in the middle of the network's TGIF programming block, between *Sabrina, the Teenage Witch* and *Boy Meets World*.

The series provided an opportunity for several members of the *Clueless* cast and crew to jump right into a new project. *New* is the right word, too; in many ways, the TV show felt wholly separate from the film, despite some obvious connections between them.

Several of the characters from the first *Clueless*—including Stacey Dash's Dionne, Donald Faison's Murray, Elisa Donovan's Amber, Wallace Shawn's Mr. Hall, and Twink Caplan's Miss Geist—made the transition (at least initially) from large screen to small. Others were altered, excised, or reborn via a new actor. Alicia Silverstone, for example, was too busy with her burgeoning film career to reprise her Cher, so Rachel Blanchard, a Canadian actress best known for Nickelodeon's *Are You Afraid of the Dark?*, signed up to fill her platform shoes.

As divergent from its source material as it may have been, *Clueless* the TV show still managed to generate new merchandising opportunities for Viacom, three seasons' worth of television (one on ABC and two on UPN), and the chance for several members of the *Clueless* family to hang out on the quad together, at least for a little while longer.

Adam Schroeder, coproducer, *Clueless* the movie and the TV series: We all decided we didn't want to do a sequel to it because, I don't know—*Clueless* goes to college? Eh. We could have! But Amy had developed this as the TV show *No Worries* and she was really interested in TV and we thought this could be a really great TV show. So we sold it to Paramount TV as a straight-to-series. Not as a pilot, but as a straight-to-series . . . It was a very different kind of experience.

Amy Heckerling, writer-director: We knew that [Alicia Silverstone] wasn't going to be in it, and we knew that we wouldn't have Paul Rudd. Although he came and did me a favor and was a guest on one episode. Brittany and Breckin [were, too].

Elisa Donovan, Amber: It was great for me because I had a lot more to do. They really incorporated Amber into the show in a much bigger way.

Danny Silverberg, second assistant director on *Clueless* the movie, first assistant director on *Clueless* the series, director of one episode: Sean Holland had a much bigger part in the series, and he's just a sweetheart of a guy. And Donald—it was really nice to have that kind of a homecoming with them.

Mona May, costume designer: I was the designer on season one because we really wanted to translate exactly what we did in the film to the small screen. We wanted to make sure we are as true as we can be to the film, even though it's such a different medium and it's so much faster.

Adam Schroeder: There was a lot of ancillary stuff to do with [the TV show]. I think that's where the Contempo Casuals tie-in thing [came from]. And there were books.

There was indeed a promotional tie-in with Wet Seal, which by then also owned all the Contempo Casuals stores. Although the film had already generated some tie-in books, the series unleashed a new stream of Clueless*-related young-adult fiction that synched up with the show. (In the interest of full disclosure: those titles were issued by the same publisher behind this book, Simon & Schuster.) Viacom Consumer Products, the merchandising division of Paramount's parent company, signed licensing agreements with other partners, including the toy behemoth Mattel, allowing the company to create numerous, largely fashion-focused* Clueless *products, including a CD-ROM game and a trio of dolls based on Cher, Dionne, and Amber.*

Nancy Zwiers, former senior vice president of marketing at Mattel: We were always looking for likenesses to overlay on top of Barbie.

When *Clueless* kind of hit its stride in the pop culture, we thought it would be a perfect fit for Barbie because of a couple of things. Number one, the main characters were very much of an aspirational age, teenager, for girls who like Barbie. You know, they imagine what it's like to be a teenager. Secondly, they were really into fashion.

Elisa Donovan: I remember talking to the Mattel executives and saying, "I would really like it if we could make mine be anatomically correct, in the sense that I don't want to have a Barbie body." I'm still very outspoken about women's issues and anorexia and eating disorders and I felt like, I don't want to perpetuate this idea. So can't we make it so that they look like our body shapes? And they looked at me like, *You must be smoking crack.*

Nancy Zwiers: I seem to remember that the property so captured the imagination of the [doll's] designers that they pretty much nailed it. It wasn't a painful process like it can sometimes be.

Elisa Donovan: You have to do this photo shoot where they take, I mean, like hundreds of photos of your head so that they get your exact profile and they get, really, the shape of your face. So even though there is kind of a stock similarity to most of them, they still do something—like if you look at mine, it has my nose, it has my eyes.

Stacey Dash, Dionne: They made a mold of my face and what's weird is that the Barbie, because I have a lump—I have a very specific nose . . . but they got my nose right on the Barbie. If you look at the Barbie, the Barbie has my nose. It's just bizarre. It's crazy.

Elisa Donovan: We were, oh my God, standing in front of my trailer when they were finally done and one of the executives was like, "Look what we have!" And they opened the top of the box and out comes your little doll. . . . It was a very bizarre, bizarre experience.

While merchandise opportunities were booming, Clueless *ultimately did not perform as well in the ratings department as* ABC *hoped. Heckerling also wasn't as happy in this TV-ified version of Cher's world as she had been in the film version. A few members of the original* Clueless *family, including Heckerling and May, opted to move on in the midst of or just after the first season.*

Amy Heckerling: It was a lot of fun to do and it was nice that we all got to stay together for a while. But just the nature of the beast is that you have a network and a studio and it kind of gets into their Friday night schedule of very kid-oriented stuff. You know, not that there's anything wrong with that. But I was kind of already over [it], ready to move on, after the first six episodes.

Adam Schroeder, coproducer: It was almost as if, when we got to make it as a TV show, the movie didn't exist. It was just, "Oh we're going to do this TV show about a Beverly Hills high school where it's a comedy." All the kind of smart, sophisticated humor, the Amy Heckerling humor, was maybe not what [people at ABC] were looking for.

Amy Heckerling: After the first six episodes I was gone, and Tim O'Donnell [who became the show runner and executive producer] came in and it sort of turned into a different animal.

Wallace Shawn, Mr. Hall: The TV show was a lot of fun at first. It was great. But when the new people came in it became much less fun for me because they really would have wanted to change my character.

Stacey Dash: It was awesome. It was fun to do. And then Amy left and it got kind of weird, because of course her vision wasn't there anymore, and she wasn't there anymore, and it got kind of strange.

Twink Caplan: Amy needed to move on to do other things. She wanted to write stuff and we stayed at Paramount with a development deal. . . . It was, I guess, time to move on.

ABC canceled Clueless *after its first season. However, the series had enough of an audience to entice UPN, Paramount's television network, to pick it up for two more seasons.*

Danny Silverberg: There definitely was a tonal shift to the show. It became more of a poppy TV show, rather than Amy's quirky spin on teen life. But the show itself was a very enjoyable experience.

Elisa Donovan: The irony is I think that the shows got a lot better in the second and third seasons. They just moved better and they were more right for television. But then less people, even, watched it because it was a smaller network and it was a new network and it just had a different audience. But we had a great time.

Kate Schellenbach, drummer, Luscious Jackson: [In one episode] Cher was doing a report for her women's studies class on Luscious Jackson. So they got tickets to see us perform. Everything about that is just so funny to me. So we did one of those scenes, these classic teen movie scenes where you're the band playing at the club or the high school or whatever.

Elisa Donovan: I loved the episodes where Donald and Sean and I would go on these capers together. Amber was always trying to coerce the two of them to do her bidding in one way or another. [In] one episode we kidnapped a tiger? I think it was a rival school's mascot or something?

Amy Heckerling: I loved the episodes that have Breckin and Paul Rudd in them, just because it was so fun to have them.

Paul Rudd, Josh (and Sonny for one TV episode): I remember [my character] was Sonny, because it was Sonny and Cher. I remember he was like a biker guy, kind of a cool dude. And that Amy directed it. I also remember thinking that Rachel, the girl who played Alicia's part, was really good, also really kind of nailed it. And thinking: *Wow, she's really talented and kind of reminds me a little bit of Alicia.*

Amy Heckerling: The one where Cher gets a bad haircut . . . Bronson [Pinchot] is one of the hairdressers. Herb Hall from the school, he is one of the hairdressers. That was fun.

Adam Schroeder: Brittany came back to do an episode. That was great. And there was also an episode that Breckin came back to do. Those were really fun and special. But I couldn't tell you what they were about if you had a gun to my head.

The Most Coveted *Clueless* Gadgets Circa 1997

All the *Clueless* dolls, clothes, books, and assorted paraphernalia may have seemed pretty rad to the average ten-year-old in 1997. But out of all the "As if!" tie-in merch that flooded the marketplace during that period, perhaps the most coveted items were these "high-tech" ones.

The *Clueless* Hands-Free Phone

To be clear—and I know this sounds *insane*—this was not a cell phone. It was just a $29.99 landline phone that came with a headset for hands-free gabbing. But wait: there was more. It also had a special eavesdropper detector that would activate a security alert if your little brother had the audacity to listen in on the other extension, *and* buttons that would automatically insert three *Clueless* phrases ("As if!" "Whatever," and "I'm Audi") into any conversation, *and* a voice changer that, to quote from the back of the box, "lets you change your voice in five ways—from high and breathless to normal to low and sultry." (Um, does normal really count as one of the five ways?) It should be surprising to no one that, during the 1997 holiday shopping season, these phones were as coveted as Sing & Snore Ernie and Tamagotchi virtual pets.

Clueless CD-ROM

Also for a mere $29.99, you could pop this disc into your PC—don't worry, it's compatible with Windows 95—and, among other things, create your own virtual closet and engage in computer-game versions of makeovers. Who said you can't buy a sense of control in a world full of chaos?

Dear Diary . . . *Clueless* Organizer

This *Clueless*-ized version of the popular digital organizer, manufactured, like the hands-free phone, by Tiger Electronics, claimed to be for "ultra hip girls." And it obviously was ultra hip because its features had names like "Wassup?" mode (otherwise known as the ability to schedule events on a calendar) and "Way Cool Happenings." Oh, and it allowed users to save a list of "Trendy Stuff" that contained as many as fifty (!!) characters. Suck on that, iPhone.

The Impact of *Clueless* on: The Careers of Cast and Crew

Clueless was, without question, a game changer for every single person who worked on it, both on-camera and off. For members of the cast and crew, the film placed a noteworthy credit on their résumés and, often, swung open the doors to opportunities in Hollywood that they could not access before. (In the specific case of Alicia Silverstone—who was at her absolute white-hottest career-wise after *Clueless*—those new opportunities included an incredibly lucrative multimovie deal and the chance to don a Batgirl suit.) When a film becomes a hit and, as *Clueless* did, a cultural phenomenon, the actors and artists behind it quickly realize that their association with it will attract a lot of attention. What those same actors and artists couldn't possibly have known in 1995 is that twenty years later, attention would still be paid.

Steven Jordan, production designer: I mean, that movie—I think it was great for all of us. Everybody fell forward on that.

Donald Faison, Murray: It started my career, man. I wouldn't have anything that I have today if it wasn't for Amy and *Clueless* and Scott Rudin and all of them. I'm honest with you when I tell you this: my career really took a big step forward. It wasn't just like a baby step. It was like a giant leap forward after getting that movie.

Breckin Meyer, Travis: You walk upstairs one step at a time and there were a couple of movies that let me jump three or four steps. I think *Clueless* was one of them.[26]

---

26 Interview with the *West Australian*, July 25, 2014.

Elisa Donovan, Amber: Suddenly you have all of these people that are very interested in meeting you. You're put on lists . . . People knew who I was. And then, I started working consistently.

Stacey Dash, Dionne: I got recognized a lot more. I still do, to this day, which I'm very proud of.

Nicole Bilderback, Summer: [For] feature films, it was definitely easier to get in and be a real contender for other big parts in studio films.

Donald Faison: Forest Whitaker told me he hired me for *Waiting to Exhale* because Amy hired him, back in the day, for *Fast Times*. When he found out I was doing *Clueless*, Amy's project, he was like, "Well, you should do this project then" . . . After he auditioned a bunch of people, he said to his assistant: "I think I'm going to go with Amy's kid."

Danny Silverberg, second assistant director: I owe a lot to this movie because that was the show that gave me my first-AD career.

Debra Chiate, editor: A lot of doors opened up. . . . Paramount was really good to me.

Mona May, costume designer: It kick-started my career. I did a lot of movies that had a lot of visual impact—*The Wedding Singer, Never Been Kissed, Romy and Michele* . . . movies that also are very memorable for fashion, and also movies that are beloved by a lot of people.

Bill Pope, director of photography: Since then I wandered via the Wachowskis into action and Sam [Raimi] sort of went into action, so people think of me as a particular cinematographer. Eventually, someone will come up on a set and say, "Dude, you did *Clueless*." Yeah, those are the best. It doesn't get any better than that. They go, "Wow." They don't know how to put it together, but there's respect. There's genuine respect right there.

Steven Jordan: It's sort of a double-edged sword because when you do something that has a success like that, people are looking for the same project again: "Do what you did in *Clueless*."

David Kitay, composer: I've always been really stupid about my career. I've done some really stupid things, and they've paid off accordingly.

Right out of *Clueless*, there was an opportunity to record a Susanna Hoffs record, [the singer] from the Bangles. So some other folks and I did that for about a year. . . . I walked out of *Clueless*, [and] instead of trying to catch every movie I could and build that up, I disappeared and turned into a record producer for, like, a year and a half. . . . You know, you can't really design the path you're on. I guess you could, but you have to go with what you think is the right thing at the moment.

*Perhaps the two people under the most pressure to decide on the "right" thing in the post-*Clueless *moment were the women most publicly poised to capitalize on it: Alicia Silverstone and Amy Heckerling. After attending a Shakespeare boot camp in Massachusetts during the summer of '95, Silverstone went in one splashy direction: she signed a deal with Columbia Pictures that* Variety *reported would net her $10 million, commit her to star in two films (the first being* Excess Baggage, *with Benicio Del Toro), and land her a three-year first-look production deal. At eighteen, she instantly became one of the higher-paid actresses in Hollywood, and report-*

edly, one of the town's youngest producers ever, which meant that her subsequent career moves—particularly her decision to play Batgirl in Joel Schumacher's Batman and Robin*—would be closely scrutinized.*

Alan Friedman, makeup supervisor: Alicia had stopped by [the *Clueless* TV show set] after a *Batman* fitting—it must have been a year or so after [*Clueless*]. This person who was now playing Batgirl, I don't think could have played the part of Cher anymore. Whatever the naïveté, whatever that moment in time was . . . she was not the same person.

The present-day Alicia, twenty years later, looks more like Cher than she did shortly after [the movie]. She got into the Hollywood grind of two or three bad movies and wearing a rubber suit. She was a little exhausted at that point.

Amy Heckerling: I love Alicia and I want the best for her. But she was also on her trajectory. She went from the movie to Shakespeare camp. She was very young and still learning. The studio system—they really suck people in and spit them out.

Alicia Silverstone: At the time, becoming a producer sounded really interesting and exciting, but the woman I am now knows that you can't grow as an artist if you're becoming a businessperson. And you can't grow as an artist if you're becoming a famous person instead of an actress. If you asked me to produce something now, I'd be like, "Why?" I would rather write books about healing people and changing their lives. I'd rather inspire people to be their best, healthiest selves.[27]

---

27 Conversation with Amy Heckerling, *Bullett* magazine, fall 2012 issue.

According to Ken Stovitz, Heckerling's agent, she, too, was inundated with offers. But the writer-director's approach was almost the opposite of her young star's: she chose to play it low-key.

Ken Stovitz, Amy Heckerling's agent: Everybody was interested in her. Everybody came out of the woodwork and said we wanted [*Clueless*], why didn't I give it to them? Why didn't I elect to sell it to them? She was offered a lot. We set up a lot of stuff, but the truth is she just mostly wanted to do her thing. It just made her hot again, which is how fickle [Hollywood is]. Like they forgot that she was talented before.

Amy Heckerling: I manage to stay in my own little universe regardless.

Ken Stovitz: She said, "You know what? I really love this thing and let me do the TV show."

Heckerling didn't stick with the Clueless *TV show for long. As she considered her next directing project,* Romy and Michele's High School Reunion *popped up as a possibility.*

Amy Heckerling: I was trying to figure out what I wanted to be writing next and I was shown that script. We had some meetings. I was at the reading. [The writer, Robin Schiff,] was struggling with a situation I had, that a studio had made drafts that she wasn't happy with. She liked the original and when I told them that the other draft was the better one that she liked also, I think she was happy about that. But I felt like, okay, if you do girls that people think are not that bright or whatever, that will be it forever. Maybe I shouldn't do this, exactly, next, as much as I love the movie.

After leaving Clueless *the series, Heckerling, along with several people who worked on* Clueless *(May, Kitay, Jordan, Friedman, and choreographer Mary Ann Kellogg), moved on to* A Night at the Roxbury, *the feature-length take on the* Saturday Night Live *sketch featuring Will Ferrell and Chris Kattan as head-bobbing singles-bar scammers. Heckerling coproduced the movie alongside Lorne Michaels. It's also been widely reported, both online and by people who worked on the comedy, that she ghost-directed it, but that's something Heckerling won't confirm. In fact, try to talk to Heckerling about her choices post-*Clueless*—a period that led to some frustrating experiences at the box office and with simply getting to make the movies she wanted to make, period—and she'll do her best to change the subject.*

Amy Heckerling: A bunch of crappy things happened that I don't even want to think about. I just have to think about the future.

She's also tired of being asked whether or not her gender has anything to do with some of the seemingly unnecessary struggles she's endured. Some of her friends and colleagues, however, are a bit more vocal on the subject.

Amy Heckerling: I've been asked that question [about gender] since I was twenty-three. And I don't know what to say. You can get bitter and then you can get angry. And anger isn't good for your work. So what am I supposed to do? It's not like I had the choice of being a man or a woman.

Amy Wells, set dresser: It seems to me that women directors just get so crapped on. After a film like that, the world should have opened up to her.

Gayle Nachlis, executive director of Women in Film and former talent agent at the William Morris Agency: I think many of the studios' executives looked at [*Clueless*] like it was a fluke, that we women still can't be a lucrative market, even though there were a lot of other movies out there to prove [otherwise]: *First Wives Club*. *Waiting to Exhale* was another one.

Now it's all kind of coming back around again with the serialized [YA] novels, like *The Hunger Games* and *Twilight* and *Divergent*. But [women are] not getting the directing jobs.

David Kitay: People have never given [Amy] the respect she deserves for being one of the highest-grossing female directors in history.[28] The weird thing for her is that it's not about her being a female, or this or that. She's just frickin' talented.

Stacey Dash: What I love about her is that she doesn't take any shit. She won't just do a film to do a film. She will do what she wants.

Paul Rudd, like Heckerling, also made a conscious decision to pursue projects that really spoke to him. Immediately after Clueless *wrapped, he moved to New York City, snagged a part in a Baz Luhrmann film, and focused his energy on Broadway theater for a while.*

Paul Rudd, Josh: I heard they were doing *Romeo + Juliet*. I thought, I can do Shakespeare. I wanted to get in on that, and I love that movie. I loved *Strictly Ballroom*, which was Baz

28 As of March 2015, Box Office Mojo's list of the top-grossing directors of all time (which has not been adjusted for inflation) ranks Heckerling at number 160 based on her box office returns, behind fellow women such as Betty Thomas (101), Nancy Meyers (104), and Nora Ephron (114), but, as of this writing, ahead of Judd Apatow (161), Spike Lee (162), John Hughes (184), Robert Redford (216), and Wes Anderson (248).

Luhrmann's other [film]. So I really tried to get an audition for that and then got a part in that movie. That, I'm sure, happened because I was in *Clueless*.

Then I got a job in a play. So *Clueless* came out, and I had some other opportunities for some other movies and things like that. And I didn't do any of them, and instead did a play for a year. Under the understanding: this is amazing. *This is a Broadway play and I'm only—I'm in my twenties. I don't know much. I want to learn. I just want to get better. So I think this is the way to do it.*

My agents, they were just super-confused by some of my choices at the time. Like: why would you move to New York right when this movie's coming out? Because at that time, too, it was especially like: "No. You have to live in LA. Why would you want to do that? This movie came out, and there's some opportunities to do some other things now, and other movies. Don't you want to take advantage of that? Why would you tie yourself up to do a play for a year?" But I was very clear in those decisions.

Jeremy Sisto also grappled with how to establish himself as an actor whose range extends beyond Elton.

Jeremy Sisto, Elton: Before you have something like that, a hit, you have a little bit more leverage, I guess, as an actor, before they see you in a specific way. You try to stake your claim and I was doing all these weird, intense movies at the time that all kind of bombed or didn't work for whatever reason. And then the hit was this big comedy. So I was probably a little concerned that I was going to be stuck in that sort of world.

I never wanted to do comedy at that age. Now I'm like: whatever. At the time, I was a young actor and I wanted to be brooding, and doing a big Hollywood comedy was like, *What am I doing?* I felt too responsible for the whole thing, when really, it's such a lucky thing to get any kind of career in this business that I should have just shut up and enjoyed the ride. But I was like, *How do I make this work?* For me, it was just a weird stepping-stone that I was trying to figure out how to deal with.

*Hollywood success brings a certain heat. Because they were still so young, some of the actors weren't quite sure how to handle it. Though most of them worked steadily, on the spin-off TV series and/or other projects, the post-*Clueless *period led to soul-searching, big life decisions and, sometimes, frustration.*

Justin Walker, Christian: I did a bunch of TV pilots. I did a bunch of crappy movies, which I wish, to this day, I didn't do. But I was young. I was naive. I had an "I can make anything work" mentality. I needed to work. I needed to make money. I needed to survive. There began this very, very difficult process of being famous but not working. At least not working all the time, and that is very hard to justify.

You can hear in my voice [that] it was a very difficult, frustrating process.

I was up for everything. *Everything*. Pretty much every teen movie that came out within two or three years of [*Clueless*] . . . *I Know What You Did Last Summer*, *Scary Movie*, any of that stuff. A lot of which my peers were in, and in some cases I was going up against them.

Stacey Dash: I was getting a lot of teen movie offers but I didn't want to do teen movies. I then got married—I got married, actually, during the [TV] series and then got divorced and then got married again and had a baby. So I just took a lot of time off through that period of time to raise my daughter, and didn't really get back into the fold of things until four or five years ago.

Susan Mohun, Heather: I actually left LA to go to graduate school in Northern California just because I came from a theater background and I thought *Clueless* would be a great opener. And it was, and it wasn't. I did a few more things. I never had a good agent. I was not good at selling myself.

Amy was wonderful. She had me read with Paul for a lot of different roles, but then she did *Clueless* the TV show. So all the things that she was going to do were kind of put on hold and then it didn't pan out. Which is totally fine. I have a great life.

Sometimes it wasn't so much to read so that we could get cast, it was just to do a reading for something that she wanted to hear, to see if she liked the script. I'd say Paul and I did that a few more times. Then I did a reading of *Romy and Michele*—I believe she was going to direct it—and then I think what happened was they offered her *Clueless* the TV show. So she did not do *Romy and Michele*, which was too bad for me. . . . I think I read for the part of one of the snobby friends. Then I remember her saying that I was too old for *Clueless* the TV show because they were going for kids that were actually high school age. I think I was twenty-four or twenty-five. Which I totally understood. . . . She was incredibly nice and normal and funny and really great. I have to say, of all the people I worked with, she was the most sane and totally no airs at all.

Justin Walker: I remember exactly where and when [I was first recognized in public]. I was in the produce section of Ralph's supermarket in Toluca Lake, California, which is right over the hill, right near where I stayed when they flew me out for the screen test. People started looking at me in the produce section and I thought, *Oh my God*.

Now, it's very, very, very, very much worth noting that being famous [for playing] a gay teenager carried a lot of mixed reactions. A lot.

I was the guest of honor at the soapbox derby in Akron, Ohio. I can't remember the year, but it was within probably two, maybe three years of the movie coming out. There was a lot of partying that went on. And as I was walking down [through] the actual event, waving to the crowd, grand marshal kind of thing, a guy standing on the side of the road yelled out to me: "Hey, you're that faggot from *Clueless*, right?"

A lot of the friends that I had in college, typically American masculine friends, people that I was very happy to tell, "Hey, this [movie] happened." There was a fair amount of, "Yeah, *but* . . ." This is the bizarre result of all of this at the time.

Elisa Donovan: You then realize, *Maybe from here on out, I'm always going to have to be aware of people looking at me*. That anonymity thing is gone. It's just how it is. But the beginning of understanding that is very disorienting and disruptive if you don't really have a grip on who you are. And then if you believe that you're that important, like people pretend you are, you've really got problems. [*Laughs*]

Donovan is right about the anonymity thing being gone; two decades later, members of the cast and crew are still often approached by giddy Clueless *fans. No matter what choices they've made in their careers or what turns their lives have taken, that has been a constant, for everyone.*

Alicia Silverstone: I was at the American Music Awards [recently], and it was amazing to have so many people come over to me that were so excited, as if they had just seen [*Clueless*]. Some of them were really young and some of them were, like, Katy Perry. . . . There were people responding [to me] as if that movie had just come out or something.

Breckin Meyer: I get the tardy speech from *Clueless* a lot. It's always nice when someone does it because I don't remember it exactly.

To this day, I have no idea what people are talking about when they come up and they just say: "Rollin' with the Homies." Every time someone comes up, it takes me a second to realize what they're talking about. They do the hand gesture, which to me—that signals rough waters to me.

Wallace Shawn, Mr. Hall: Oh, [people recognize me from *Clueless*] an incredible amount. I mean, there are *Princess Bride* fans; I meet people every day who are *Princess Bride* fans. The *Clueless* fans who I see, I would say, every other day, are a delightful group of people of all ages. And they're good people, rather smart, and I enjoy being congratulated for that.

Dan Hedaya, Mel: Yesterday I went to just go for a checkup. It was a relatively young woman who was the doctor and she paused and she looked at me for a moment, and she said, "Are you the dad from *Clueless*?" I said, "Yeah. Was I a good dad?" And her eyes just—she said, "I love that movie." She's twenty-six, -seven, so she was seven years old when the movie was made. It just keeps going from one generation to the next. It's pretty amazing.

Barry Berg, coproducer and unit production manager: I was in one of the remote areas of Alaska scouting locations some years ago, waiting for a plane on a dirt runway. There was just a lady in a Quonset hut and that was sort of the terminal, in the middle of nowhere. It was me, and I had an assistant with me. All of a sudden, out of the blue, this lady's daughter shows up from God knows where—because again, we were in the middle of nowhere—with a DVD of *Clueless* and wanted me to sign it. It is nonstop. People are constantly asking me about it. Really. It's a phenomenon.

Twink Caplan, associate producer and Miss Geist: I was at somebody's party and Paris Hilton came up to me and said something—"Miss Geist, you're hot." I said, "Oh, okay, that's good to know."

Susan Mohun: I'm teaching third grade right now. I was on yard duty yesterday, ironically, and this eighth-grade girl twirling her hair comes up to me and she was like, "Um, were you in Clueless?" I said, "Yes, that's so weird. That was so long ago. How do you even know that?" She said, "I recognize you. But, like, what are you doing *here*? This is a schoolyard with my *school*." I said, "Yeah, you know, that was a long time ago."

Adam Schroeder, coproducer: Three years ago, I read a script and was developing it with these guys, and I went to go meet the director for the first time. I met him on the Fox lot. We're sitting there talking and he was a young guy. . . . He says to me, "We've met before." I'm like, *Oh, geez*. I never want to dis anybody. But he was very young, like twenty-five or twenty-six.

He said that he was Amy Heckerling's daughter's—Mollie's—best friend from the time we were making *Clueless*, all through junior high school and high school. He stayed friends with her for all these years. I'd met him as a kid. . . . Here was this little, used to be an eight-year-old kid, and I ended up producing his first movie, called *Chronicle*.

Now I'm actually developing a movie with Mollie. She wrote this fantastic script and we're developing it together and I hope to make that next year. I've come full circle.

Justin Walker: I don't spend a lot of time thinking about [*Clueless*] by any stretch. I mean, I'm involved in eight million things at one time, always. But talking about it now, it's like, you miss them. We all saw each other for this reunion for *Entertainment Weekly* magazine. I guess it was about a year and a half ago? I loved seeing them. I didn't particularly like getting together to talk about something from twenty years ago. But I liked seeing them.

Paul Rudd: I'd come back to LA and I stayed with Breckin and Donald. Donald and Breckin; we got to be really tight after the movie. Alicia I'd see occasionally. Brittany I saw a few times. There was always kind of this weird thing where, it's like going to school with somebody. Whenever we see each other now, it's like, *Wow. That was a while ago. People really liked that. And we had no idea what we were doing.*

Stacey Dash: I just let [my eleven-year-old daughter] watch it for the first time. And I have a Barbie, so I just gave her the Barbie. She's very proud. She wears a [*Clueless*] T-shirt. I guess they were selling them at Forever 21 or something. She wears the T-shirt to every sleepover she goes to because it's me, Cher, and Tai. So she's very proud.

It feels good to be able to be part of a film that my daughter can watch, and my granddaughter can watch one day.

Susan Mohun: I did show [my kids] the one part [of *Clueless*] I was in and they're like, "Is that all? Is there more?" "No, that's pretty much it." They're like: "Oh, okay. Can we go to the park?"

Remembering Brittany Murphy

Watching *Clueless* has always been a light, fun experience. But if there's one thing about the movie that now elicits a twinge of sadness, it's the fact that Brittany Murphy, such a burst of bubbly, innocent energy in the movie, is no longer here.

Murphy died on December 20, 2009; according to the LA County Coroner's Office, her death was caused by pneumonia, with anemia and the effects of multiple prescription drugs playing secondary roles. She was only thirty-two.

In any interview for this book in which Brittany Murphy's name came up—and given the importance of her role in the film, it came up in most of them—those who knew her spoke of her with great fondness and a continuing sense of sadness that she's gone. Repeatedly, colleagues and friends said Murphy was very much the wide-eyed new girl in Hollywood when she played Tai in *Clueless*. She later gave herself a makeover of sorts and took on more leading-lady roles in films such as *Don't Say a Word* and *8 Mile*. But those who knew her and loved her say that her generosity of spirit never got a makeover. Because it didn't need one.

Breckin Meyer, Travis: We did *King of the Hill* for eight years together after *Clueless*. She played the character of Joseph, but when Joseph went through puberty, I took over. She still stayed on as Luanne. So for eight years we were working twice a week on *King of the Hill*. She was amazing. She was so sweet and so much fun, and especially that character in *Clueless*—it was so easy for not just the audience, but also for Travis to fall in love with her because she's just adorable. She's so much fun. Even when she says that line, "You're a virgin who can't drive," and it's such a dis to Cher, you're still like, "God, she's so *cute*." Look at the way that little mouth moves. She's doing that Marisa

Tomei–from–*My Cousin Vinny* thing, which is adorably weird. Brittany was unbelievable in that film and then backed it up with some amazing stuff after that. It continues to suck that she's not here.

Paul Rudd, Josh: She was very, very nice. *Really* nice. Whenever I'd see her years after, whether it would be at an audition or just at a dinner or a party or something, it was always so great to see her. She was always very smiley and, you know: big hugs and smiles. Just a lovely girl.

Alicia Silverstone, Cher: The audition I remember the most was when Brittany Murphy came in. I didn't know if I was really allowed to express my opinion on casting choices, but I couldn't help myself after she read. She was so brilliant. It's so weird to think she's not around anymore. It seems very abstract.

Amy Heckerling, writer-director: She was like a puppy: just a ball of energy, and happy. Everybody loved her. I don't think there was a person in the whole cast and crew that wasn't just crazy about her.

Mona May, costume designer: There was something about her that really was already there, some kind of a star power or talent that you immediately knew. She just was really, really good. That character [in *Clueless*] became so alive. It wasn't a farce. It was truly this young girl trying to find herself.

Elisa Donovan, Amber: She was so young, and I don't just mean in age. And fiercely talented.

She didn't like to be in the hair and makeup chair, which

nobody really does. But with Amber, I was in there half the day, all the time, so everybody would come in and out and I'd still be sitting in there. She was shooting something and they wanted her to go in for touch-ups before she went back to set and they were doing my hair and she said: "No, no, I'm fine, I'm fine, I'm fine, I'm just going to do it myself." And she would grab the curling iron and was trying to curl her hair really quick and they said, "What are you—what are you doing?" And she was always very energetic and flittery. And she just burned the side of her head. I mean, it was sizzling with this curling iron. And then everybody's freaking out because now they've got to cover up the burn on her head that she's just got. [*Laughing*] She said, "Oh it's fine, it's fine, it's fine. Everything's fine." She had a lot of energy.

Nicole Bilderback, Summer: She was always a delight. She was always so pleasant and funky and fun, and she was a unique, beautiful spirit. And funny. Really funny.

Justin Walker, Christian: Brittany Murphy was the most disarmingly over-the-top sweetheart that you could ever meet in your life. At that time in her life, she was always with her mom, and her mom was like that, too. I don't know anything about her personal life after that. What I do know is that that path did not match the person that I knew.

Jeremy Sisto, Elton: I liked her a lot. She obviously had a very positive energy. . . . I feel like when she was in *Clueless*, she was this kid that was kind of real, I don't know, not Hollywood at all. She never became Hollywood, but I remember seeing her and she started looking more and more glamorous every time I saw her. So it was kind of like she was one of those kids—like all of us, I guess—that grew up in the Hollywood world. And I was kind of there, too, so I always had a bond with her.

Stacey Dash, Dionne: She didn't have a bad bone in her body. She had a contagious laugh. . . . It's a tragic loss. It didn't have to happen. And that's what's most tragic about it.

I think she had a concept of Hollywood and she wanted to fit into that concept, as opposed to being herself, you know, and making Hollywood conform to who she was. Which they would have, because she was so talented. This is what Hollywood does to you. It makes you feel like you have to be someone other than who you are. And that's unfortunate.

Amy Heckerling: I felt like there was pressure from Hollywood to have a certain look and a certain way you had to be in order to be a star. I always missed the way that she looked when we were shooting. But she was always the most adorable, wonderful person. We all miss her so much. . . . Her talents never really got to be fully shown, the amount and the range that she had.

Kate Schellenbach, drummer, Luscious Jackson: Brittany Murphy was super, super nice and she came over and was hanging out with us [on the set of the "Here" music video].

At the time, our band was obsessed with the Judds, which was a very random thing to be obsessed with. There was going to be a Lifetime movie of the Judds' life story on that day and we all really wanted to watch it and somehow Brittany Murphy got involved in this quest to find the television so we could watch the Lifetime movie. I don't recall if we ever saw it. But I just remember she was just really sweet and social. . . . Later, I worked in television. I worked as an interview producer, a celebrity segment producer, on talk shows.

I started working at *Ellen*, and Brittany Murphy ended up

being one of my guests that I had produced. I had a preinterview with her and said, "Oh, you and I have met before," and I mentioned the video and stuff and she remembered everything. She was like, "Oh my God!" You know, it's sad to me now because she was such a sweet girl, and super engaged and one of those people who has no filter, where they just glom onto anyone who is around. Like they're too nice, in a way.

Donald Faison, Murray: When we did the movie, she was an actual teenager and I got to know her as a young adult, also. She was so loving and happy. And she had that spark. Hollywood starlets try to get that, but it was just natural for her. There was something about Brittany's spirit. Yeah, man, it is tough to believe that she's gone. One, because she was so young, and two, because it just seemed like she had a lot more to do on this side of things. Wherever she's at now—if there is an afterlife, I'm sure she's there rockin' out and making the most out of it. She was such an awesome person.

Amy Heckerling: I have the Brittany Murphy silver Doc Martens that she wore to the dance. They fit me. I just like having a piece of her. She means, and she meant, so much to me.

Five Key Post-*Clueless* Teen Movies

As the 1990s began, the eighties teen movie boom had more or less gone bust. While TV shows about adolescents hit big during that period—*Beverly Hills 90210*, *Saved by the Bell*, *Party of Five*, and, oh so briefly, *My So-Called Life*—the high school movie genre that reached peak, John Hughes–ian heights in the mideighties had more or less petered out in the mainstream by 1995.

But after the success of *Clueless* and, in 1996, Wes Craven's *Scream*, the teen movie genre started to inhale and exhale again.

With the teen population swelling—in 1997, there were 38.2 million "kids in America," according to the *New York Times*, a number that was still growing—studios realized they had a ripe audience for high school movies. By 1999, nary a weekend went by without at least one pubescent-oriented motion picture opening in theaters.

Many of the films released during the '90s/early '00s coming-of-age wave are notable for their quality, their box office success, or sometimes both. But these five should be at the top of any *Clueless* fan's Netflix queue, because the fingerprints of Cher and co. are all over them.

Can't Hardly Wait (1998)

As a last-night-of-high-school movie, this was more like a nineties-set version of *American Graffiti* or *Dazed and Confused*. But the presence of several *Clueless* faces—including Donald Faison, Breckin Meyer, and Nicole Bilderback—makes it impossible to watch without being reminded of Bronson Alcott High.

10 Things I Hate About You (1999)

Following on the heels of *She's All That* (based on George Bernard Shaw's *Pygmalion*) and *Cruel Intentions* (a modernized *Dangerous Liaisons*), this update of Shakespeare's *The Taming of the Shrew* was part of the classics-redux trend that *Clueless* kick-started. This nineties take on the Bard definitely feels like something from the Amy Heckerling or John Hughes canon.

Dick (1999)

A comedy about two teen besties (Kirsten Dunst and Michelle Williams) who are smarter than they look and sound, and whose shenanigans update a different sort of classic tale: the story of the Watergate scandal, with *Clueless*'s Dan Hedaya as Richard Nixon. The only possible explanation for this widely praised film's weak box office performance is that people were too embarrassed to say its name out loud. ("Have you seen *Dick*? Oh my God, I loooove *Dick*.")

Bring It On (2000)

What Amy Heckerling did for the Valley Girl, screenwriter Jessica Bendinger and director Peyton Reed did for the American cheerleader, creating Torrance Shipman (Dunst, again), a rally girl with intelligence and determination to match all the sparkle in her fingers. Like *Clueless, Bring It On* focuses on Caucasian and African-American young women, and introduces a male romantic lead (Jesse Bradford's Cliff) who, with his Clash T-shirts and antiestablishment attitude, is basically Josh in non-Rudd form.

Mean Girls (2004)

What happens when you breed the dark, catty undertones of *Heathers* with the bright color palette and smart writing of *Clueless*? You get a true classic of the genre that is *Clueless*'s closest cousin, in terms of nonstop online quotability and its exalted status in the teen-movie pantheon.

The Impact of *Clueless* on: Fashion

Clueless was hardly the first movie to prove that costumes can sometimes pop off a screen and become a phenomenon in their own right. For decades, the worlds of film and fashion have collided and given birth to iconic ensembles and the sort of sartorial genius that get widely imitated in the real world. Think of Audrey Hepburn's *Breakfast at Tiffany's* LBD, Diane Keaton's necktie-and-vest ensembles in *Annie Hall*, or even the casual off-the-shoulderness of Jennifer Beals's ripped sweatshirt in *Flashdance*.

But there isn't a single high school or teen movie in the modern era, and probably ever, that had a greater impact on fashion than *Clueless*. This film immediately affected what regular, non–Beverly Hills kids wanted to wear, what was being sold in stores, and what designers decided to include in their collections. And it's still doing that today. In terms of its fashion influence and the longevity of that influence, *Clueless* is simply without peer.

July/August 1995: *Within weeks of its July 19 release, the cultural significance of the* Clueless *look is established. An article in the fashion industry bible* Women's Wear Daily *proclaims it "the fashion movie of the year," while an August piece in the* New York Times *says* Clueless *is being "heralded as the fashion film of the moment," even though it also satirized those who fixate on clothes and makeup.*

Mona May, costume designer: The world has to be ready to receive something and embrace it and want it. I think girls were ready. The one theme [I hear] when I speak to women, all over and all ages, from especially I would say twenty-five and up—girls [who] were at a young age when the movie came out—is how it changed them. How they wanted to emulate it, how they wanted to be the girls . . . just how the style opened them up.

It shocks me in the most wonderful way, that film and character and the fashion can have that impact on the psyche.

Deborah Nadoolman Landis, costume designer, founding director and chair of UCLA's David C. Copley Center for the Study of Costume Design: Some actresses you can keep putting more clothes on or putting more plaid and more color and more texture and more pattern on and other actresses just can't tolerate it because they're overwhelmed by it. And in this film, Alicia Silverstone always looks right. Somehow, she always looks right. Whether she's wearing her crazy multipiece, layered outfits with her kneesocks, or whether she's wearing that gorgeous white dress when she comes in to see her dad. The clothes never overwhelm her, and that's a triumph.

Wallace Shawn, Mr. Hall: The costumes, in many cases, were meant to be funny. But then people started imitating them in real life.

Jessica Morgan, cofounder and cowriter of the fashion and celebrity blog Go Fug Yourself: I have always been into the sort of preppy thing—grunge was *very not me*—so [Cher's] style was very appealing to me. I wore a lot of pleated skirts and sweater vests and kneesocks and chunky-heeled Mary Janes that next year. *A lot*.

Lena Dunham, star and creator of HBO's *Girls*: It was such a big deal to me that I wore kneesocks and a mini-backpack to school every single day of fifth grade, and it wasn't making me any friends.[29]

October 1995: *The Oliver by Valentino spring 1996 collection, dubbed the* Clueless *line, is unveiled during Milan Fashion Week. According to the* New York Times, *it features plenty of pastel and chiffon, as well as models showing off apparel while "chatting on pink cellular phones." In the US that same month, California designers show off their spring/summer collections, many of which are dominated by a Cher-ish femininity.* Teen *magazine fashion editor Bonnie McAllister tells the* Los Angeles Times: *"It has a lot to do with the movie* Clueless. *Girlie girls are back in a big way. Hair and makeup are done, and the clothes are feminine. Grunge is gone."*

29 *New York Times* interview, March 7, 2012.

Mona May: I think that really was the beginning of allowing girls to be girly [again]. I think that was a moment that gave women permission to be more themselves. You can be feminine. You can be girly. You can be cute and it's okay. It's fun. I think that's a very important word, too—you can have fun with this.

1995–1996: *After Bloomingdale's publicly acknowledged that it missed the opportunity to be out in front on the* Clueless *trend—"I only wish I had done a tie-in," senior vice president Kal Ruttenstein told* Women's Wear Daily, *adding that the movie would be "required viewing for our junior buyers"—the department store runs some* Clueless*-connected advertising and creates an in-store* Clueless *boutique, according to the* New York Times, Newsday, *and the recollections of* Clueless *producer Adam Schroeder. Later, in a December 1996 story on the synergy between the fashion and film worlds, Hollywood marketing consultant Sandra Ruch tells the* New York Times *that* Clueless *"set a pattern" that both industries are hoping to replicate.*

Kimberley Gordon, founder and designer of the Wildfox fashion line: At the time that the movie was being written, before it came out, grunge was the big thing. That was pretty much what everybody was showing and wearing. It was a lot of really baggy clothes, sort of hip-hop, really oversize jeans and oxfords, very cool, like, tomboy style. It was sort of antifeminine. When the movie came out, it wasn't like [Mona] had followed some trend of this extreme feminine schoolgirl style. The movie came out and it wasn't even there. Then all of a sudden, you start seeing a lot more bright colors and a lot more young girls embracing it.

I'm sure there's a little bit of prediction there. She probably was in tune with that. Even if you look back at old pictures of Kate Moss, there are some really cool old, girly photos of her in these little baby-doll dresses. I think it really hit right around when *Clueless* hit. That's why it's so interesting: [*Clueless*] sort of changed things.

August 1996: *In conjunction with the forthcoming debut of* Clueless *the TV series, the Wet Seal/Contempo Casuals retail chain announces a* Clueless *tie-in that involved the sale of* Clueless-*branded merchandise, including caps and T-shirts, as well as in-store promotions in all 365 of its US Wet Seal and Contempo Casuals stores.*

Emily Weiss, founder of fashion and beauty website Into the Gloss: I grew up in Connecticut, and on the first day of sixth grade—conservative Connecticut public school, where lacrosse and field hockey were big—I showed up in thigh-high stockings, a plaid miniskirt from Contempo Casuals, and loafers, and I had a feather-topped pen. The entire *Clueless* look.[30]

Kimberley Gordon: Even stores that I shopped in did a huge turnover in the way that they sold things. Suddenly brights were in, little cropped mini-Ts and kneesocks and plaid skirts. It was this whole wave of fashion that came through. Even being thirteen, I noticed, and I think that's pretty amazing if a movie can influence fashion to a degree where it can affect a young teenage girl.

December 1998: *Britney Spears's music video for ". . . Baby One More Time"—in which Spears dons a midriff-baring schoolgirl uniform before switching into an outfit reminiscent of Sporty Spice—becomes one of the most popular clips on MTV. It's hardly the blatant* Clueless *homage that the "Fancy" video would pull off nearly two decades later, but still: Spears in over-the-knee socks and fluffy*

30 Buzzfeed interview, June 3, 2013.

pink hairpieces unquestionably looks like a more cheaply dressed version of Cher Horowitz.

2008: *Knee-high socks and other* Clueless*-style looks come back in style, thanks in part to the popularity of the CW's* Gossip Girl, *which certainly overlaps with* Clueless *in the Venn diagram of teen pop culture from the past twenty-five years.*

Heather Cocks, cofounder and writer, Go Fug Yourself: The movie definitely opened my eyes to the idea that in some ways, nothing ever really goes out of style—or that you can take something old and spin it into something new. Cher's iconic plaid mini and thigh socks and heeled loafers were a nineties take on an old classic. It was all familiar clothing with a twist, which is what the fashion industry has to do every six months to stay fresh. But I also recognized a lot of it as veering into parody. The movie walked such a fine line of social commentary and social satire, and the costumes did the most amazing job of enhancing that. If the clothes opened my eyes to anything, maybe it was that—the way that the clothes in a movie can communicate, too.

2010: *The influence of* Clueless *on young, up-and-coming fashion designers becomes increasingly apparent. Handbag and apparel designer Rebecca Minkoff creates a spring/summer 2010 line inspired by* Clueless, *right down to a black leather pleated skirt named after the movie. Fashion news websites such as Fashionista and Refinery29 point to the 2010 collections of numerous designers—including Alexander Wang, Miu Miu, Prada, and shoe designer Robert Clergerie—as evidence of a* Clueless *revival. Is some of this revival-spotting happening, in part, because style bloggers tend to be women who grew up on* Clueless *and immediately think of it every time they see the slightest hint of a plaid pattern? Maybe. Still: it's worth noting* *that in two separate conversations in* Interview *magazine and* Vanity Fair, *Wang cited* Clueless *as his favorite film of all time.*

Heather Cocks: I think it's possible that *Clueless* just encouraged people to let their fashion-freak flags fly, so to speak. People wore *crazy* stuff in that movie and made it work for them, within that world, and that kind of erased some of people's barriers. After that, I think nothing seemed too insane to try.

2010 to present: *Mainstream stores begin to carry* Clueless *merchandise in greater abundance. Girly online retailer ModCloth sells a fit-and-flare hot-pink skirt named after* Clueless *and lands a shout-out in a 2010 issue of* Lucky *magazine; Urban Outfitters starts to sell T-shirts with obvious* Clueless *references, like "You're a Virgin Who Can't Drive," emblazoned across them; and in 2012, Topshop, the fashion and accessories store, issues a bright pink lip pencil named after* Clueless. *Because, obviously, anything that draws attention to your mouth is good.*

Sarah Pitre, director of national programming, Alamo Drafthouse: The nineties is sort of back in terms of fashion trends. So hilariously, if anybody wore one of those outfits, they would look normal. They wouldn't look "What are you doing from the nineties?" So I think the fashion doesn't feel dated.

Heather Cocks: Amber's outfits made me laugh the hardest. She was a delight. At one point—I think in the scene where Cher is taking photos of the whole group—she's in a striped ensemble that *would* technically be a long-underwear onesie if it joined up, but it's actually a turtleneck and then matching leggings/socks that go almost all the way up. It's amazing. I would so wear that under my ski clothes. If I ever skied.

2010: *Calvin Klein issues a new version of Cher's famous Calvin Klein slip dress that "looks like underwear," after Ilaria Urbinati—celebrity stylist, owner of LA boutique Confederacy, and, apparently, quite the* Clueless *fangirl—urges Calvin Klein creative director Francisco Costa to do so.*

Sarah Pitre: The Calvin Klein dress is a classic. Girls could wear that right now and they would look fresh off the runway.

Amanda Hess, writer, Slate: There's so many aspects of it that are held up as ridiculous. Like her clothes-matching system or her response to her dad who is trying to belittle her clothing because it's too small and she says: "It's a Calvin Klein dress." Her response is simultaneously hilarious—that this is her response to going out as a teenager wearing something that is probably inappropriate—but it's also not super dismissive of that idea that fashion is, for a lot of girls, a way for them to express their creativity. So [the movie] is toeing this strange line where a lot of stuff that these girls are engaged in is hyper-ridiculous, but also, there is something about it that is really freeing.

2013: *The* Clueless *revival continues on runways and in various design collections. Versace's fall 2013 line is noted for its* Clueless *vibe, thanks to certain ensembles splashed in screaming yellow plaid, while Wildfox's spring 2013 lookbook, created with permission via a licensing arrangement with Paramount, is one mega-homage to* Clueless, *complete with the requisite knee-highs and Mary Janes, as well as a sweater emblazoned with the phrase "As If" and a Tai-esque model holding a binder with Marvin the Martian drawings on it.*

Kimberley Gordon: The sweater that says "As If" on it sold like crazy. That's a testament [to the movie] right there, because that came right from it.

Mona May: I think we get too sophisticated too early. . . . It's hard to find yourself, who you are, and [*Clueless*] was like the thread of: You know what? Just being a girl is a great thing. You can play with fashion. Like with your dolls. But you can do it now [as] you.

The Impact of *Clueless* on: Girl Power and Progressiveness

The moment that most defines *Clueless*—that clarifies who Cher Horowitz is, unleashes its most repeated catchphrase, and, subtextually, in retrospect, proclaims how much this movie would mean to girls and women—occurs roughly four minutes into the film, when Cher brutally rebuffs a guy in a backward baseball cap who's trying to put his arm around her.

"Get off of me!" she shouts as she pushes him, hard. "Ugh—as *if*!"

At its most basic, this moment tells us that Cher is not interested in typical high school boys and, therefore, is unlike most girls we've seen in typical high school movies. But it's also a powerful image of 1990s-era girl power. When Alicia Silverstone's Cher rejects that dude-bro, she's not only asserting herself. She's literally shoving the boys outside of the frame and announcing that she, like all those girls Gwen Stefani was just singing about on the movie's soundtrack moments ago, is ready for her close-up.

Clueless arrived on the pop culture landscape at the "Just a Girl" moment following the rise of the punk-feminist Riot Grrrl movement but before the ascendance of the Spice Girls' bubblegum version of femme power. It was a time when female voices were being heard more loudly on Capitol Hill (1992 became the so-called Year of the Woman, after a then-historic four female senators were elected to Congress), on radios and MTV (in addition to the domination of TLC and Mariah Carey, the early nineties marked the rise of shockingly candid alt-rockers like Liz Phair, Alanis Morissette, and Courtney Love), and in the pages of *Sassy* magazine.

Admittedly, it's hard to imagine Cher Horowitz in the front row at a Bikini Kill show. I'm also pretty sure that when writer Rebecca Walker coined the term *third-wave feminism*, she didn't mean to encourage girls to cajole their teachers into giving them better grades. But at a time when women were finding new ways to express themselves, Cher's über-confidence struck a deep chord with girls and women who were torn between their ambitious impulses and their love of party dresses and fluffy pens.

As Susan Douglas points out in her book *The Rise of Enlightened Sexism*, the movie "marked a turning point in the depiction of girls and women in film and TV," ushering in a "new girliness." The complicated, simultaneously cynical and optimistic third-wave feminist *Clueless* sensibility—which stamps down aggressively on all hints of misogyny and celebrates the value of female relationships, all while displaying girly, mascara-and-miniskirt flair—has been co-opted in tons of films and TV shows over the past twenty years, including *Legally Blonde*, *The Powerpuff Girls*, *Sex and the City*, and *The Mindy Project*. There are so many, in fact, that Sarah Pitre, director of national programming at the Alamo Drafthouse, built an entire successful film series, called Girlie Night, around these kinds of offerings.

While stereotypical boys may have been shoved out of *Clueless*'s frame, the movie also allowed other underrepresented groups to make their way into the picture. At a time when black and white characters were pretty much segregated in the cinematic landscape (as they still are), *Clueless* showed us a friendship between a white girl and an African-American girl in which both were strong, supportive equals. With Justin Walker's Christian, Amy Heckerling demonstrated that straight and gay kids could commingle in a similarly positive way. *Clueless* is a mainstream movie that could hardly be described as radical. But in its treatment of gender, race, and sexual orientation, it led by example in a way that Hollywood, even today, rarely manages to follow.

Dr. Devoney Looser, professor of English at Arizona State University and Jane Austen scholar: I think, like Naomi Wolf and the power feminist, which really isn't all that different from leaning in, [*Clueless* conveys] this idea that the system stinks but if you just make yourself a better person and a stronger person, you'll make your way, honey. I think that is a positive message. It's definitely looking on the bright side. If [feminism] stopped there, politically, that would be very troubling to me.

Amy Heckerling, writer-director: [Cher's] not [a feminist] in terms of, she's going to go out and organize everybody to get equal pay. But she will be influenced by Josh as far as the rights and wrongs of the world as she sees them. And she'll fight with him on some stuff, but she will be active in others. She does have the power.

I don't know if you're ever around little girls. Before they reach puberty and the estrogen-weakling hormone starts going through them, they are just as powerful as little boys. They can be as bossy, they can control things, they can figure they're running everything. That pre-childbearing, "love me, love me, and stay with me while I sit on the egg" kind of drug that goes through women—in the best of all possible worlds, in my brain, women wouldn't have that change. Little girls would stay with the power that they feel through their teen years and their twenties.

Sarah Pitre, director of national programming, Alamo Drafthouse: I think she has some shallow interests, but I think at the end of the day, Cher is not self-absorbed at all.

I would say Cher is definitely empowered. It's just that some of her ambition leads her to the mall.

Ta-Nehisi Coates, national correspondent, *The Atlantic*: I think the seriousness with which [Amy Heckerling] took women, which I imagine has gone remarked upon—*Fast Times* is really stunning to me in that respect. It came out in '82, and it's a really, really aggressively feminist movie, and I mean that in the best way. I was sort of shocked by the politics of that. It's less so in *Clueless*, but it's there. You know what I mean? She doesn't just sort of make fun of this ditzy girl. She's not your stupid ha-ha-ha-ha. She takes, I guess what they would cast in a lot of teen movies as the subject of derision, and gives her all sorts of complexity.

Kerensa Cadenas, pop culture writer and editor: She's flawed and not perfect. I think maybe that is the most empowering thing of all about her. There's definitely aspects of her that you wouldn't want to emulate, but I think she's figuring it out, too. I feel like Cher looking back would be like, "Oh, that thing when I tried to convince my teachers to give me an A was probably not a really good call."

There's so much about her that is really positive. I think she's like a real person, and that's one of the things I like best about her. She could have been such a caricature of a flighty Valley Girl and she's not.

Alicia Silverstone, Cher: Cher was smart and helpful and passionate and creative and very full of heart. I think she sends the message that you really can change, especially if you have the willingness and earnestness to do it.

Amanda Hess, writer, Slate: I could empathize with [Cher] and could see the way that she put herself forward in class in a way that I couldn't, maybe, exactly model. But I liked that about her. It seemed like, even if I wasn't going to look like her or have her clothes, that might be something I wanted to be able to do, which was go in front of my class and speak about things that were important to me and that are actually important to the world. Even though it's in this crazy, satirical context, there was something that was empowering about that. Because I didn't see a lot of models of girls standing up for themselves at that time.

When I was in middle school I had some sort of humanities class where we were being introduced to this idea of critical reading. The assignment was to take a song that you liked and explain it to the class. And I talked about "Supermodel." The movie must have come out a few years before that. But at a time when I was like, "I don't even know what to choose because I don't have any thoughts about anything and I don't know what I can say about anything," that song was what I chose because I was like, "Oh, this is the song that has some sort of turn in it that has an interesting commentary that I can talk about."

Kimberley Gordon, founder and designer, Wildfox: I think it lets girls know you don't have to be a stereotype to be someone that is a role model or someone that you can believe in, especially as a woman. We live in such a sexist world that in order to be certain things in life, it's almost like you have to become a stereotype of that thing in order to succeed.

It's allowing girls not to have to live by these stereotypes, which is feminist, in a way.

Dr. Devoney Looser: I think there's some ways in which *Clueless* was at the vanguard of that. That is, reworking a lot of these stereotypes in ways that had more feminist potential.

Amanda Hess: I do think *Clueless* as this blockbuster version of nineties femininity was more rich and complicated than a lot of what we saw in mainstream movies for the next ten years. The idea that people are now going back to that speaks to how bad that type of stuff got as much as how good *Clueless* is on its merits.

Kerensa Cadenas: One thing that stands out for me every time I watch *Clueless* is the friendship between Cher and Dionne. Like if you watch *The Hunger Games*, Katniss has no female friends. Homegirl could definitely use, like, a buddy.

Clueless seems diverse in the landscape of more recent teen movies. To me, at least. At the time watching it, it didn't make any difference to me. I didn't think anything of it. It seemed: oh, that's normal life. I had a gay best friend when I was in seventh grade who came out to me when I was in ninth grade.

Matt Kane, director of entertainment media, GLAAD: *Clueless* was obviously in a lot of ways a cultural touchstone for a generation, and I think the fact that Christian was a part of it really said something about a certain kind of cultural awakening that was happening at the time, especially among the younger generation in terms of LGBT issues. The fact that he was very casually brought into the story and his sexual orientation, after it was revealed in the story, really wasn't made to be

 that big of a deal suggests that there was a sea change happening in the way that young people thought about sexual orientation and how much it actually mattered in terms of the quality of the person.

The character of Christian was, in a lot of ways, very non-stereotypical. He sort of had that very unique, retro style to him and wasn't afraid to jump up and get in someone's face to protect a friend.

Paul Rudd, Josh: That they were making a movie and one of the characters was gay and he was a really cool character—I mean, that hadn't really been seen before, especially in a high school movie. I remember thinking that was really great, and I thought that was a great character.

Amy Heckerling: I got a letter from GLAAD that was very happy. He stood up to the bullies that could have possibly hurt Tai. They were glad to see he was doing something brave besides, you know, he's my new shopping friend.

Matt Kane: I think that was a really great example of a director deciding we're just going to introduce this character very casually and not make that big of a deal about it.

Justin Walker, Christian: When you come out, so to speak, in your first role, that is what people label you as, whether they're being in any way, shape, or form homophobic or stereotypical or any of that. What people called me was, for the most part, "He's the gay guy from *Clueless*." I'm not here to tell you that it kept me from getting parts at all. I'm here to tell you that it was a factor in every part of my life.

Would I do it again? The answer to that question is, without hesitation. [I would do] it for me, and for the movie, and for what it might have meant to other people and other roles and teenagers questioning their sexuality at that point in their lives. All of that without a doubt . . . is bigger than my personal experiences in and around all that.

Matt Kane: There are certainly a lot of straight people I've met over the years who cite *Clueless* as being one of the first films that they ever saw that introduced them to the concept of a gay person, actually showed them one on-screen. These are usually people who were seeing it when they were quite young. For that, I think it really did help introduce a whole generation to the fact that gay people are people, too. And that generation has grown up to become very supportive, especially compared to where their parents are politically.

Ta-Nehisi Coates: African-Americans pop up in teen movies, as sort of these side characters that are kind of there. Have you seen *Not Another Teen Movie*? That spoofs it and basically gets it down. I don't know, [the African-American characters] just seemed really, really human in *Clueless*. Very, very well-integrated. Very, very believable.

This is a difficult thing to do. Maybe it's not so difficult, actually. Let me rephrase that: I don't think it's actually difficult at all. It requires that you see a kind of humanity in black people and not see black culture as either something that's animalistic or something that you can't touch with a ten-foot pole.

I think they were able to manage that pretty well [in *Clueless*]: to have African-American characters, in that world, accepted as themselves. As their own, human selves. And that's not a small thing.

Stacey Dash, Dionne: That was Amy, Amy's genius—race doesn't matter.

Wallace Shawn, Mr. Hall: I think [*Clueless*] presents a somewhat believable fantasy of America as a decent country and Americans as people who are capable of being good people and learning how to be better people. This is a very nice idea that is very agreeable. I mean, because it's not phony. For example, there are hundreds of films and television shows that supposedly show, let's say, gay people and straight people, black people and white people, Christians, Jews, all getting along. But they feel fake. They feel phony.

In *Clueless* somehow [Amy] makes you believe it. You think, yes, this could happen somehow. This could be possible. If we change in the right ways, this could be possible.

So "Fancy": The Story Behind Iggy Azalea's *Clueless* Music Video

Few things have confirmed the continued cultural significance of *Clueless* as loudly and clearly as the 2014 music video for Iggy Azalea's "Fancy," a three-minute re-creation of *Clueless* in which Azalea stars as a rhyme-dropping version of Cher Horowitz.

"Fancy" the song was inescapable during the spring and summer of that year. It slid into the number one spot on the Billboard Hot 100 chart in early June and stayed there through the week of July 19, a week that, coincidentally, marked the nineteenth anniversary of *Clueless*. But the music video was a sensation in its own right. Its release last March resulted in tons of media coverage and even earned some Twitter love from Alicia Silverstone herself.

The official version of the video, also featuring artist (and *Clueless* fan) Charli XCX, has been viewed on YouTube more than 398 million times as of this writing. Every time someone watches it, what she sees is a meticulously detailed homage to *Clueless* that re-creates multiple scenes from the film, including the Haitians debate, the tennis court scene, the freeway debacle, and the Val party, along with the Cher and Dionne plaid ensembles; the pink, fluffy pens; and Murray's Kangol hat and fake braces. Azalea and her team took the verisimilitude so far that they actually shot the video's high school scenes at Grant High School, where most of the interior school scenes in the real *Clueless* were filmed.

Director X, director of the "Fancy" video: We were going back and forth over a bunch of ideas. Nothing was clicking. Then suddenly she realized that *Clueless* was it. She really knows her audience and that generation. When I was working on it and I would say to someone, "Oh yeah, it's *Clueless*," all these girls in her age range would just lose their minds: "Oh my God, *Clueless*!"

Iggy Azalea: *Clueless*, to me growing up, was just that stereotypical LA Valley Girl movie. And it was very hard for me as a kid to know what was real and what wasn't real. Is that really how people in LA dress? Do they really talk like that? I didn't know—the line was very blurred, I wasn't sure. So it's something that really always stuck in my head.[31]

Director X: We shot the video over two days and prepped it for just a couple days. A normal prep and shoot, it was nothing out of the ordinary. . . . Her stylist is very detail oriented. That's her permanent team, so it wasn't the usual, like, "Hey, hire a stylist." This is someone who's always around Iggy and so those ideas were able to flow and get a true, real understanding of what she needed. On that end of things, they were off to the races the moment this idea became a reality.

Iggy Azalea: A lot of the costumes that weren't replicas and we didn't have made, we had either gotten from movie costuming houses, like the Universal back lots and Sony back lots—we got a lot of the costumes from there.[32]

 31, 32 Fuse.tv interview, May 14, 2014.

Director X: I approached even how I shot it very much the way *Clueless* was done. . . . You know, I was making *Clueless*. We were making—well, I wouldn't say a parody, almost like an homage. I just had to do my homework and look at what was really going on in that flick. So as much as possible, we were trying to put people in the right places. When it comes to this kind of thing, I always think about Weird Al Yankovic, where you're redoing, like, "Beat It." He did shot for shot. When he does your video, he does your video. So that was my inspiration on that side.

Iggy Azalea: I've just always wanted to re-create *Clueless*. I think all girls do. Even a little bit, even if you deny it, you want to. I've just been looking for an excuse and "Fancy" seemed like an excuse. "Fancy," to me, seemed like the kind of song that Cher would listen to.[33]

Amy Heckerling, writer-director of *Clueless*: People would send me the Iggy Azalea video and go, "Oh, are you angry?" No, that's nice to see. That's funny. I mean, you know, I think it's cool that somebody appreciates that. How can you not like that?

Twenty Years Later: Why *Clueless* Endures

Two full and tumultuous decades in American culture have passed since the summer that *Clueless* burst into theaters. But the platform-shoe prints of this comedy of nineties manners can still be seen all over popular culture.

In every TV show and movie that adopts a young-skewing female point of view—*Pitch Perfect*, HBO's *Girls*, *New Girl*, *The Mindy Project*, *Suburgatory* (especially the episodes that reunited Alicia Silverstone with Jeremy Sisto), and others—hints of *Clueless* can be found. Its influence can be seen, too,

33 MTV News interview, March 14, 2014.

in the myriad modernized Jane Austen tales that followed in its wake, including *Bridget Jones's Diary*, *The Jane Austen Book Club*, *Bride and Prejudice*, the Hindi rom-com *Aisha* (which is far more *Clueless* than *Emma*), *Austenland*, and *The Lizzie Bennet Diaries*. "*Clueless* deserves to be much, much more recognized for its influence on popular culture related to Austen," notes Austen scholar Dr. Juliette Wells.

On social media, the *Clueless* effect has resulted in scads of Tumblrs fire-hosed with "As if" GIFs or branded with names like "In Cher Horowitz We Trust"; Instagram feeds filled with *Clueless* screen shots or ladies dressed in Cher-wear for Halloween and New Year's; and tweets peppered with *Clueless* quotes or, in the case of the @modernclueless Twitter feed created by writers Jessica Blankenship and Ella Cerón, devoted exclusively to 140-character, Cher Horowitz–ian interpretations of current events. That account, by the way, has more than twenty-eight thousand followers. (Sample tweet: "Cher: I'm captain of the Ebola epidemic relief. Mel: I don't think they need your skis.")

The fashion choices, music videos, and/or social media profiles of some of the biggest contemporary pop stars—from Charli XCX to Rihanna to Katy Perry to Iggy Azalea—point to a continued *Clueless* fixation, as do the number of *Clueless*-related blog posts, listicles, and quizzes that pour forth on the regular from outlets like Buzzfeed, Bustle, Jezebel, and (yes) Vulture.

Pretty soon, the *Clueless* legacy may make its mark on a new cultural frontier: the stage. Amy Heckerling has written the book and lyrics for a long-gestating musical version of *Clueless*. At the time this is being written, the Dodgers—the play-producing team behind Broadway hits such as *Matilda*, *Jersey Boys*, and *Urinetown*—are in the process of signing on to produce; Kristin Hanggi, who directed the original production of *Rock of Ages*, is on board to direct; *Clueless* composer David Kitay has been working on some of the musical arrangements with Heckerling; and the aforementioned Katy Perry has expressed interest in playing Cher, though, at this pre-publication moment, that's not a done deal. "It's a jukebox musical, so it's got songs from the past," Heckerling says. Kitay adds, "It's really a totally original slant on that that I don't think anybody's ever done before."

Clearly *Clueless* isn't going anywhere. Which raises a question that was posed during just about every interview conducted during the writing of this book: what makes this movie so enduring?

In keeping with the complex mix of satire, broad comedy, cultural commentary, and earnest teen romance at work in the movie itself, there are multiple answers to this question.

In the book *X vs. Y*, a back-and-forth exchange of pop cultural arguments written by sisters Eve and Leonora Epstein, the X-er, Eve, suggests that *Clueless* appeals to her generation as well as her younger sister's because the relationship between Cher and Josh is essentially "the story of Generation Y (Cher) falling in love with Generation X (Josh)." I heart this idea *hard*.

There's also the notion that the movie's fantasy captured certain elements of our future reality, which gives *Clueless* a currency and timelessness that other teen movies lack.

Taking that a step further, I also offer this: *Clueless* operates on a level that mirrors the way we process information in the era of digital media. We are all reinventers now. We immediately turn TV moments into GIFs, filter our Instagram photos so they'll look more evocative, post our own versions of movie trailers on YouTube, even, in extraordinarily rare cases, self-publish *Twilight* fan fiction that goes on to become bestselling works of mainstream erotica. Every piece of pop culture we encounter is an opportunity for reinterpretation.

As music supervisor Karyn Rachtman implied, *Clueless* is steeped in a nondigital version of that kind of updating. It samples from preexisting things—*Emma*'s story structure, slang from the UCLA dictionary, nineties pop culture references, schoolgirl plaid, seventies and eighties pop songs, the iconography from other movies—then reworks them in a way that creates something totally new, different, and original.

Clueless was at the forefront in so many ways. And for so many reasons, that's very likely where it will continue to stay. Not "as if"; for sure.

Adam Schroeder, coproducer: I keep on thinking, *Wow, it's such an old movie* and I wonder, *Does it feel dated?* But whenever I talk to friends with kids, or relatives and [their] kids, they all have discovered the movie in the last twenty years and it kind of plays just as if it were contemporary, even with twenty years having gone by.

Alicia Silverstone, Cher: It was always a movie that spoke to many different generations. I remember when it came out, parents really loved it. Because, you know, they had to see it with their kids three thousand times and they would say, "Actually, I really like that movie." Amy makes movies for both. It's got all the young teenybopper things going on but it's also got super-clever ideas spread through there as well.

Danny Silverberg, second assistant director: I've got kids. They're not young anymore, but they're twenty and seventeen. They have seen the movie a dozen times. I didn't even realize that. My daughter told me, "Oh yeah, we watch this all the time." It's a sleepover movie, when friends come over after school—they've seen it over and over again.

It's still very relevant to what teenagers are doing.

Sherry Lansing, former chair and CEO of Paramount Pictures: Much of who you are as a young girl is still who you are as an adult, even though you've had experience. But I think for women—and maybe for men as well, but I can only speak for myself—we all remember that and it still strikes a chord for us. Here I was, clearly not the demographic, but it turns out that the demographic was everybody.

Alan Friedman, makeup supervisor: I have a wedding business [doing makeup] up in Northern California, in wine country. And I can't tell you how many times I will go to a location to work with a group of young ladies and that's been part of the festivities. If there hasn't been a male stripper getting naked, there's certainly been *Clueless* on disc.

Bill Pope, director of photography: Like Amy and the fountain in *Gigi*, there's something that touched [fans]. And it goes right into their iconography.

Charlie Lyne, director of the teen movie documentary *Beyond Clueless*: What *Clueless* really did in my eyes, in terms of restoring faith in that [teen] genre, was show that there was a market for films that were very fiercely set in the here and now and felt like they were for actual teenage audiences.

Sarah Pitre, director of national programming, Alamo Drafthouse, founder of the Girlie Night movie series: It's also super nostalgic for those of us that were in high school in the nineties. To me, it's like a guilty pleasure without the guilt because it does have substance and it did make an impact on our culture. I have a ton of guilty pleasures and I'm not ashamed of them. But I would never call *Clueless* a guilty pleasure. It's just a freaking good movie.

Stacey Dash, Dionne: It was the first of its kind. They tried to do some [teen movies like it] after that but, I feel, failed. They never got it just right like *Clueless* did.

Amanda Hess, writer, Slate: *Clueless* . . . has so many smart things to say about consumerism, I think, and it is really kind to its characters even when it is mocking them. I think especially for someone like Tavi [Gevinson] or the people who are in her community that she has created, they really are drawn to that. They're still really in this teen world that, in a lot of ways, is like ruled by this consumerist culture. There are parts of it that they want to engage in and parts they want to push back against. That movie is like a great gateway for understanding how that might be possible.

Wallace Shawn, Mr. Hall: The movie is both a satire and, in a way, a sort of celebration of these characters. And I can't really explain this, but people love it who see it as a satire, and people love it who see it as a celebration. Their actual feelings as they watch the movie may be not that different, I don't know. It's a sort of mysterious phenomenon.

Paul Rudd: *The Breakfast Club* and those movies were major movies to me and all of my friends, probably for the same reason that *Clueless* is major to some other people. They saw that movie at an age when it's like, *Oh, I'm that age and there's not a lot of movies about kids my age that are like this*. I don't know what it is. But then they kind of grow up with a feeling of nostalgia. You know, you see it at a certain age and you like it. Then you see it a few times. I mean, [*Clueless*] was a multi-viewing kind of movie. I've met many parents that said, "God, we played that DVD in our house so much." Or videotape, probably, at the time. It becomes a part of your childhood and then as you get older, you just have such warm feelings about something like that.

It's an amazing thing to be in a movie that somebody is that passionate about, or has actually meant something like that to somebody. As to why, I don't question why. But I certainly am appreciative [that] it does hold such affection for so many people.

Amanda Hess: That was the first Paul Rudd movie that I had ever seen and I think he definitely imprinted on me and other girls of my generation, where he became just, like, the ideal male actor. We're all still following Paul Rudd's career partly because of that.

Amy Wells, set dresser: It's so funny because I'll see Paul Rudd now, and I just cannot believe—how can someone continually be that gorgeous for an entire lifetime?

I worked with Jon Hamm, who's a good friend of his, for a long time. I always said Jon Hamm was the most gorgeous creature on Earth. As I look at Paul Rudd, I realize: No. It's actually Paul Rudd.

Michelle Manning, Paramount executive who oversaw production and also produced *Sixteen Candles* and *The Breakfast Club*: I think that what Amy Heckerling, Cameron Crowe, John Hughes—what they all did very well was talk to kids, because they were kids in their hearts. It wasn't like: here's what I think you sound like . . . It was: here's what you sound like and here's the issues that are relevant to you. I think that makes kids want to listen, you know.

[John and Amy,] they were both, at whatever age they happened to be—and probably still to this day, with Amy—they're teenagers. I mean, they are teenagers. They would hang with the kids [on set] as if they were one of them. There was never a feeling of "I'm the director and the writer, so I'm the boss." It was always like, "I'm just one of you and let's hang out and let's be teenagers together."

Paul Rudd: One of the things that Amy does better than anybody is represent kids and teenagers and the stuff that they go through, but not talk down to them in any way. Because she loves kids and respects their thoughts about things, and what's important to them, and their insecurities, and everything. I think she captures that in a really sweet way in this movie.

Jeremy Sisto, Elton: Amy is just a genius and [*Clueless*] was one of her amazing ideas. It's pretty exciting to be a part of something like that, but it's really—for me it feels like the thing that's amazing about it is her. That she had this idea and she wrote the script and she created these characters.

Twink Caplan, associate producer and Miss Geist: Amy made a place for all of us, in a certain time, in an era that will never be forgotten, just like [George Lucas] did with *American Graffiti*. You know, there are those standout times that make you always remember you're part of something so much bigger. You're the face of somebody's childhood, or just something that they'll remember.

Jessica Morgan, cofounder and cowriter, Go Fug Yourself: I think that there are a lot of movies that are really funny in context, but you can take lines out of *Clueless* and it's still amusing. Which lends itself to maximum real-life quotability. Regardless of context, "You're just a virgin who can't drive" is basically the meanest thing you can humanly say to a teenager.

Heather Cocks, cofounder and cowriter, Go Fug Yourself: There will never be a day when Jess tells me her foot hurts that I don't reply, "Do you want to go to the nurse?"

Kate Schellenbach, drummer, Luscious Jackson: I also like the way it doesn't put down anybody. Like there's the stoner, but then he's sort of included, and then there's the gay kid who—there's no gay slurs, which is kind of amazing.

For all of us who have kids and we're constantly trying to find things on Netflix for them to watch . . . when you find something like *Clueless*, you're like, "Thank God, it's something I can watch with my kid." I think we all get a little something out of it.

Jace Alexander, Mugger: I have three kids so I'm constantly looking for movies. They're always saying, "Let's watch a comedy, let's watch a comedy." Then I start scrolling through these massive lists of old comedies and I just scroll past all of them because they're not really that good. They're not really that funny, and they don't make you feel good, most of them. This one has that little touch of magic to it, you know? It really does.

Dan Hedaya: I think there's a purity to the movie. It's clean-cut. It's not vulgar. . . . Mostly, when I think about it, it feels like a very pure movie. There's nothing cynical about it.

Paul Rudd: And Alicia's so good in it. She just carries the thing. She's incredible in it.

Elisa Donovan, Amber: Once in a while, when all the stars are aligned and all of the right people are involved, this beautiful thing happens. And I think that that is what happened with this movie. It doesn't happen all the time. There are like a handful of movies that have that kind of longevity, especially for comedies, because comedies are so difficult to make.

Mona May, costume designer: Maybe to some people it would be silly to say, "Oh my God, you did *Clueless*." To me, it's very serious because it's my work. It's my own expression of my art. I will never feel tired of talking about it. I will always feel proud of it no matter what. My friends laugh that I'll have a boa on my grave, you know. A pink boa on my grave.

Bill Pope: In the end, you're left with exactly what Amy wanted you to be left with: you're happy.

Amy Heckerling: I'm happiest when I'm in that sort of fantasy land. That happy, youthful, optimistic place where somebody can see what's good in people and see what's good in the world. Maybe you have to be an idiot to be like that. Not an idiot. But clueless.

Biographical Notes for All *Clueless* Sources Quoted in This Book

• • •

Jace Alexander, otherwise known as the mugger from *Clueless*, is a television producer and director whose credits include NBC's *The Blacklist*, the MTV comedy *I Just Want My Pants Back*, and USA's *Royal Pains*.

Iggy Azalea is a pop and hip-hop artist whose 2014 debut studio album, *The New Classic*, yielded multiple hits, the biggest being "Fancy."

Dicky Barrett is the front man for the Mighty Mighty Bosstones, who frequently perform live and released their most recent CD, *The Magic of Youth*, in 2011. Barrett also can be heard regularly as the announcer on *Jimmy Kimmel Live!*

Barry Berg's recent producing projects include the History miniseries *Hatfields & McCoys*, which starred Kevin Costner, and History's *Texas Rising*, which debuted on the network in May 2015.

Nicole Bilderback followed her work as Summer in *Clueless* with roles in numerous films and TV shows, including *Can't Hardly Wait*, *Dawson's Creek*, *Bring It On*, and *The Mentalist*.

She recently starred opposite Vivica A. Fox and Zoë Bell in *Mercenaries*.

Dr. Inger S. B. Brodey has been a professor for thirteen years at the University of North Carolina–Chapel Hill, where she teaches comparative literature and also serves as director of the comparative literature program. She regularly teaches seminars on Jane Austen and co-organizes UNC's annual Jane Austen Summer Program.

Kerensa Cadenas is a writer and editor focused on pop culture. Her work has appeared in Women and Hollywood, the Hairpin, Bitch Media, and *The Week*.

Twink Caplan has appeared in a variety of film and TV projects since her work as a producer and costar of *Clueless*, including *I Could Never Be Your Woman*, *Tim and Eric's Billion Dollar Movie*, and, more recently, an independent film called *Noirland*. She also was in an episode of *Community* in which she played—you guessed it—a teacher (this time, of dance).

Josh Caterer is a worship leader at a church in Barrington, Illinois. He also writes and records Christian music as a solo artist, and still plays gigs a few times a year with the Smoking Popes, a band that counts Josh's brothers, Eli and Matt, as members.

Debra Chiate's editing credits, in addition to *Clueless*, include *Harriet the Spy*, *Never Been Kissed*, *Loser*, *The House Bunny*, *Vamps*, and *Movie 43*.

Ta-Nehisi Coates is the National Magazine Award–winning national correspondent for *The Atlantic*, author of the memoir *The Beautiful Struggle* (Spiegel & Grau, 2008), and a journalist-in-residence at the City University of New York's Graduate School of Journalism. His next book, *Tremble for My Country*, will be released in October 2015.

Heather Cocks and **Jessica Morgan**, a.k.a. the Fug Girls, have been writing the celebrity fashion and entertainment site Go Fug Yourself (which, of course, is sprinkled with *Clueless* references) since they cofounded it in 2004. They've also published two young adult novels, *Spoiled* and *Messy* (Little Brown Books for Young Readers, 2012), and a third for grown-up adults called *The Royal We* (Grand Central Publishing, 2015).

Arthur Cohen was the worldwide marketing chief for Paramount Pictures for fourteen years, overseeing the campaigns for 272 movies, including the second-biggest moneymaker of all time: *Titanic*. He left that post in 2003. Currently, he says, "I'm a private equity manager. But it's my equity."

Coolio is a hip-hop artist and reality TV star who had numerous megahits in the nineties, including "Fantastic Voyage," "Gangsta's Paradise," and "1 2 3 4 (Sumpin' New)." He has since appeared in the Oxygen network series *Coolio's Rules*. He also wrote a cookbook called *Cookin' with Coolio* (Atria Books, 2009), related to the Web series of the same name. He continues to tour and perform live.

Jill Cunniff, Gabby Glaser, and **Kate Schellenbach** are still performing and making music as Luscious Jackson. In 2013, they released two crowd-funded CDs: *Magic Hour* and one for kids called *Baby DJ*. They have also been performing live shows, including the 2014 Bumbershoot music festival in Seattle.

Stacey Dash has appeared in numerous film and TV projects post-*Clueless*, most notably BET's series *The Game* and the VH1 series *Single Ladies*. She is now a regular commentator for Fox News. Her first book, *There Goes My Social Life* (Regnery Publishing), will be released in July 2015.

Director X has made music videos for numerous high-profile hip-hop and pop artists. In addition to Iggy Azalea, he's directed videos for Drake, Nicki Minaj, Justin Bieber, Usher, R. Kelly, Jay Z, and Kanye West.

Elisa Donovan is an actress who appears in the ongoing *The Dog Who Saved . . .* series of holiday films as well as other indie and TV movies. A wife and the mother of a daughter, Scarlett Avery, she also writes a parenting blog for People.com and narrates the audiobook versions of Sheryl Sandberg's *Lean In* and *Lean In for Graduates*.

Lena Dunham is the creator, executive producer, and star of the HBO series *Girls* and author of the book *Not That Kind of Girl: A Young Woman Tells You What She's "Learned"* (Random House, 2014).

Donald Faison appeared in numerous movies post-*Clueless*, including *Waiting to Exhale*, *Remember the Titans*, *Uptown Girls* (with Brittany Murphy), *Kick-Ass 2*, and Zach Braff's *Wish I Was Here*. Aside from *Clueless*, he is best known for his role as Turk on TV's *Scrubs*, which ran for nine seasons, first on NBC and later on ABC. He can currently be seen on TV Land's *The Exes*.

Carrie Frazier became a senior vice president and head of casting at HBO in 1998. She worked there for fourteen years, supervising and/or participating in the casting of numerous projects, including *Gia*, *Game Change*, *Temple Grandin*, and the HBO series *Game of Thrones* and *In Treatment*. She currently works as a consultant on various film projects.

Alan Friedman worked on makeup for *A Very Brady Sequel*, *A Night at the Roxbury*, and the Reese Witherspoon/Paul Rudd romance *Overnight Delivery*, among others. These days he works as a wedding and event makeup artist, a public speaker, and an instructor.

Kimberley Gordon is the creative director and cofounder of Wildfox, a vintage-inspired clothing line born in 2007. Wildfox clothes are sold online and in department stores, including Bloomingdale's and Nordstrom.

Richard Graves continues to work as a first assistant director; some of his film credits include *The Wrestler*, *(500) Days of Summer*, *The Amazing Spider-Man*, and *Noah*.

Herb Hall retired in 2014 after more than forty years of teaching, twenty-eight of them at Beverly Hills High School. Over the years at Beverly, he was chairman of the theater department, a speech coach, and a teacher of theater as well as English, speech, and film, all while pursuing acting on the side.

Amy Heckerling has directed *Loser*, *I Could Never Be Your Woman*, and *Vamps* since *Clueless*, as well as episodes of TV shows *The Office*, *Gossip Girl*, *Suburgatory*, and *The Carrie Diaries*. She's currently working on bringing her musical version of *Clueless* to the stage.

Dan Hedaya is a veteran actor of stage, television, and film whose credits include *Blood Simple*, *Cheers*, *The Usual Suspects*,

The First Wives Club, and, more recently, *The Humbling* with Al Pacino and *The Mindy Project*. He is also a longtime painter of abstract art.

Amanda Hess is a staff writer for Slate and a National Magazine Award winner. She has written about culture, women, Hollywood, technology, and a host of other things for *Pacific Standard*, *Wired*, *Elle*, *Details*, *ESPN the Magazine*, and elsewhere. She was a contributor to *The Book of Jezebel* (Hachette Book Group, 2013).

Steven Jordan continues to work as a production designer, having overseen the visual style on movies such as *Never Been Kissed* and *Loser*, as well as many TV series, including *Fringe*, *Enlightened*, and *Parenthood.*

Matt Kane is the director of entertainment media for GLAAD, a media watchdog organization focused on equality and fairness for the LGBTQ community and accuracy in the way its stories are told.

Mary Ann Kellogg, who began her career as a dancer with Twyla Tharp's company, has acted as choreographer on a vast array of film and TV projects, including *Mad Men*, *A Night at the Roxbury*, *Superstar*, *The Guru*, *Gilmore Girls*, *The Mindy Project*, and *Saving Mr. Banks*.

David Kitay has composed music for many film and TV projects, including *Mad About You*, *Ghost World*, *The Ice Harvest*, and Amy Heckerling's *Vamps*. He's currently working with Heckerling to arrange music for the *Clueless* musical.

Kokin is a hat designer and maker in New York City whose hats have been featured in the pages of fashion magazines, as well as on other films and TV shows in addition to *Clueless*, including *Dr. T and the Women*, *Sex and the City*, and *Gossip Girl*.

Deborah Nadoolman Landis is the founding director and chair of the David C. Copley Center for the Study of Costume Design at UCLA and a woman who has created some iconic costumes of her own, for projects that include *Raiders of the Lost Ark*, *National Lampoon's Animal House*, and the video for Michael Jackson's "Thriller." She has also written several books about Hollywood costumes.

Sherry Lansing became the first-ever female head of a major movie studio as the president of 20th Century Fox in 1980. Beginning in 1992, she was chairman and CEO of Paramount Pictures for more than twelve years, ushering films such as *Titanic*, *Election*, and *Mean Girls* to the big screen. She's currently the CEO of the Sherry Lansing Foundation, a nonprofit devoted to cancer research, health, public education, and encore career opportunities.

Dr. Devoney Looser is a professor of English at Arizona State University and a lifetime member of the Jane Austen Society of North America. She also plays roller derby under the pseudonym Stone Cold Jane Austen.

David Lowery is still singing and playing guitar with the band Cracker, who released a new CD, *Berkeley to Bakersfield*, in 2014, and has tour dates scheduled in 2015.

Charlie Lyne is a British freelance writer and filmmaker who directed the documentary *Beyond Clueless*, an impressionistic look at the common tropes and themes in the teen movies released after *Clueless*.

Michelle Manning was an executive at Paramount for more than a decade. She was copresident of production when she left the studio in 2004 to become an independent producer. Her credits include *The Eye*, starring Jessica Alba, and, more recently, the independent film *Jenny's Wedding*, starring Katherine Heigl and Tom Wilkinson.

Mona May has been a costume designer for more than twenty years, creating the ensembles for such films as *The Wedding Singer*, *A Night at the Roxbury*, *Enchanted*, *The House Bunny*, *American Reunion*, and the Lifetime Whitney Houston biopic *Whitney*, directed by Angela Bassett.

Charlie Messenger cast extras for several movies after *Clueless*, including 1998's *The Parent Trap* and *The Green Mile*, before closing his agency's doors in 2002. A former actor, he is back at it again, currently doing background work and commercials.

Breckin Meyer has done plenty (and, presumably, rarely been tardy) since *Clueless*. He's played roles in a number of comedies (and a few dramas) over the years, including *54*, *Go*, *Road Trip*, and the *Garfield* movies. He recently starred on the TNT series *Franklin & Bash* alongside Mark-Paul Gosselaar; he also does voice work and has written for the Emmy Award–winning stop-motion-animation series *Robot Chicken*.

Susan Mohun is a teacher who has taught theater and other subjects at the high school and grammar school levels. She's married with two children, lives in San Francisco, and would love to get back into acting again in the not-too-distant future.

Gayle Nachlis is the executive director of Women in Film, a nonprofit organization focused on creating equal opportunities for and portrayals of women in all forms of media. Prior to that, she spent nearly thirty years at the William Morris Agency as a talent agent and vice president.

Brian Nelson, onetime guitarist for Velocity Girl, now works in IT at a charter school in Washington, DC. Velocity Girl reunited and played a few gigs around 2000, according to Nelson, but never fully regrouped after that.

Ron Orbach does not give driving lessons, but he's still acting on stage and screen. His Broadway credits include *Laughter on the 23rd Floor*, *Dance of the Vampires*, and *Soul Doctor*. He also has appeared on television in episodes of *Law & Order* (opposite his cousin, the now-late Jerry Orbach) and, more recently, *Girls*.

Nina Paskowitz has styled the hair of many high-profile celebrities (Keanu Reeves, Ben Stiller) and has been the lead stylist on numerous films and television shows, including *Iron Man*, *The Five-Year Engagement*, and NBC's *Parenthood*.

Sarah Pitre is the director of national programming for the Alamo Drafthouse cinemas, where she has instituted such "lady-centric" events as Girlie Night and Afternoon Tea. She also cofounded the young adult literature website Forever Young Adult.

Bill Pope is a cinematographer who has been the director of photography on numerous memorable movies over the past twenty years, including all three films in the *Matrix* trilogy, *Spider-Man 2* and *3*, *Team America: World Police*, *Scott Pilgrim vs. the World*, and the pilot episode of *Freaks and Geeks*.

Karyn Rachtman earned producer credits on several soundtracks following *Clueless*, including *Romeo + Juliet*, *Boogie Nights*, and *Moulin Rouge*. She recently coproduced, with Pras Michel, the documentary *Sweet Micky for President*, about the 2010 presidential election in Haiti.

Dr. Joan Klingel Ray was a professor of English at the University of Colorado–Colorado Springs for more than thirty-four years when she retired in 2012. She is a former president of the Jane Austen Society of North America and the author of the book *Jane Austen for Dummies* (Wiley Publishing, 2006).

Marcia Ross became the executive vice president of casting for the Walt Disney Studios Motion Picture Group shortly after *Clueless* was released. She held that position for fourteen years, supervising the casting of many productions and acting as casting director on such films as *10 Things I Hate About You*, *The Princess Diaries*, *Enchanted*, and *The Muppets*. She has her own casting agency, Marcia Ross Casting, and produces films via her production company, Floating World Pictures.

Paul Rudd told Elizabeth Banks she tasted like a burger in *Wet Hot American Summer*, made "Do you know how I know you're gay?" an inquisitive catchphrase in *The 40-Year-Old Virgin*, unleashed the power of Sex Panther cologne in *Anchorman*, and introduced the word "jobin" into the lexicon in *I Love You, Man*. He's also been in tons of other films, TV shows, and plays, will star as Ant-Man in the 2015 Marvel blockbuster, and seemingly stopped aging at some point in 1996.

Adam Schroeder has produced many major Hollywood films since *Clueless*, including *The Truman Show*, *South Park: Bigger, Longer, and Uncut*, *Zoolander*, and *Chronicle*. He's currently producing the sci-fi action film *Convergence*, slated to star Paul Wesley of TV's *The Vampire Diaries*.

Kim Shattuck is the lead singer and guitarist for the Muffs, who released a new CD in 2014 called *Whoop Dee Doo* and will be playing gigs in LA and beyond in 2015. Shattuck also briefly played bass with the Pixies in 2013.

Wallace Shawn is an actor, screenwriter, and playwright whose post-*Clueless* credits include the *Toy Story* movies (he's the voice of Rex), Woody Allen's *The Curse of the Jade Scorpion*, *Vamps*, *Gossip Girl*, and *Admission*. His film *A Master Builder*—which he adapted from the play by Henrik Ibsen and starred in—was released in 2014.

Danny Silverberg made the transition from second AD to first AD post-*Clueless* and has amassed numerous credits in that capacity, *Hairspray*, several episodes of *Glee*, and *Pitch Perfect 2* among them.

Alicia Silverstone continues to act, appearing in movies (*Beauty Shop*, *Butter*, *Vamps*, *Who Gets the Dog?*), TV shows (*Miss Match*, *Children's Hospital*, *Suburgatory*), and plays, on Broadway (*The Graduate*, *Time Stands Still*, and *The Performers*) and elsewhere. She has built the Kind Life, a Web community focused on vegan life and environmental issues, and is the author of two books: *The Kind Diet* (Rodale Books, 2011) and *The Kind Mama* (Rodale Books, 2014).

Jeremy Sisto has starred in numerous films and TV series, including *Thirteen*, *Six Feet Under*, *Law & Order*, *Suburgatory*, and A&E's *The Returned*.

Jill Sobule released a new album in 2014 called *Dottie's Charms*, still performs on a regular basis, and composed the music and lyrics for a new version of *Yentl*, staged in 2014 at Washington, DC's Theater J.

Jeffrey T. Spellman has continued to work as a location manager or supervisor, mostly in the television world, where he's scouted locations for *Buffy the Vampire Slayer* and *Joan of Arcadia*, and currently scouts for *Criminal Minds*.

Ken Stovitz is a talent agent at Paradigm and has represented Amy Heckerling for more than two decades. He's also a producer whose credits include *Seven Pounds* and the 2010 version of *The Karate Kid*. You also may recognize him as Mike from David Lynch's *Blue Velvet*.

Justin Walker is vice president of the Hollywood Dell Civic Association and the chairman of the executive committee of the Cheremoya Foundation, a nonprofit that supports Hollywood's Cheremoya Elementary School. Contrary to Internet reports that he's involved in running a restaurant—"That was a business that I haven't been involved in for eight years"—he is focused on another line of work that he says he cannot discuss. "It's not something I can talk about because of the nature of the business. What I can tell you is that it's a thrill a minute and I'm extremely proud of it and it is not lascivious in any way."

Karl Wallinger is the musician and songwriter behind World Party, which has been performing live in recent years following Wallinger's recovery from a severe brain aneurysm in 2001. More tour dates, and possibly a new CD, are expected in 2015.

Emily Weiss is the founder of the beauty website Into the Gloss and a line of beauty products called Glossier.

Amy Wells has worked as a set dresser on a number of projects since *Clueless*, including *Mad Men*, *A Single Man*, the Paul Thomas Anderson features *The Master* and *Inherent Vice*, and ABC's *Scandal*.

Dr. Juliette Wells is an associate English professor and chair of the English department at Goucher College in Towson, Maryland, home of the largest Jane Austen collection in North America. She's also a member of the board of directors for the Jane Austen Society of North America and author of the book *Everybody's Jane: Austen in the Popular Imagination* (Bloomsbury Academic, 2011).

Dean Wilson worked as a prop master or assistant prop master on several films after *Clueless*, including *Three Kings* and *Mystic River*; he retired from the business in 2012.

Nancy Zwiers is a former senior vice president of marketing for Mattel and the founder and CEO of Funosophy, a brand-building consulting and invention firm that specializes in toys and entertainment.

Acknowledgments

Tardiness is not something you can do all on your own. Many, many people contributed to my tardiness. I'd like to thank my parents, for never giving me a ride to school; the LA city bus driver, for taking a chance on an unknown kid; and last but not least—what, you honestly thought I could resist reprinting part of Travis Birkenstock's tardiness speech in the acknowledgments of this book? *As if!*

But in all seriousness, what Travis says, in part, is also true of writing an oral history. It's not something you can do all on your own. Many, many people contributed.

Let's start at the beginning: I am so thankful to John Sellers, my editor at Vulture (and these days, at Esquire.com), who assigned me the Val party oral history that would, eventually, lead to this book. He was extraordinarily supportive and helpful as I wrote this and I appreciated it enormously. I also want to give shout-outs to Josh Wolk and Gilbert Cruz, my other editors at Vulture when the *Clueless* piece and book project came into being, who were highly encouraging as well.

If there's an LA city bus driver in this situation, it has to be my agent, Allison Hunter, who is not only originally from California, but also took a chance on an unknown kid by suggesting that I should write a book about *Clueless*. Not only did she make this whole oral history happen, she also used the phrase "I think everything is going to work out" more times than I can count during the occasionally stressful writing process. Every time she said it, she sounded so calm and confident that I always believed her. Turns out she also was right. Thank you, Allison, for everything.

I feel very, very lucky to have had Lauren Spiegel at Touchstone as my editor. Lauren was always flexible, enthusiastic, and savvy about how to make the book the best it could be. She also knew just when to pepper an e-mail with a *Clueless* reference, which is a must-have skill for every successful young woman. My thanks also to Miya Kunangai, Jessica Roth, and everyone at Touchstone and Simon & Schuster who worked to make the book the shiny, happy thing it is, from the eagle-eyed copy editors to the inspired designers to everyone in publicity and marketing who couldn't wait to start spreading the word about *As If!*

Of course, there would have been no word to spread if it weren't for the many, many sources who willingly and generously agreed to be interviewed as part of this project. I am forever grateful to each and every one of them. There are a few, in particular, to whom I want to express extra gratitude. First and foremost, my heartfelt thanks to Amy Heckerling. Without her, there would be no *Clueless* and, obviously, no book. She devoted hours of her time to answering numerous, often hyper-specific questions and always did so with patience, good humor, and total humility. Thank you so, so much, Amy.

My thanks to everyone on the *Clueless* team who went above and beyond by sharing old photos, tracking down information, and doing whatever they could, without reservation, to assist me with the book. In particular: Mona May, Richard Graves (and Ben Waller and Ralph Bertelle at Paramount), Danny Silverberg, Alan Friedman, Adam Schroeder, Marcia Ross, Dicky Barrett, and Nicole Bilderback. I'm incredibly appreciative of the contributions from every single cast member, but especially those who carefully answered e-mail follow-up questions (Elisa Donovan); carved out time to talk for quite a while on a Saturday (Paul Rudd); answered the phone at ludicrously early hours (Twink Caplan); spoke at great length with no hesitation and tremendous candor (Justin Walker); and kindly had lunch with me and picked up the bill (Wallace Shawn). Many thanks also to the experts: the Jane Austen scholars, the musicians (ladies of Luscious Jackson, you *rock*!), journalists, *Clueless* fans, and industry insiders, including Sherry Lansing, Carrie Frazier, and Arthur Cohen, whose insights proved invaluable.

In many cases, interviews would not have happened if a middleman or middlewoman, publicist, manager, sibling, spouse, daughter, or, in one case, Amy Friedman and Molly Winston at Theater J in Washington, DC, hadn't faciliated and helped put wheels in motion. Your efforts meant so much.

One of the hardest things about doing an oral history like this one is—and here's where all the journalists start nodding in weary recognition—*all the transcribing*. Desiré Moses and Katherine Reis Williams provided much-needed assistance by transcribing many interviews from spoken word into written. Ladies: you single-handedly saved my fingertips, and at least some of my sanity.

I specifically quote from several books and other sources in *As If!* but want to acknowledge the ones that proved most useful and edifying in my research, including: *Jane Austen and Co.*, edited by Suzanne R. Pucci and James Thompson; *Jane Austen in Hollywood*, edited by Linda Troost and Sayre Greenfield; *Teen Movies: American Youth on Screen* by Timothy Shary; *X vs. Y: A Culture War, a Love Story* by Eve and Leonora Epstein; *The Rise of Enlightened Sexism: How Pop Culture Took Us from Girl Power to Girls Gone Wild* by Susan J. Douglas; myriad *Entertainment Weekly*, *New York Times*, and *New York* magazine articles that have been written about *Clueless* over the years; the special features on the Blu-ray release of *Clueless*; and, of course, *Emma* by Jane Austen.

I owe one forever to Neeraj Bewtra and Barb Deli, who hooked me up with a place to stay while doing book-related research in New York. Many thanks to them and all of my friends who listened to me jibber-jabber about *Clueless*, including Leah Kramer, Sarah Gershman, Patrick Kraich, Barbara Berlin, and Neil Cantor, who were always extra-interested in knowing how the book was going. Thanks also to my freelance writing support group, Libby Copeland, Tammy Kennon, and Liz Kelly Nelson, who are the best therapists/cheerleaders an author could have.

Finally, the family. Thank you to my parents, Don and Linda, who fostered my love of reading and writing and would have been so excited to read this; to my brother and permanent life coach, Tim Chaney, my sister-in-law, Monica, and my nephew, Drew; and to my husband Rob, who kept the household running, switched up his schedule when interviews threw monkey wrenches into our plans, and continued to prove that he's the most generous human being on the planet, which is super-convenient since I'm married to him. Last but in no way least: thank you to my son, Luke, who tolerated the fact that I talked a lot about *Clueless* even though he's not old enough to see it yet. Thanks for being understanding when Mommy said she had to work on this (and she said that *a lot*). In two or three years, you can finally see the movie that inspired this book. I'm pretty sure you're going to *love* it.

—Jen Chaney